James A. Brakken's

The Annotated
Early Life Among the Indians

—— • ——

Reminiscences

from the Life of

Benj. G. Armstrong

1892

— • —

— ● —

To the Ojibwe people,
with optimism that your history
will be forever remembered
and someday better understood.

————— ● —————

And in memory of
Professor John Anderson,
contributor to this book,
who taught us even little birds
can soar high in the sky
above the Earth Mother.
May your wisdom and faith sail
on forever within the four winds.

— ● —

James A. Brakken's

THE ANNOTATED
EARLY LIFE AMONG THE INDIANS

REMINISCENCES

FROM THE LIFE OF

BENJ. G. ARMSTRONG
1892

Badger Valley Publishing
James A. Brakken
45255 East Cable Lake Road
Cable, Wisconsin 54821
715-798-3163

Badger Valley Publishing

An independent publisher for independent authors.

TREASUREOFNAMAKAGON@GMAIL.COM   BADGERVALLEY.COM

MEGWITCH!

To Dr. John Little Bird Anderson, professor, historian, tribal chairman, master of Ojibwe culture, college president, and so much more. May you always know I truly valued your advice and treasured your friendship.

Albeit a bit late, I thank you, Benjamin Armstrong, for being a champion to your people and for having the good sense to put your thoughts on paper. Few do. Everyone should.

Thank you Eric Schubring, musician, friend, philosopher, and WOJB-FM newscaster, for suggesting I consider publishing this annotated version of Benjamin Armstrong's 1892 memoir. Such a wonderful idea!

Anne and Mario of Cable Lake, thank you twice! First, for rescuing the only signed copy of Armstrong's book I've had the pleasure to hold and, second, for lending it to me for this project.

To Tory Stroshane of the Ashland Historical Society and to all historical society volunteers in the western Great Lakes region, thank you for keeping our history alive.

For your on-the-mark suggestions and proofreading, I thank Lorna, Howie, and my brutal but delightful Yarnspinners writing critique group. You help me keep the wheels of the cart behind the mule and usually on the right trail.

Above all, thank you Sybil, my love, my wife, my partner in life, for your unfaltering confidence in my work, for your incredible patience, and for contributing in so many ways.

TABLE OF CONTENTS

FOREWORD

I come from a family line steeped in Ojibwe, Oneida, and Scottish history—a DNA tree that goes back hundreds of years—from the Island of Lewis in Scotland to Sorel, Quebec, then to the Great Lakes region where my Ojibwe ancestors made their home for centuries more. And where family, tribal, and settler histories intertwine with cultural, economic, and political relationships today.

In spite of early genocidal policies of the U.S. government and European disease that killed thousands, the Ojibwe side of this family tree continues to flourish in the 21st century, providing a pathway for new opportunities on an ever-changing landscape.

Essentially, history is like the seven blind men touching the elephant. Recalled events become meaningful to the people who experienced them. Shared, written memories allow all to peek into the past from many angles—to revisit ancient lore and oral stories handed down.

My family—and probably yours—rubbed elbows with much of the history offered within the Armstrong memoir. Reviewing his story, correcting a few errors, and adding context gives us a fresh view of a controversial but nostalgic period in U.S. history and the history of the Ojibwe Nation tribes.

We can't change history. We can only learn from it. And *The Annotated Early Life Among the Indians* contributes to a clearer picture of our past, setting parts of the record straight. Perhaps it might guide all of us as we move forward.

Our elders often challenged us to know where we came from in order to know where we need to go. To all who thrive on understanding our past, I invite you to enjoy this new addition to the literary library of our collective history.

Paul DeMain (Skabewis)
CEO of Indian Country Communications, Inc.
Oneida/Ojibwe - Bear Clan

Early Life Among the Indians

Reminiscences from the Life of Benj. G. Armstrong
Annotated by James A. Brakken

In his own words, this is the 1892 memoir of Benjamin Green Armstrong, a trader, woodsman, and a man whose drive to protect his friends, the Ojibwe people, knew no bounds. His efforts to assist them included persuading the government to honor treaties granting them the right to gather fish, game, rice, and other bounty from the lands they ceded to the government in the mid-19th century. Perhaps his greatest accomplishment occurred in 1852, when he led a small contingent of Ojibwe leaders to Washington, hoping to convince President Millard Fillmore to honor past treaties. The effort was successful and avoided a war between the Lake Superior Ojibwe and the United States.

Introduction

In 1833, a thirteen-year-old Alabama boy fell from a horse. Benjamin Green Armstrong's injuries resulted in respiratory problems causing a doctor to recommend a move to a different climate. Young Armstrong chose the woodlands and waters of western Lake Superior and found friends among the Ojibwe people who lived there. They helped him recuperate. He learned their language. They shared their customs and traditions. He became their interpreter. They taught him skills in trapping, hunting, and fishing. He became a trader. And, unlike other white traders in the region, he made sure the Ojibwe people were treated with fairness and respect. Although never employed by the government, Benjamin Armstrong's life work benefitted Native Americans far more than any government Indian agent did.

Armstrong married the niece of Great Buffalo. Chief of

chiefs, Buffalo was perhaps the most respected of the 19th century leaders in the western Great Lakes region. Chief Buffalo, who considered Ben Armstrong his adopted son, was steadfast and proud. Unlike leaders of most other bands, he advocated peaceful coexistence with the Sioux and other Indian Nations as well as with the whites. Yet, as Armstrong's words reveal, when Buffalo's people were threatened by Sioux warriors, he responded with the skills and leadership of a great military general. And when faced with treaty violations and abusive government policies that could result in disease and starvation for his people, Great Buffalo chose to face war with the United States rather than risk their certain death. Although it seemed inevitable, Benjamin Armstrong prevented that war by making a bold, eleventh-hour effort to help the chiefs of the Great Lakes bands persuade Washington officials to adhere to the promises they made to the Ojibwe.

That decision and Armstrong's council to the Natives of northern Wisconsin not only saved innumerable lives, but also resulted in a new agreement, the Treaty of 1854. It includes language that continues to protect Native American entitlements. In fact, today's tribal right to hunt, fish, and gather wild rice on land they once ceded to the United States government and the right to live in their homelands can be traced directly to Benjamin Armstrong's efforts on behalf of the Great Lakes Ojibwe people.

Today, few people know of the "Ojibwe Trail of Tears," also called the "Wisconsin Death March." It began with the treaties of 1837 and 1842 and the U.S. Commissioner of Indian Affairs offering allotments of food, supplies, and money to the Ojibwe people in trade for timber and mineral rights on millions of acres in Wisconsin, Upper Michigan, and Minnesota. In a surreptitious 1849 attempt to relocate the five Great Lakes bands of Ojibwe, the Commissioner announced they'd have to travel hundreds of miles west to Sandy Lake, Minnesota, to collect their promised allotments. Three thousand Ojibwe arrived there in October to find no food, supplies, or payments waiting. By early winter, hundreds of men, women, and children had perished from starvation and disease. The others returned home on foot, with more dying along the way. Chief Buffalo vowed to fight and die in their homelands rather than starve in the government's death camps.

In desperation for his friends and hoping to avoid war, Benjamin Armstrong urged Great Buffalo to join him on a journey to the nation's capital. Respecting the knowledge and intuition of his adopted son, the chief agreed. Buffalo, Armstrong, Chief O-sho-ga and three Ojibwe dignitaries left by canoe the following summer, hoping to persuade President Millard Fillmore to honor the treaties and avoid an uprising and many more deaths. Government agents and officials repeatedly told them to turn back. Yet, they persevered. By the time they reached New York City, they had but one dime left. Armstrong was able to raise the money needed to complete the journey by presenting themselves to curious, high society New Yorkers.

Against all odds, they succeeded in meeting with President Fillmore in Washington. Appalled at how the Indian Affairs Commission had treated the Great Lakes Ojibwe, Fillmore pledged to honor the treaties and create one more— an agreement giving them permanent right to remain in their homelands and receive their promised allotments in La Pointe on Madeline Island. The party of seven returned by train to La Crosse, Wisconsin, then canoed the rivers north to their homes.

In appreciation for Benjamin Armstrong's efforts to help them, the chiefs of the five Lake Superior tribes insisted the new treaty award him one square mile of land for a new home. That land encompassed an area now known as the City of Duluth and included the harbor and Minnesota Point, later renamed Park Point.

But Benjamin Armstrong's memoir is more than an account of his defense of the Ojibwe. His story encompasses more than six decades of life as a woodsman and trader working in northwestern Wisconsin, Upper Michigan, and northern Minnesota during a time when the pelts of beaver, mink, otter, and other furbearers represented the greatest economic export of a developing nation. It was also a time when the fur trade declined and industrialists' interests shifted to timber, minerals, and the abundant lands controlled by Native Americans.

In his own words, Benjamin Armstrong gives us a first-hand account of the Ojibwe people's plight. He also offers a detailed depiction of 19th century life in the western Great Lakes states when hardworking European settlers and American businessmen descended on the north, cultures clashing and life changing forever.

~~~

The Trail to Native American Discontent
James Brakken

The following historical background is intended to help readers better understand attitudes, actions, and conflicts between Native Americans and European descendants settling in the Midwest during the 19th century.

Early conflict

Indian nations in the upper Midwest fought over hunting territories for hundreds of years before the incursion of white trappers and traders in the 17th and 18th centuries. The Sioux and Ojibwe met on many Wisconsin and Minnesota battlefields. Pride and concern for survival of their people fueled the wars, as did the desire for revenge for a fallen brave's life. As European immigrants moved westward, Native American resistance to white settlers, although rarer than portrayed in popular media, did exist.

The French and Indian War and the War of 1812

Greatly outnumbered by the British during the French and Indian War (1754 - 1763), France recruited and armed eastern Native warriors. Although a significant factor in the fighting, Native support was not enough to assure France of victory. England prevailed and French territories extending beyond the Great Lakes came under British rule. The ensuing treaty ceded the French territories known as New France to England. This gave the British ownership of lands stretching far west of Lake Superior.

Six decades later, British military leaders feared too many Americans moving westward would result in the eventual loss of Britain's lands. As the French had done earlier, they armed and supported those Native American tribes willing to attack

American settlers. With the aid of Native warriors, the British hoped to create a buffer territory too dangerous for Americans to inhabit. Although there were other factors, this was one cause of the War of 1812. But, when the British were defeated on both land and sea, the British sued for peace. Their plan for an Indian-held barrier state in the American Northwest Territory (the area from Ohio to Wisconsin) failed to survive during the resulting peace negotiations. After the 1814 signing of the Treaty of Ghent, British rule of the Northwest Territory (formerly New France) was transferred to the Americans. British military recruitment and support of Native American warriors ceased. No longer threatened by attack, settlers soon moved beyond Ohio and into southern Wisconsin and northern Illinois to mine the lead deposits found there. Other settlers sought out land to farm.

The Winnebago War

Following the War of 1812, the Winnebago (Ho-Chunk) people objected to the influx of so many American settlers. Several young braves, including Red Bird and Little Buffalo, fostered this discontent, recruiting a small band of warriors who then harassed the settlers. Most of these incidents posed little threat and went unnoticed by the government. Then, in 1826, Red Bird and his fellow warriors attacked and killed a French trader, Pierre Methode, his Potawatomi wife, and their children near Prairie du Chien, Wisconsin. Their scalps, including one from a three-year-old child, were used by Red Bird to encourage other Winnebagos to fight for their lands. The 1826 murders of the Methode family caused many settlers to leave the lead mining region of southern Wisconsin and northern Illinois (then part of Michigan and Missouri Territories) for safety. The ensuing, brief struggle became known as the Winnebago War.

The government responded to Red Bird's aggression with

700 mounted militia soldiers and 800 U.S. Army Regulars who converged on southern Wisconsin to quell the small uprising. They were accompanied by 50 mixed-blood militiamen and 120 Menominee warriors who supported the government cause. Outnumbered, most Winnebagos refused to support Red Bird. In 1827, Chief Decorah delivered both Red Bird and Little Buffalo to the Army, along with four other dissidents.

This may have ended the strife, had not other hostile Winnebago warriors spread word that these six surrendered warriors had been handed over to their enemies, the Sioux, for execution. Though this rumor was untrue, it resulted in a second Winnebago assault on white settlers and another quick response from the Army, finally quelling the aggression.

Red Bird died in prison awaiting trial. The others were tried and found guilty. Hanging was the mandatory punishment. Fearing this would set off more Indian hostility, President John Quincy Adams stayed their sentences.

Though the Winnebago War amounted to little more than a few attacks on settlers and quick response from the Army, it changed U.S. policy. President Adams, who had previously encouraged peaceful assimilation of all Native Americans into society, changed his mind and his method. In his final State of the Union Address, Adams declared Native Americans could not be civilized. To accommodate settlement of the United States, he urged they be taken from their homelands and placed on reservations, a policy later termed as Indian Removal. His successor, Andrew Jackson, agreed, beginning decades of maltreatment of Native Americans by the government and inevitable discontent among the tribes.

The Black Hawk War

Although treaties between Native Americans and the United States allowed only minerals to be mined and trees to be harvested on tribal lands, the conditions of the treaties were often violated by government officials and ignored by the settlers. Subsidies guaranteed to tribal members by the treaties were not always delivered or were deficient in quality and quantity. Indian agents and their trader friends often benefitted more than the intended Native recipients. As more and more settlers poured into the lead mining region, they crowded the indigenous people away from lands that once provided game and grain. Starvation and illness soon plagued many of the tribes.

To compound matters, when establishing the treaties, representatives of the United States were frequently misunderstood by the Natives. Interpreters skilled in speaking often could not read or write. The resulting treaties rarely said what the Native people thought they did. In many cases, elders who signed documents for mineral and timber rights later learned they had agreed to leave the land forever. Bitterness and mistrust of the government grew.

In 1831, after rejecting advice from the Army to move from southern Illinois to lands west of the Mississippi, Black Hawk (Ma-ka-tai-me-she-kia-kiak), Chief of the Sauk Nation, rallied six hundred of his people to resist. His band consisted of 200 young, able-bodied men and 400 elders, women, and children. Chief Blackhawk wrongly thought he would have support from the British far to the north in Canada. Because he made this claim to the settlers, the Army labeled his small force the "British Band." The presence of so many women, children, and elderly among Black Hawk's followers clearly indicates they were not a serious threat to settlers or soldiers. Rather, they had gathered more in protest than as an act of hostility. Nevertheless, the U.S. Army regarded this as an act of war.

The War Department assigned General Henry Atkinson to quell what they now regarded as an Indian uprising. His soldiers forced Black Hawk's band to move from their homes to land west of the Mississippi. But Blackhawk and his people soon returned, hoping to settle near what is today Rockford, Illinois. The soldiers then pushed them north and their skirmishes resulted in several deaths on both sides. Atkinson stepped up the effort to end what he perceived to be a threat to all Wisconsin settlers, especially those who now mined southwest Wisconsin lead, an important military commodity.

Frustrated by the Army's persistence to force them westward, and seeking revenge for the earlier deaths of their brothers, a handful of renegade warriors attacked settlers in northern Illinois and southern Wisconsin. This resulted in another 2,100 militia volunteering to fight Black Hawk.

On May 18, 1832, a group of Atkinson's men encountered Black Hawk's band near what is now Stillman, Illinois. Carrying a white flag, three of Black Hawk's men approached, presumably to talk. The three were taken prisoner by the soldiers who then fired upon the other Sauks. Until this time, Chief Black Hawk had not been committed to war. Now, with his men captured while under a flag of truce, he sought revenge. That evening, Black Hawk and his warriors attacked, killing twelve militiamen and forcing the rest to retreat. This routing of General Atkinson's soldiers convinced President Andrew Jackson and his Secretary of War, Lewis Cass, to quickly crush the British Band. Jackson gave the order to make an example of Chief Black Hawk, believing this would eliminate any future threat of uprising from other tribes.

Unaware of the War Department's new plans, Black Hawk remained in southern Wisconsin. Factions of his British Band attacked settlers, killing, scalping, and mutilating them. By June, General Atkinson had amassed a force he termed the "Army of the Frontier," consisting of 629 army regulars and 3,196 mounted militia. His officers included a young Abraham Lincoln and the son of Alexander Hamilton.

A number of skirmishes followed and on June 20, about 100 Sauk warriors attacked the fort at Blue Mounds, Wisconsin, killing five soldiers. On June 25, another skirmish left nine of his people and five soldiers dead. Short on food and supplies, Black Hawk led his people northward. Now fewer than 600 in number, they sought a safe place to encamp.

On July 21, the militia surprised Black Hawk at the present site of Sauk Prairie, Wisconsin. In the Battle of Wisconsin Heights, the British Band lost nearly 70 warriors, the Army only one. The battle, however, was regarded as a success for Black Hawk because it gave most of his other followers time to escape.

Knowing he was outnumbered by trained, well-equipped soldiers, Chief Black Hawk sent a message to General Atkinson, explaining that the British Band would cease fighting and again cross the Mississippi River as earlier directed. After instructing his people to prepare for the crossing, Black Hawk and several others went on ahead. General Atkinson ignored the message and had the messenger arrested.

On August 1, 1832, Atkinson ordered a gunboat, the *Warrior*, up the Mississippi to its confluence with the Bad Axe River where the British Band prepared to cross into Minnesota. The fleeing Sauks now numbered about 140 warriors and 360 women, children, and elderly. Although Black Hawk's people waved a white flag of truce, soldiers on the gunboat opened fire with cannon and muskets.

General Atkinson lost fourteen men in the Battle of the Bad Axe. However, his soldiers slaughtered 260 men, women, and children. Of those, most drowned after being shot while swimming or rafting across the river in a desperate attempt to reach safety. Atkinson's soldiers showed no mercy, scalping many of the dead and turning the battle into a bloody massacre. Around 70 Sauk survivors reached the Minnesota side of the Mississippi River, only to be hunted down and killed by Sioux and Ho-chunk warriors siding with the government.

The Black Hawk War resulted in the deaths of 77 white

settlers and soldiers and over 500 Natives.

Chief Black Hawk surrendered to the Indian Agent at Prairie du Chien on August 27, 1832, along with several other Sauk leaders. Most were released. Chief Black Hawk and two others were taken to Washington on the orders of President Jackson who met with them before sending them to the prison at Fort Monroe, West Virginia. There they were treated with respect, visited by dignitaries and military leaders, and even posed for portraits by several artists.

Their term of "punishment" lasted only two weeks. Afterward, to convince them of the futility of resisting white settlement of the upper Midwest, they were shown the nature and extent of European development in the eastern states. Black Hawk and the others were escorted to Baltimore, Philadelphia, and New York City where they met more dignitaries, saw plays, attended social functions, and toured a Navy warship and several factories.

Although future years would see some discontent among Native Americans in the Western Great Lakes States, the Black Hawk War marked the end of armed resistance east of the Mississippi River, ushering in white settlement of Wisconsin and neighboring states.

~~~

The 1990s "Walleye War"
James A. Brakken

In the 1842 La Pointe treaty negotiations between the USA and the Lake Superior Ojibwe bands, the government recognized the Ojibwes' right to the lands earlier claimed by France and England. U.S. leaders desired to promote the harvest of timber and extraction of minerals, knowing this was important to the settlement of the Midwest. The government sent negotiators who offered supplies, money, and assistance from blacksmiths, teachers, and doctors in trade for timber and mineral rights. A key component of the agreement was the Ojibwes' right to forever hunt, fish, and gather food and other bounty from the land. Satisfied with the terms of the treaties, the Ojibwe ceded their lands to the government in the trade. The Treaty of 1854, also signed in La Pointe, established land reservations for the northern Wisconsin bands, thus ensuring their permanent future residency.

In 1908, the State of Wisconsin claimed it had the right to suspend the treaty rights in the interest of managing fish and game. The federal courts maintained the Ojibwe had legal right to hunt and fish on federal lands, but the courts did not address hunting and fishing on private or state-owned lands.

In 1974, Fred and Mike Tribble of the Lac Courte Oreilles band used spears to harvest fish through the ice on an off-reservation lake in Sawyer County. Although the treaty gave them the right to take fish on this public water, both were cited for poaching. The tribe filed suit. A U.S. District Court decision upheld the tribal right to hunt and fish throughout its former territories. The State appealed without success. Wisconsin's Attorney General then appealed to the U.S. Supreme Court who let the lower court's decision stand.

On August 21, 1987, after detailed scientific testimony, U.S. District Court Judge Barbara Crabb approved a natural resource code adopted by the six Ojibwe tribal governments. This allowed final federal approval permitting tribal members to harvest walleye and other fish on public waters off reservation.

Many non-natives mistakenly believed the courts had granted all new spearfishing rights to the tribes. Actually, the right of Ojibwe tribal members to hunt, fish, and gather *always* existed, even though it had not been exercised for decades.

The following spring at Butternut Lake in Price County, tribal fishermen prepared to fish. For centuries, their ancestors had attached torches to the bows of their canoes to attract and spear fish. Now they used flashlights, steel spears, and aluminum boats. White protesters tried to block the landing. Racial slurs, obscenities, and threats were followed by rocks and beer bottles thrown by the protesters. Local police refused to intercede. The standoff continued until a team of officers was called in from Superior, 100 miles away. Under threat of arrest, the crowd reluctantly allowed the fishermen to proceed.

During the next few weeks, the six tribal bands of the Lake Superior Ojibwe practiced their spearfishing. Protests across northern Wisconsin increased. Two protest groups were formed: Protect America's Rights and Resources and Stop Treaty Rights Abuse. The latter organized some of the largest and most violent boat landing protests. They argued spearfishing threatened their livelihoods and walleye population declines would hurt northern Wisconsin tourism. In reality, licensed anglers took a far greater percentage of walleye than the tribal fishermen, yet the fish population still remains stable due to increases in fish stocking by both the DNR and the tribal fish hatcheries.

Spring spearfishing protests continued during the following years. In 1991, Judge Crabb issued an injunction against those engaged in violent behavior on or near lakes where the Ojibwe speared. The DNR and the tribes then worked together to establish sustainable quotas of walleyes for larger lakes in the ceded territory and the tribes agreed to not spear on small lakes deemed susceptible to overharvest. When they learned that spearing their quotas on some lakes would cause those lakes to be closed to non-native anglers, the tribal governments agreed to not spear or take their quota on those lakes.

In his 1996 run for governor, Tommy Thompson tried again to abrogate the 19th century treaty rights but failed. The Wisconsin Legislature later passed a law protecting all hunters and anglers against harassment. They also directed all public schools to incorporate Native American history and culture in their curricula. It includes information about the tribe's permanent right to hunt, fish, and gather, rights reserved in 1837, 1842 and 1854 when Natives traded away hundreds of thousands of acres of land to the government.

Although some state-licensed anglers still have hard feelings about the treaty rights, protests are now rare. Sport fishing groups that once opposed exercise of tribal treaty rights have since joined with the tribes to protect the northern Wisconsin fishery from mining industry attempts to alter the landscape, including lakes, streams, and watersheds. Fred and Mike Tribble are revered for their courage to stand up for their rights and The Lake Superior Ojibwe bands continue to work with the State of Wisconsin to reduce tensions and manage fish populations in northern Wisconsin.

~~~

Regarding Use of the Term Indian
James A. Brakken

In his memoir, Benjamin Armstrong often uses the term Indian.

History tells us when Christopher Columbus landed in 1492, he thought he'd discovered India so he called the people he met "Indians." Ever since, Europeans have referred to the people indigenous to most of the western hemisphere as Indians, although many of them prefer to be regarded as Anishinabe which translates into "first people."

In the mid-1960s, some Anishinabe objected to the term Indian because their ancestors were not from India. In the interest of political correctness, the mainstream news media began using another term—Native American, or Native. The obvious problem is that anyone who is born and raised in a place is native to that place, regardless of ethnic origin. If born in the U.S., you are "native" to America. Capitalizing aside, the term Native or Native American remains as objectionable to some Anishinabe as the word Indian is to others.

To complicate matters, we have been misled by historians. India did not exist when Columbus landed. Hindustan did. Yet, Columbus did not call his new acquaintances Hindu or Hindustanis. Some historians believe he referred to them—in Spanish—as "people in God," or "people *en Dios.*" They claim as the Spanish moved across the continents, this transformed into "indios" then "Indians."

Although it would be convenient to find a single, best word for descendants of the Original People native to the western hemisphere when Europeans arrived, it may be better to allow each individual to choose. After all, isn't the New World known for encouraging individuality? And those who prefer Indian should use the expression with pride, for this is the term used with honor by Great Buffalo and his fellow chiefs of the Ojibwe bands, as well as Benjamin Armstrong, Buffalo's adopted son. It would be wrong to dishonor them by saying they were wrong in their choice to use the term Indians, just as it is wrong to dishonor those wishing to be called Natives, Native Americans, or Anishinabe. Let the Original People be original—with pride.

~~~

On the Accuracy of the Armstrong Memoir
James A. Brakken

At the age of 71, due to his failing eyesight, Benjamin Armstrong dictated the following account of his life to a friend, Thomas Wentworth. Both lived and worked in the Lake Superior port city of Ashland, Wisconsin, during a time when that city thrived due to the white pine timber harvest, mining, and the shipping trade. The Armstrong manuscript was delivered to Arthur. W. Bowran, an Ashland printer who set the type and printed a hardcover edition.

In his preface, Armstrong apologizes for not being certain of some dates and places. In fact, a number of his recollections occur at the wrong time or place. Like many "as told to" memoirs, Armstrong's story tends to ramble. During the course of the work, he recalls people and places earlier overlooked, causing his memoir to jump back and forth in time. Problems are compounded with Wentworth's apparent "subconscious editing" of the text and Bowron's less-than-perfect typesetting. Today, these qualities, along with the memoir being written in a late-19th century vernacular, add to the flavor and charm of the book. They also offer a unique north country authenticity to the author's life story.

~~~

Other Notes

The Marr and Richards Engraving Company of Milwaukee, Wisconsin, provided the illustrations for Armstrong's book. John Marr and George Richards were partners and created thousands of etchings and wood engravings for publications in the late 19th century. Rather than sign their own names, they chose to sign their works with the company name. The images for this memoir, some based on photographs and others on imagination, were etched into copper plates before being shipped to Arthur Bowron, the Ashland printer.

This is the only annotated version of the complete Armstrong manuscript in print today. It assures his memoir will never be lost to time. In addition to being a fascinating view of 19th century Native American life in the western Great Lakes wilderness, his story offers narratives about those who lived there, including the author, Benjamin Green Armstrong, a true friend of the Ojibwe people.

Other than James Brakken's notes on Armstrong's words, the only changes made in this 2016 version of the original book are a few spelling corrections, several punctuation modifications, and elimination of some mistakes made in A. W. Bowron's typesetting. Therefore, any errors you discover in Armstrong's story are from the original 1892 text.

The following is Benjamin Armstrong's memoir as dictated in his own words and style to Thomas Wentworth of Ashland, Wisconsin, in 1891. James Brakken's notes and commentary appear in italics. They clarify some of Armstrong's statements, offer background information, and provide insight into how the treaties affect life in northern Wisconsin today.

Benjamin G. Armstrong

Thomas P. Wentworth

EARLY LIFE AMONG THE INDIANS

·

REMINISCENCES

FROM THE LIFE OF

BENJ. G. ARMSTRONG

TREATIES

OF

1835, 1837, 1842

AND

1854.

Habits and Customs of the Red Men
of the Forest

Incidents, Biographical Sketches,

Battles, &c.

DICTATED TO AND WRITTEN BY

THOS. P. WENTWORTH

ASHLAND, WISCONSIN

1892

PRESS OF A. W. BOWRON,
ASHLAND, WISCONSIN

Contents

PREFACE

This undertaking I begin, not without misgivings about my ability to finish a well-connected history of my recollections. I kept no dates at any time, and must rely wholly upon my memory at seventy-one years of age.

Those of my white associates in the early days, who are still living, are not within reach to assist me by rehearsals of former times.

Those of the older Indians who could assist me, could I converse with them, have passed beyond the Great River, and the younger ones, of whom there are many not far distant, could not assist me in the most essential portions of the work.

Therefore, without assistance and assuring the reader that the dates will be essentially correct, and that a strict adherence to fact will be followed, and with the hope that a generous public will make due allowance for the lapse of years, I am,

Your obedient servant,

THE AUTHOR

Early Indian History

Chapter I

———— • ————

The First Treaty – The Removal Order – Treaties of 1837 and 1842
- A Trip to Washington - In New York City with Only One Dime –
At the Brokers Residence

My earliest recollections in the northern Wisconsin and
Minnesota territories dates back to 1835, at which time General
Cass and others on the part of the Government, with different tribes
of Indians, the Potawatomies, Winnebagos, Chippewas, Sac &
Foxes and the Sioux; at Prairie du Chien, met in open council, to
define and agree upon boundary lines between the Sac and Foxes
and the Chippewas. The boundary or division of territory as agreed
upon and established by this council was the Mississippi River
from Prairie du Chien north to the mouth of the Crow Wing River,
thence to its source. The Sac and Foxes and the Sioux were
recognized to be the owners of all territory lying west of the
Mississippi and south of the Crow Wing River. The Chippewa*, by
this treaty, were recognized as the owners of all lands east of the
Mississippi in the territories of Minnesota and Wisconsin, and north
of the Mississippi to the British Possessions, also Lake Superior
Country on both sides of the lake to Sault Ste. Marie and beyond.
The other tribes mentioned in this council had no interest in the
above divided territory from the fact that their possessions were
east and south of the Chippewas' Country, and over their title there
was no dispute. The division lines were agreed to as described and
a treaty signed; when all shook hands and covenanted with each
other to live and peace for all time to come.**

Chippewa, Chippeway, Ojibwe, and Ojibwa are all variations of the same term and are often mispronounced with a short a in the final syllable. The accurate pronunciation is "CHIP-e-way" or "o JIB-way."

Today, Chippewa, with a short a, is a common and acceptable mispronunciation of the original term, Chippeway. Most who visit the Chippewa Flowage or Chippewa River, or live in Chippewa Falls, the city found in Chippewa County, might disagree.

**Lewis Cass, Michigan Territorial Governor, and the Governor of Missouri Territory, William Clark, called for a council of the tribes at Prairie du Chien, Wisconsin in 1825, not 1835. The primary purpose of the conference was to end the centuries-old war between the Sioux and the Ojibwe and establish a boundary line between their lands. Armstrong was five years old then. Thus, the memory he relates here is probably that of another council held ten years later. It is unlikely either Governor Cass or Governor Clark attended in 1835.*

In 1837 the Government entered into a treaty with the Chippewas of the Mississippi and the St. Croix Rivers at St. Peter, Minnesota, Col Snelling, of the army, and Maj. Walker, of Missouri, being the commissioners on the part of the Government, and it appears that at the commencement of this council the anxiety on the part of the commissioners to perfect a treaty was so great that statements were made by them favorable to the Indians, and understood perfectly by them, that were not afterwards incorporated by the treaty. The Indians were told by these commissioners that the great father had sent them to buy their pine timber and their minerals that were hidden in the earth, and that the great father was very anxious to dig the mineral, for of such material he made guns and knives for the Indians, and copper kettles in which to boil their sugar sap. "Timber you make but little use of, it is the pine your great white father wants to build many steamboats, to bring your goods to you and to take you to Washington bye-and-bye to see your Great Father and meet him face to face. He does not want your lands; it is too cold up here for farming. He just wants enough of it to build little towns where soldiers stop, mining camps for miners, sawmill sites and logging camps. The timber that is best for you the Great Father does not care about. The maple tree that you make your sugar from, the birch tree that you get bark from for your canoes and from which you make your sugar pails for you sugar sap, the cedar from which you get material for making canoes, oars and paddles, your great father cares nothing for. It is the pine and minerals that he wants and he has sent us here to make a bargain with you for it," the commissioners said. And further, the Indians were told and distinctly understood that they were not to be disturbed in their possession of their lands so long as their men behaved themselves. They were also told that the Chippewas had always been good Indians and the Great Father thought very much of them on that account, and with these promises fairly and distinctly understood they signed the treaty that ceded to the government all their territory lying east of the Mississippi, embracing the St. Croix district and east to the Chippewa River, but to my knowledge the Indians never knew that they had cede their lands until 1849, when they were asked to remove there from.

In 1842 Robert Steward, on the part of the government, perfected a treaty at La Pointe, on Lake Superior, in which the Chippewas of the St. Croix and Superior country ceded all that portion of their territory, from the boundary of the former treaty of 1837, which the Chippewas of the Mississippi and St. Croix Indians, east and along the south shore of the lake to the Chocolate River, Michigan, territory. No conversation that was had at this time gave the Indians an inkling or caused them to mistrust that they were ceding away their lands, but supposed they were simply

3

selling the pine and minerals, as they had in the treaty of 1837, and when they were told, in 1849, to move on and thereby abandon their burying grounds – the dearest thing to an Indian known – they began to hold councils and to ask each as to how they had understood the treaties, and all understood them the same, that was: That they were never to be disturbed if they behaved themselves. Messengers were sent out to all of the different bands in every part of their country to get the understanding of all the people, and to inquire if any depredation had been committed by any of their young men, or what could be the reason for such a sudden order to move. This was kept up for a year but no reason could be assigned by the Indians for the removal order.*

The Treaty of 1842 made at La Pointe stipulated that the Indians should receive their annuities at La Pointe of a period of twenty-five years. Now by reason of a non-compliance with the order to move away, the annuity payment at La Pointe had been stopped and a new agency at Sandy Lake, near the Mississippi River, and their annuities taken there, and the Indians told to go there for them, and to bring along their women and children, to remain there, and all that did not would be deprived of their pay and annuities.

*Rich copper deposits found in the Keweenaw Peninsula caused mining interests to pressure the government into seeking mineral rights on Native lands. A new treaty provided the mineral rights and also allowed for the removal of Natives from their lands "at the pleasure of the president." President Zachary Taylor ordered the removal of all Native people from the ceded territory to lands west of the Mississippi River. To prompt this move, the Ojibwes' allotments would be given to them at Sandy Lake, 155 miles to the west of La Pointe, the previously agreed distribution place. Thus began the atrocity known as the Wisconsin Trail of Tears.

In the fall of 1851 and after all the messengers had returned that had been sent out to inquire after the cause of the removal orders, the chiefs gathered in council, and after the subject and thoroughly canvassed, agreed that representatives from all parts of the country should be sent to the new agency and see what the results of such a visit would be. A delegation was made up, consisting of about 500 men in all. They reached the new agency about September 10th of that year. The agent there informed them that rations should be furnished to them until such time as he could get the goods and money from St. Paul.

Some time in the latter part of the month we were surprised to hear that the new agency had burned down, and as the word came to us, "had taken the goods and money into the ashes." The agent immediately started down the river and we saw no more of him for some time. Crowds of Indians and a few white men soon gathered around the burnt remains of the agency and waited until it should cool down, when a thorough search was made in the ashes for melted coins that must be there if the story was true that goods and money had gone down together. They scraped and scratched in vain. All that was ever found in that ruin in the shape of metal was two fifty-cent silver pieces. The Indians, having no chance to talk with the agent, could find nothing, which they wished to know. They camped around the commissary department and were fed on the very worst class of sour, musty pork heads, jaws, shoulders and shanks, rotten corned beef and the poorest quality of flour that could possibly be milled. In the course of the next month no fewer than 150 Indians had died from the use of these rotten provisions, and the remainder resolved to stay no longer, and started back for La Pointe.

At Fond du Lac, Minnesota, some of the employees of the American Fur Company urged the Indians to halt there and wait for the agent to come and finally showed them a message from the agent requesting them to stop at Fond du Lac, and stated that he had procured money and goods and would pay them off at that

5

point, which he did during winter of 1851. About 500 Indians gathered there and were paid, each receiving 4 dollars in money and a very small goods annuity. Before preparing to leave for home the Indians wanted to know of the agent, John S. Waters*, what he was going to do with the remainder of the money and goods. He answered that he was going to keep it and those who should come there for it would get their share and those that did not would get nothing. The Indians were now thoroughly disgusted and discouraged, and piling their little bundles of annuity goods into two piles agreed with each other that a game of lacrosse should be played on the ice for the whole stock. The Lake Superior Indians were to choose twenty men from among them and the Interior Indians the same number. The game was played, lasting three days and resulting in a victory for the Interior Indians. During all this time councils were being held and dissatisfaction was showing itself on every hand. Threats were freely indulged in by the younger and more resolute members of the band, who thought while they tamely submitted to outrage their case would never grow better. But the older and more considerate ones could not see the case as they did, but all plainly saw that there was no way of redress at the present and they were compelled to put up with just such treatment as the agent saw fit to inflict on them. They now all realized that they had been induced to sign treaties that they did not understand, and had been imposed upon. They saw that when the annuities were brought and they were asked to touch the pen, they had only received what the agent had seen fit to give them, and certainly not what was their dues. They had lost 150 warriors on this one trip alone by being fed on unwholesome provisions, and they reasoned among themselves: Is this what our Great Father intended? If so we may as well go to our old home and there be slaughtered where we can be buried by the side of our relatives and friends.

6

J. S. Watrous, Indian Affairs Agent, had a widespread reputation for taking advantage of his position and even accused by a St. Paul judge of gambling with and distributing spirits to the Indians as well as cohabiting with their women. Watrous also partnered with his trader friends to exploit the Ojibwe people. Although his greed and unforgivable lack of concern for Indians was deplorable, Watrous was not alone—many Indian agents displayed similar behavior.

Representing the Chiefs of the Great Lakes tribes, Chief Great Buffalo formally accused Indian Affairs Agent, J. S. Watrous, of the grave neglect at Sandy Lake that killed many of their people. In Buffalo's eyes as well as the other chiefs', Watrous was the government official primarily responsible for their removal to Sandy Lake. They claimed he knew full-well that the allotments would never arrive and the long journey would be disastrous. The five tribal chiefs felt it was his doing that they were denied their money and supplies, fed spoiled food, and deprived of reasonable shelter—all resulting in the illness and death of hundreds of their people. However, the root of the removal of the Ojibwe and the appalling, outrageous treatment they received at Sandy Lake originated not in Wisconsin, but in the highest government offices in Washington, DC.

These talks were kept up after they had returned to La Pointe. I attended many of them and being familiar with the language, I saw that great trouble was brewing and if something was not quickly done trouble of a serious nature would soon follow. At last I told them if they would stop where they were I would take a party of chiefs to Washington, where they could meet the Great Father and tell their troubles to his face. Chief Buffalo and other leading chieftains of the country at once agreed to the plan, and early in the spring a party of six men were selected, and April 15, 1852, was appointed as the day to start. Chiefs Buffalo* and O-sho-ga with four braves and myself made up the party.

*Chief Great Buffalo was also known as Kechwaishke, Beshkike, and Le Boef.

Washington Delegation, June 22, 1852*

On the day of starting and before noon, there were gathered at the beach at old La Pointe, Indians by the score to witness the departure. We left in a new birch bark canoe, which was made for the occasion and called a four-fathom boat, twenty-four feet long with six paddles. The four braves did most of the paddling, assisted at times by O-sho-ga and sometimes by Buffalo. I sat at the stern and directed the course of the craft. We made the mouth of the Montreal River, the dividing line between Wisconsin and Michigan, the first night, where we went ashore and camped without covering, except our blankets. We carried a small amount of provisions with us, some crackers, sugar and coffee, and depended on game and fish for meat. The next night, having followed along the beach all day, we encamped at Iron River.

*Benjamin Armstrong is easily identified in the above engraving and the one on page 45. Unfortunately, historians cannot agree on which figure is Chief Buffalo.

No incidents of importance happened and on the third day out from La Pointe. At 10 am we landed our bark at Ontonagon where we spent two days in circulating a petition I had prepared asking that the Indians might be left and remain in their own country and the order for their removal be reconsidered. I did not find a single man who refused to sign it which showed the feeling of the people nearest the Indians upon the subject. From Ontonagon we went to Portage Lake Houghton and Hancock and visited the various copper mines and all there signed the petition. Among the signers I would occasionally meet a man who claimed personal acquaintance with the President and said the President would recognize the signature when he saw it which I found to be so on presenting the petition to President Fillmore. Among them was Thomas Hanna a merchant at Ontonagon, Capt. Roberts of the Minnesota mine, and Douglas of the firm of Douglas & Sheldon, Portage Lake.

Met on the Trip to Washington

Along the coast from Portage Lake we encountered a number of severe storms which caused us to go ashore and we thereby lost considerable time. Stopping at Marquette I also circulated the petition and procured a great many signatures. Leaving there, nothing was to be seen except the rocky coast until we reached Sault Ste Marie where we arrived in the afternoon and remained all the next day getting my petition signed by all who were disposed. Among others who signed it was a Mr Brown who was then editing a paper there. He also claimed personal acquaintance with the President and gave me two or three letters of introduction to parties in New York City and requested me to call on them when I reached the city saying they would be much pleased to see the Indian chieftains from this country and that they would assist me in case I needed assistance which I found to be true.

The second day at the Soo the officers from the fort came to me with the intelligence that no delegation of Indians would be allowed to go to Washington without first getting permission from the government to do so as they had orders to stop and turn back all delegations of Indians that should attempt to come this way en route to Washington. This was to me a stunner. In what a predicament I found myself. To give up this trip would be to abandon the last hope of keeping that turbulent spirit of the young warriors within bounds. Now they were peaceably inclined and would remain so until our mission should decide their course. They were now living on the hope that our efforts would obtain for them the righting of a grievous wrong but to return without anything accomplished and with the information that the great father's officers had turned us back would be to rekindle the fire that was smoldering into an open revolt for revenge. I talked with the officers patiently and long and explained the situation of affairs in the Indian country and certainly it was no pleasant task for me to undertake without pay or hope of reward to take this delegation through and that I should never have attempted it if I had not considered it necessary to secure the safety of the white settlers in that country and that although I would not resist an officer or disobey an order of the government, I should go as far as I could with my Indians and until I was stopped by an officer, then I would simply say to the Indians, "I am prevented from going further. I have done all I can. I will send you as near home as I can get conveyances for you, but for the present I shall remain away from that country" The officers at the Soo finally told me to go on but they said you will certainly be stopped at some place probably at Detroit. The Indian agent there and the marshal will certainly oppose your going further. But I was determined to try and as soon as I could get a boat for Detroit we started. It was the steamer *Northerner* and when we landed in Detroit, sure enough we were met by the Indian Agent and told that we could go no further, at any rate until the next day, or until he could talk with me at his office. He then sent us to a hotel, saying he would see that our bill was paid until that next day. About 7:30 that evening I was called to his office and had a little talk with him and the Marshal. I stated to them the facts as they existed in the northwest, and our object in going to Washington, and if we were turned back I would not consider that a white man's life would be safe in the Indian Country, under the present state of excitement; that our returning without seeing the President would start a fire that would not soon be quenched. They finally consented to my passing as they hardly thought they could afford to arrest me, considering the petitions I had and the circumstances I had related. "But," they also added, "we do not think you will ever reach Washington with your delegation."

I thanked them for allowing us to proceed and the next morning sailed for Buffalo, where we made close connections with the first railroad cars any of us had ever seen and proceeded to Albany, at which place we took the steamer *Mayflower*, I think. At any rate the boat we took was burned the same season and was commanded by Captain St. John.

We landed in New York City without mishap and I had just only one ten-cent silver piece of money left. By giving the bus driver some of the Indian trinkets I persuaded him to haul the party and baggage to the American House, which then stood a block or so from Barnum's Theatre. Here I told the landlord of my financial embarrassment and that we must stay overnight at any rate and in some way the necessary money to pay the bill should be raised. I found this landlord a prince of good fellows and was always glad that I met him. I told him of the letters I had to parties in the city and should I fail in getting assistance from them I should exhibit my fellows and in this way raise the necessary funds to pay my bill and carry us to our destination. He thought the scheme a good one, and that himself and me were just the ones to carry it out. Immediately after supper I started out in search of the parties to whom I had letters of introduction, and with the landlord's help in giving me directions, I soon found one of them, a stock broker, whose name I cannot remember, or the street on which he lived. He returned with me to the hotel, and after looking the Indians over, he said, "You are all right. Stay where you are and I will see that you have money to carry you through." The next day I put the Indians on exhibition at the hotel, and a great many people came to see them, most of whom contributed freely to the fund to carry us to our destination. On the second evening of the exhibition this stockbroker came with his wife to the show, and upon taking his leave, invited me to bring my delegation to his house the next afternoon, where a number of ladies of their acquaintance could see them without the embarrassment they would feel at the show room. To this I assented, and the landlord being present, said he would assist in furnishing the conveyance. But when the bus was brought up in front of the house for the purpose of taking the Indians aboard, the crowd became so dense that it was found impossible to get them in it, and it was with some difficulty that they were gotten back to their room. We saw it would not be possible for them to get across the city on foot or by any means yet devised. I dispatched a note to the broker stating how matters stood, and in less than half an hour himself and his wife were at the hotel, and the ready wit of this little lady soon had a plan arranged by which the Indians could be safely taken from the house and to her home without detection or annoyance. The plan was to postpone the supper she had arranged for the afternoon until the evening, and that after dark the bus could be placed in the alley back of the hotel and the Indians got into it without being observed. The plan was carefully carried

12

out by the landlord. The crowd was frustrated and by 9 p.m. we were whirling through the streets with shaded bus windows to the house of the broker, which we reached without any interruption, and were met at the door by the little lady whose tact had made the visit possible, and I hope she may now be living and read this account of that visit, which was nearly thirty-nine years ago. We found some thirty or forty young people present to see us, and I think a few old persons. The supper was prepared and all were anxious to see the red men of the forest at a white man's table. You can imagine my own feelings on this occasion, for, like the Indians, I had been brought up in a wilderness, entirely unaccustomed to the society of refined and educated people, and here I was surrounded by them and the luxuries of a finished home, and with the conduct of my wards to be accounted for, I was forced to an awkward apology, which was, however, received with that graciousness of manner that made me feel almost at home. Being thus assured and advised that our visit was contemplated for the purpose of seeing us as nearly in our native ways and customs as was possible, and that no offense would be taken from any breach of etiquette, but, on the contrary, they should be highly gratified if we would proceed in all things as was our habit in the wilderness, and the hostess addressing me, said it was the wish of those present that in eating their supper the Indians would conform strictly to their own habits, to insure which, as supper was then being put in readiness for them, I told the Indians that when the meal had been set before them on the table, whey should rise up and pushing their chairs back, themselves upon the floor, taking with them only the plate of food and their knife. They did this nicely, and the meal was taken in true Indian style, much to the gratification of the assemblage. When the meal was completed each placed his knife and plate back upon the table, and moving back towards the walls of the room seated himself upon the floor in true Indian fashion.

As the party had now seen enough to furnish them with tea table chat, they ate their supper and after they finished requested a

13

speech from the Indians, at least that each one should say something that they might hear and which I could interpret to the party. Chief O-sho-ga spoke first, thanking the people for their kindness. Buffalo came next and said he was getting old and was impressed by the manners of white people and showed considerable feeling at the nice way in which they had been treated there and generally upon the route. Our hostess, seeing that I spoke the language fluently, requested that I make them a speech in the Chippewa tongue. To do this so they would understand it best I told them a story in the Indian tongue. It was a little story about a monkey which I had often told the Indians at home and it was a fable that always caused great merriment among them, for a monkey was, in their estimation, the cutest and most wonderful creature in the world, an opinion that they hold to the present time. This speech proved to be the hit of the evening, for I had no sooner commenced (though my conversation was directed to the white people), that the Indians began to laugh and cut up all manner of pranks, which, combined with the ludicrousness of the story itself, caused a general uproar of laughter by all present and once, if never again, the fashionably dressed and beautiful ladies of New York City vied with each other and with the dusky aborigines of the west in trying to show which one of all enjoyed best the festivities. The rest of the evening until about two o'clock next morning was spent answering questions about our western home and its people, when we returned to the hotel please and happy over the evening's entertainment.

CHAPTER II

———————— • ————————

After a few days more in New York City I had raised the
necessary funds to redeem the trinkets pledged with the 'bus driver
and to pay my hotel bills, etc., and on the 22d day of June, 1852,
we had the good fortune to arrive in Washington.

I took my party to the Metropolitan Hotel and engaged a
room on the first floor near the office for the Indians as they said
they did not like to get up to high in a white man's house. As they
required but a couple mattresses for their lodgings they were soon
made comfortable. I requested the steward to serve their meals in
their room, as I did not wish to take them into the dining room
among distinguished people and their meals were thus served.

The morning following our arrival I set out in search of the
Interior Department of the Government to find the Commissioner
of Indian Affairs, to request an interview with him which he
declined to grant and said: "I want you to take your Indians away
on the next train west as they have come here without permission
and I do not want to see you or hear of your Indians again. I
undertook to make explanations but he would not listen to me and
ordered me from his office. I went to the sidewalk completely
discouraged for my present means was insufficient to take them
home. I paced up and down the sidewalk pondering over what was
best to do when a gentleman came along and of him I inquired the
way to the office of the Secretary of the Interior. He passed right
along saying, "This way sir; this way sir;" and I followed him. He
entered a side door just back of the Indian Commissioner's office
and up a short flight of stairs and going in behind a railing divested
himself of hat and cane and said:

15

"What can I do for you sir?"

I told him who I was what my party consisted of where we came from and the object of our visit as briefly as possible He replied that I must go and see the Commissioner of Indian Affairs just down stairs I told him I had been there and the treatment I had received at his hands then he said:

"Did you have permission to come and why did you not go to your agent in the west for permission?"

I then attempted to explain that we had been to the agent but could get no satisfaction but he stopped me in the middle of my explanation saying:

"I can do nothing for you. You must go to the Indian Commissioner," and turning, began a conversation with his clerk who was there when we went in.

I walked out more discouraged than ever and could not imagine what next I could do. I wandered around the city and to the Capitol thinking I might find someone I had seen before but in this I failed and returned to the hotel where in the office I found Buffalo surrounded by a crowd who were trying to make him understand them and among them was the steward of the house. On my entering the office and Buffalo recognizing me, the assemblage, seeing I knew him, turned their attention to me, asking who he was, etc., to all of which questions I answered as briefly as possible, by stating that he was the head chief of the Chippewas of the Northwest. The steward then asked: "Why don't you take him into the dining room with you? Certainly such a distinguished man as he, the head of the Chippewa people, should have at least that privilege." I did so and as we passed into the dining room we were shown to a table in one corner of the room, which was unoccupied. We had only been seated a few moments when a couple of gentlemen who had been occupying seats in another part of the dining room came over and sat at our table and said that if there were no objections they would like to talk with us. They asked about the party, where from, the object of the visit, etc. I answered

16

them briefly, supposing them to be reporters and I did not care to give them too much information. One of these gentlemen asked what room we had, say that himself and one or two others would like to call on us right after dinner. I directed them where to come and said I would be there to meet them.

About 2 o'clock they came, and then for the first time I knew who those gentlemen were. One was Senator Briggs* of New York, and the others were members of President Fillmore's cabinet, and after I told them fully what had taken me there, and the difficulties I had met with, and they consulted a little while aside, Senator Briggs said:

"We will undertake to get you and your people an interview with the President, and will notify you here when a meeting can be arranged." During the afternoon I was notified that an interview had been arranged for the next afternoon at 3 o'clock. During the evening Senator Briggs and other friends called, and the whole matter was talked over and preparations were made for the interview the following day, which were continued the next day until the hour set for the interview.

*Armstrong recalls incorrectly here, for George Briggs was a New York Representative, not a Senator.

When we were assembled, Buffalo's first request was that all be seated, as he had the pipe of peace to present, and hope that all who were present would partake of smoke from the pipe. The pipe, a new one brought for the purpose, was filled and lighted by Buffalo and passed to the President who took two or three draughts from it, and smiling said, "Who is the next?" at which Buffalo pointed out Senator Briggs and desired he should be next. The Senator smoked the pipe and then passed it to me and others, including the Commissioner of Indians, Secretary of the Interior and several others whose names I did not learn or cannot recall. From them to Buffalo, then to O-sho-ga and from him to the four

17

braves in turn, which completed that part of the ceremony. The pipe was then taken from the stem and handed to me for safe keeping, never to be used again on any occasion. I have the pipe still in my possession and the instructions of Buffalo have been faithfully kept.

The ceremonial pipe smoked at the 1854 council by Chief Buffalo, Chief O-sho-ga, President Millard Fillmore, Benjamin Armstrong, and others returned home with Armstrong. 158 years later, in a special 2010 ceremony, Armstrong's descendants presented the pipe to the Red Cliff Band of Lake Superior Chippewa. The band welcomed back the four-foot-long pipe, a symbol of Buffalo's success in convincing the U.S. government to end tribal treaty violations and establish permanent homelands near Lake Superior for his people.

Prior to its delivery by the family to the Red Cliff Band, Christie's of New York authenticated and appraised the pipe, valuing it at $500,000. (See page 213)

The old chief now rose from his seat; the balance following his example and marched in single file to the President and general hand shaking that was begun with the President was continued by the Indians with all present. This over, Buffalo said his under chief, O-sho-ga, would state the object of our visit and he hoped the great father would quiet the excitement in his country and keep his young men peaceable. After I had this speech thoroughly interpreted, O-sho-ga began and spoke for nearly an hour. He began with the treaty of 1837 and showed plainly what the Indians understood the treaty to be. He next took up the treaty of 1842 and said he did not understand that in either treaty they had ceded away the land and he further understood in both cases that the Indians were never to be asked to remove from the lands included in those treaties, provided they were peaceable and behaved themselves and this they have done. When the order came to remove Chief Buffalo sent runners out in all directions to seek the reasons and causes for the order, but all those men returned without finding a single reason among all the Superior and Mississippi Indians why the great father had become displeased. When O-sho-ga had finished his speech I presented the petition I had brought and quickly discovered that the President did recognize some names upon it, which gave me new courage. When the reading and the examination of it had been concluded the meeting was adjourned, the President directing the Indian Commissioner to say to the landlord at the hotel that our hotel bill would be paid by the government. He also directed that we were to have the freedom of the city for a week.

The second day following this Senator Briggs informed me that the President desired another interview that day, in accordance with which request we went to the White House soon after dinner and meeting the President, he told the delegation in a brief speech that he would countermand the removal order and that the annuity payments would be made at La Pointe as before and hoped that in the future there would be no further cause for complaint. At this he handed to Buffalo a written instrument which he said would explain to his people when interpreted the promises he had made as to the removal order and the payment of the annuities at La Point and hoped when he returned home he would call his chiefs together and have all the statements therein contained explained fully to them as the words of their great father at Washington.

The reader can imagine the great load that was then removed from my shoulders for it was a pleasing termination of the long and tedious struggle I had made in behalf of the untutored but trustworthy savage.

On June 28th, 1852, we started on our return trip, going by cars (*Railroad passenger cars.*) to La Crosse, Wisconsin, thence by steamboat to St. Paul, thence by Indian trail across the country to Lake Superior. On our way from St. Paul we met bands of Indians of the Chippewa tribe to whom we explained our mission and its results, which caused great rejoicing, and before leaving, Buffalo would tell their chief to send a delegation, at the expiration of two moons, to meet him in a grand council at La Pointe, for there was many things he wanted to say to them about what he had seen and the nice manner in which he had been received and treated by the great father.

At the time appointed by Buffalo for the grand council at La Pointe, the delegates assembled and the message given Buffalo by President was interpreted, which gave the Indians great satisfaction. Before the grand council adjourned word was received that their annuities would be given to them at La Pointe about the middle of October, thus giving them time to get together to receive them. A number of messengers were immediately sent out to all parts of the territory to notify them and by the time the goods arrived, which was about October 15th, the remainder of the Indians had congregated at La Pointe. On that date the Indians were enrolled and the annuities paid and the most perfect satisfaction was apparent among all concerned. The jubilee that was held to express their gratification to the delegation that had secured a countermanding order in the removal matter was almost extravagantly profuse. The letter from the great father was explained to them all during the progress of the annuity payments and Chief Buffalo explained to the convention what he had seen; how the pipe of peace had been smoked in the great father's wigwam and as that pipe was the only emblem and reminder of their duties yet to come in keeping the peace with his white children, he requested that the pipe be retained by me. He then went on and said that there was yet one more treaty to be made with the great father and he hoped in making it they would be more careful and wise than they heretofore been and reserve a part of their land for themselves and their children. It was here that he told his people that he had selected and adopted me as a son and that I would hereafter look to treaty matters and see that in the next treaty matters they did not sell themselves out and become homeless; that as he was getting old and must soon leave his entire cares to others he hoped they would listen to me as his confidence in his adopted son was great and that when treaties were presented for them to sign they would listen to me and follow my advice, assuring them that in doing so they would not again be deceived.

After this gathering of Indians there was not much of interest in the Indian country that I can recall until the next annual payment in 1853. This payment was made at La Pointe and the Indians had been notified that commissioners would be appointed to make another treaty with them for the remainder of their territory. This was the territory lying in Minnesota west of Lake Superior; also east and west of the Mississippi River north to the territory of the Bois Fort and Pillager tribes, who are a part of the Chippewa nation, but through some arrangement between themselves, were detached from the main or more numerous body. It was at this payment that the Chippewa Indians proper desired to have one dollar each taken from their annuities to recompense me for the trouble and expense I had been to on the trip to Washington in their behalf, but I refused to accept it by reason of their very impecunious condition.

It was sometime in August 1854, before the commissioners arrived at La Pointe to make the treaty and pay the annuities of that year. Messengers were dispatched to notify all Indians of the fact that the great father had sent for them to come to La Pointe to get their money and clothing and to meet the government commissioners who wished to make another treaty with them for the territory lying west of Lake Superior and they were further instructed to have the Indians council among themselves before starting that those who came could be able to tell the wishes of any that might remain away in regards to a further treaty and disposition of their lands. Representatives came from all parts of the Chippewa country and showed a willingness to treat away the balance of their country. Henry C. Gilbert, the Indian Agent at La Pointe, formerly of Ohio, and David B. Herriman, the agent for the Chippewas of the Mississippi country, were the commissioners appointed by the government to consummate this treaty.

21

While we were waiting for the arrival of the interior Indians I had frequent talks with the commissioners and learned what their instructions were and about what they intended to offer for the lands which information I would communicate to Chief Buffalo and other head men in our immediate vicinity, and ample time was had to perfect our plans before the others should arrive, and when they did put in an appearance we were ready to submit to them our views for their approval or rejection. Knowing as I did the Indians unwillingness to give up and forsake their old burial grounds I would not agree to any proposition that would take away the remainder of their lands without a reserve sufficient to afford them homes for themselves and posterity, and as fast as they arrived I counseled with them upon the subject and to ascertain where they preferred these reserves to be located. The scheme being a new one to them it required time and much talk to get the matter before them in its proper light. Finally it was agreed by all before meeting of the council that no one would sign a treaty that did not give them reservations at different points of the country that would suit their conveniences, that should afterwards be considered their bona fide home. Maps were drawn of the different tracts that had been selected by the various chiefs for their reserves and permanent homes. The reservations were as follows: One at L'Anse Bay, one at Ontonagon, one at Lac du Flambeau, one at Courte Oreilles, one at Bad River, one at Red Cliff or Buffalo Bay, one at Fond du Lac, Minnesota, and one at Grand Portage Minnesota. The boundaries were to be as near as possible by metes and bounds of waterways and courses. This agreed to before the Mississippi Chippewas arrived and was to be brought up in the general council after they came in, but when they arrived they were accompanied by the American Fur Company and most of their employees, and we found it impossible to get them to agree to any of our plans or to come to any terms. A proposition was made by Buffalo when all were gathered in council by themselves that as they could not agree as they were, a division should be drawn, dividing the Mississippi and the Lake Superior Indians from each other altogether and each make their own treaty. After several days of counseling the proposition was agreed to, and thus the Lake Superiors were left to make their own treaty for the lands north of Lake Superior to the Mississippi and the Mississippis to make their own treaty for the lands west of the Mississippi. The council lasted several days, as I have stated, which was owing to the opposition of the American Fur Company, who were evidently opposed to having any such division made; they yielded however, but only when they saw further opposition would not avail, and the proposition of Buffalo became an Indian law. Our side was ready to treat with the commissioners in open council. Buffalo, myself, and several of the chiefs called upon them and briefly stated our case but were informed that they had no instructions to make any such treaty with us and were only instructed to buy such territory as the Lake Superiors and Mississippis then owned. Then we told them of the division of the Indians had been agreed upon and after several days they agreed to set us off the reservations as previously asked for and to guarantee that all lands embraced within those boundaries should belong to the Indians and that they would pay a nominal sum for the remainder of their possessions on the north shores. It was further agreed that the Lake Superior Indians should have two-thirds of all money appropriate for the Chippewas and the Mississippi contingent the other third. The Lake Superior Indians did not seem, through all these councils, to care so much for future annuities either in money or goods as they did for securing a home for themselves and their posterity that should be a permanent one. They also reserved a tract on land embracing about 100 acres lying across and along the eastern end of La Pointe or Madeline Island so that they would not be cut off from the fishing privilege.

It was about in the midst of the councils leading up to the Treaty of 1854 that Buffalo states to his chiefs that I had rendered them services in the past that should be rewarded by something more substantial than their thanks and good wishes, and that at different times the Indians had agreed to reward me from their annuity money but I had always refused such offers as it would be taking from their necessities and as they had had no annuity money for the two years prior to 1852 they could not well afford to pay me in this way. "And now," continued Buffalo, "I have a proposition to make to you. As he has provided us and our children with homes by getting these reservations set off for us, and as we were about to part will all the lands we possess, I have it in my power, with your consent, to provide him with a future home by giving him a piece of ground which we are about to part with. He has agreed to accept this as it will take nothing from us and make no difference with the great father whether we reserve a small tract of or territory or not, and if you agree I will proceed with him to the head of the lake and there select the piece of ground I desire him to have, that it may appear on paper when the treaty has been completed. The chiefs were unanimous in their acceptance of the proposition and told Buffalo to select a large piece of land that his children might also have a home in the future as has been provided for by ours.

This council last all night and just at break of day the old chief and myself, with four braves to row the boat, set out for the head of Lake Superior and did not stop anywhere only long enough to make and drink some tea, until we reached St. Louis Bay. We landed our canoe by the side of a flat rock quite a distance from the shore, among grass and rushes. Here we ate our lunch and when completed Buffalo and myself, with another chief, Kish-ki-to-uk, wades ashore and ascended the bank to a small level plateau where we could get a better view of the bay. Here Buffalo turned to me saying:

"Are you satisfied with this location? I want to reserve the shore of this bay from the mouth of the St. Louis River. How far that way do you want it to go?" pointing southeast, or along the south shore of the lake.

I told him we had better not try to make it too large for if we did the great father's offers at Washington might throw it out of the treaty and said: "I will be satisfied with one mile square, and let it start from the rock which we have christened Buffalo Rock, running easterly in the direction of Minnesota Point, taking in a mile square immediately northerly from the head of St. Louis Bay."

As there was no other way of describing it than by metes and bounds we tried to describe it in the treaty but Agent Gilbert, whether by, mistake or not I am unable to say, described it differently. He described it as follows: 'starting from a rock immediately above and adjoining Minnesota Point, etc."

We spent an hour or two here in looking over the plateau then went back to our canoe and set out for La Pointe. We traveled night and day until we reached home.

During our absence some of the chiefs had been talking more or less with the commissioners and immediately on our return all the Indians met in grand council when Buffalo explained to them what he had done on the trip and how and where he had selected the piece of property that I was to have reserved in the treaty for my future home and in payment for my services I had rendered them in the past. The balance of the night was spent in preparing ourselves for the meeting with the treaty makers the next day, and about 10 o'clock next morning we were in attendance before the commissioners, all prepared for a big council.

Agent Gilbert started the business by beginning a speech interpreted by the government interpreter, when Buffalo interrupted him by saying that he did not want anything interpreted to them from the English language by anyone except his adopted son for there had always been things told the Indians in the past that proved afterwards to be untrue, whether wrongly interpreted or not, and we can get it correctly, we wish to hear your words repeated by him, and when we talk to you our words can be interpreted by your own interpreter, and in this way one interpreter can watch the other and correct each other should there be mistakes. We do not want to be deceived any more as we have been in the past. We now understand that we are selling our lands as well as the timber and that the whole, with the exception of what we shall reserve, goes to the great father forever."

Commissioner of Indian Affairs, Col. Manypenny, then said to Buffalo: "What you have said meets with my own views exactly and I will now appoint your adopted son your interpreter and John Johnson, of Sault Ste. Marie, shall be the interpreter on the part of the government," then turning to the commissioners said, "How does that suit you gentlemen?" They at once gave their consent and the council proceeded.

Buffalo informed the commissioners of what he had done in regard to selecting a tract of land for me and insisted that it become a part of the treaty and that it should be patented to me directly by the government without any restrictions. Many other questions were debated at this session but no definite agreements were reached and the council was adjourned in the middle of the afternoon, Chief Buffalo asking for the adjournment that he might talk over some matter further with his people, and that night the subject of providing homes for their half-breed relations who lived in different parts of the country was brought up and discussed and all were in favor of making such a provision in the treaty. I proposed to them that as we had made provisions for ourselves and children it would be only fair that an arrangement should be made in the treaty whereby the government should provide for our mixed blood relations by giving to each person head of a family or to each single person twenty-one years of age a piece of land containing at least eighty acres which would provide homes for those now living and in the future there would be ample room on the reservations for their children, where all could live happily together. We also asked that all teachers and traders in the ceded territory who at that time were located there by license and doing business by authority of law, should each be entitled to 160 acres of land at $1.25 per acre. This was all reduced to writing and when the council met the next morning we were prepared to submit all our plans and requests to the commissioners save one, which we required more time to consider. Most of this day was consumed in speech making by the chiefs and the commissioners and in the last speech of the day, which was made by Mr. Gilbert, he said: "We have talked a great deal and evidently understand one another. You have told us what you want, and now we want time to consider your requests, while you want time as you say to consider another matter, and so we will adjourn until tomorrow and we, with your father, Col. Manypenny, will carefully examine and consider your propositions and when we meet tomorrow we will be prepared to answer you with an approval or rejection."

That evening the chiefs considered the other matter, which was to provide for the payment of the debts could not be more than $90,000 and that that amount should be taken from the Indians in bulk and divided up among their creditors in a pro-rata matter according to the amount due to any person or firm, and that this should wipe out their indebtedness. The American Fur Company had filed claims, which, in the aggregate, amounted to two, or three times this sum and were at the council heavily armed for the purpose of enforcing their claim by intimidation. This and the next day were spent in speeches pro and con but nothing was affected towards a final settlement.

Col. Manypenny came to my store and we had a long private interview relating to the treaty then under consideration and he thought that the demands of the Indians were reasonable and just and that they would be accepted by the commissioners. He also gave me considerable credit for the manner in which I had conducted the matter for the Indians, considering the terrible opposition I had to contend with. He said he had claims in his possession, which had been filed by the traders that amounted to a large sum but did not state the amount. He saw the Indians had every confidence in me and their demands were reasonable he could see no reason why the treaty could not be speedily brought to a close. He then asked if I kept a set of books. I told him I only kept a daybook or blotter showing the amount each Indian owed me. I got the books and told him to take them along with him so that he or his interpreter might question any Indian whose name appeared thereon as being indebted to me and I would accept whatever that Indian said he owed me whether it be one dollar or ten cents. He said he was certain that some traders were making claims for far more than was due them. Messrs. Gilbert and Herriman and their chief clerk, Mr. Smith, were present when Mr. Manypenny related the talk he had with me at the store. He considered the requests of the Indians fair and just, he said, and he hoped there would be no further delays in concluding the treaty and if it was drawn up and signed with the stipulations and agreements that were now understood should be incorporated in it, he would strongly recommend its ratification by the President and the Senate.

The day following the council was opened by a speech from Chief Na-gon-abe (*Spelled Nay-naw-ong-gay-be on the treaty and Na-non-ga-be on the cover of Armstrong's book)* in which he cited considerable history. "My friends," he said, "I have been chosen by our chief, Buffalo, to speak to you. Our wishes are now on papers before you. Before this it was not so. We have been many times deceived. We had no one to look out for us. The great father's officers made marks on paper with black liquor and quill. The Indian cannot do this. We depend upon our memory. We have nothing else to look to. We talk often together and keep your words clear in our minds. When you talk we all listen, then we talk it over many times. In this way it is always fresh with us. This is the way we must keep our record. In 1837 we were asked to sell our timber and minerals. In 1842 we were asked to do the same. Our white brothers told us the great father did not want the land. We should keep it to hunt on. Bye and bye we were told to go away; to go and leave our friends that were buried yesterday. Then we asked each other what it meant. Does the great father tell the truth? Does he keep his promise? We cannot help ourselves! We try to do as we agree in the treaty. We ask you what this means? You do not tell from your memory! You go to your black marks and say this is

28

what those men put down; this is what they said when they made the treaty. The men we talked with do not come back; they do not come and you tell us they did not tell us so! We ask you where they are? You say you do not know or that they are dead and gone. This is what they tell you; this is what was done. Now we have a friend who can make black marks on paper. When the council is over he will tell us what we have done. We now know what we are doing! If we get what we ask our chiefs will touch the pen, but if not we will not touch it. I am told by our chief to tell you this: "We will not touch the pen unless our friend says the paper is all right."*

*Because most Natives could not read or write at the time the treaties were negotiated, many signed with only an X. For others, simply touching the pen meant agreement with the wording in the document, a method practiced among many Indian nations in the 18th and 19th centuries. This likely came from statements made by tribal chiefs that they would not touch the pen until satisfied with the wording. Hence, witnesses to a signing regarded touching the pen as a way to show their approval of the treaty after it had been signed by their chief.

Na-gon-ab was answered by Commissioner Gilbert, saying: "You have submitted through your friend and interpreter the terms and conditions upon which you will cede away your lands. We have not had time to give them all consideration and want a little more time, as we did not know last night what your last proposition would be. Your father, Col. Manypenny, has ordered some beef cattle killed and a supply of provisions will be issued to you right away. You can now return to your lodges and get a good dinner and talk matters over among yourselves the remainder of the day and I hope you will come back tomorrow feeling good natured and happy, for your father, Col. Manypenny, will have something to say to you and will have a paper which your friend can read and explain to you."

When the council met the next day in front of the commissioner's office to hear what Col. Manypenny had to say a general good feeling prevailed and a hand-shaking round proceeded the council, which Col. Manypenny opened by saying: "My friends and children: I am glad to see you all this morning looking so good natured and happy and as if you could sit here and listen to what I have to say. We have a paper here for your friend to examine to see if it meets your approval. Myself and the commissioners, which your great father has sent here have duly considered all your requests and have concluded to accept them As the season is passing away and we are all anxious to go to our families and you to your homes I hope when you read this treaty you will find it as you expect to and according to the understandings we have had during the council Now your friend may examine the paper and while he is doing so we will take a recess until afternoon."

Chief Buffalo turning to me said: "My son we the chiefs of all the country have placed this matter entirely in your hands. Go and examine the paper and if it suits you it will suit us." Then turning to the chiefs he asked, "what do you all say to that?" The ho-ho that followed showed the entire circle was satisfied.

I went carefully through the treaty as it had been prepared and with a few exceptions found it was right. I called the attention of the commissioners to certain parts of the stipulations that were incorrect and they directed the clerk to make the changes.

The following day the Indians told the commissioners that as their friend had made objections to the treaty as it was they requested that I might again examine it before proceeding further with the council. On this examination I found that changes had been made but on sheets of paper not attached to the body of the instrument and as these sheets contained some of the most important items in the treaty I again objected and told the commissioners that I would not allow the Indians to sign it in that shape and not until the whole treaty was re written and the detached portions appeared in their proper places. I walked out and told the Indians that the treaty was not yet ready to sign and they gave up all further endeavors until next day. I met the commissioners alone in their office that afternoon and explained the objectionable points in the treaty and told them the Indians were ready to sign as soon as those objections were removed. They were soon at work putting the instrument in shape.

The next day when the Indians assembled they were told by the commissioners that all was ready and the treaty was laid upon a table and I found it just as the Indians had wanted it to be except the description of the mile square. The part relating to the mile square that was to have been reserved for me read as follows: "Chief Buffalo being desirous of providing for some of his relatives who had rendered them important services it is agreed that he may select one mile square of the ceded territory heretofore described."

"Now," said the commissioner, "we want Buffalo to designate the person or persons to whom he wishes the patents to issue." Buffalo then said, "I want them to be made out in the name of my adopted son." This closed all ceremony and the treaty was duly signed on the 30th day of September, 1854. This done the commissioners took a farewell shake of the hand with all the chief's hoping to meet them again at the annuity payment the coming year. They then boarded the steamer *North Star* for home. In the course of a few days the Indians also disappeared, some to their interior homes and some to their winter hunting grounds and a general quiet prevailed on the island.

About the second week in October, 1854, I went from La Pointe to Ontonagon in an open boat for the purpose of purchasing my winter supplies as it got too late to depend on getting them from further below. While there a company was formed for the purpose going into the new ceded territory to make claims upon lands that would be subject to entry as soon as the late treaty should be ratified. The company consisted of Samuel McWaid, William Whitesides, W.W. Kingsbury, John Johnson, Oliver Melzer, John

McFarland, Daniel S. Cash, W.W. Spaulding, all of Ontonagon, and myself. The last two named gentlemen, Daniel S. Cash and W.W. Spaulding, agreeing to furnish the company with supplies and all the necessaries, including money, to enter the lands for an equal interest and it was so stipulated that we were to share equally in all that we, or either of us might obtain. As soon as all the supplies were purchased and put aboard the schooner *Algonquin* we started for the head of the lake, stopping at La Pointe long enough for me to get my family aboard and my business matters arranged for the winter. I left my store at La Pointe in charge of Alexander Nevaux, and we all sailed for the head of Lake Superior, the site of which is now the city of Duluth. Reaching there about the first week in December – the bay of superior being closed by ice – we were compelled to make our landing at Minnesota Point and take our goods from there to the main land on the north shore in open boats, landing about one and one half miles east of Minnesota point at a place where I desired to make a preemption form myself and to establish a trading post for the winter. Here I erected a building large enough for all of us to live in, as we expected to make this our headquarters for the winter, and also a building for a trading post. The other members of the company made claims in other places, but I did no more land looking that winter.

About January 20th, 1855, I left my place at the head of the lake to go back to La Pointe and took with me the furs I had collected up to that time and I had a good place at La Pointe to dry and keep them. I took four men along to help me though and two dog trains. As we were passing down Superior Bay and when just in front of the village of West Superior a man came to us on the ice carrying a small bundle on his back and asked me if I had any objections to his going through in my company. He said the snow was deep and the weather cold and it was bad for one man to travel alone. I told him I had no objections provide he would take his turn with the other men in breaking the road for the dogs. We all went on together and camped that night at a place well known as Flag

River. We made preparations for a cold night, as the thermometer must have been twenty-five or thirty degrees below zero and the snow fully two feet deep. There were enough of us that we cut and carried a large quantity of wood, both green and dry, and shoveled the snow away to the ground with our snowshoes and built a large fire. Then we cut evergreen boughs and made a windbreak or bough camp and concluded we could put in a comfortable night. We then cooked and ate our supper and all seemed happy. I unrolled a bale of bear skins and spread them out on the ground for my bed, filled my pipe and lay down to rest while the five men with me were talking and smoking around the campfire. I was very tired and presume I was not long in falling asleep. How long I slept I cannot tell, but was awaken by something dropping into my face, which felt like a powdered substance. I sprang to my feet for I found something had got into my eyes and was smarting them badly. I rushed for the snow bank that was melting from the heat and applied handful after handful to my eyes and face. I found the application was peeling the skin off my face and the pain soon became intense. I woke up the crew and they saw by the firelight the terrible condition I was in. In an hour's time my eyeballs were so swollen that I could not close the lids and the pain did not abate. I could do nothing more than bathe my eyes until morning, which I did with tea-grounds. It seemed an age before morning came and when it did come I could not realize it, for I was TOTALLY BLIND. The party started with me at early dawn for La Pointe. The man who had joined us the day before went no further, but returned to Superior, which was a great surprise to the men of our party, who frequently during the day would say: "There is something about this matter that is not right," and I never could learn afterward of his having communicated the fact of my accident to any one or to assign any reason or excuse for turning back, which cause us to suspect he had a hand in the blinding, but as I could get nothing in the matter. This man was found dead in his cabin a few months afterwards.

At La Pointe I got such treatment as could be procured from the Indians, which allayed the inflammation but did not restore the sight. I remained at La Pointe about ten days, and then returned home with the dog train to my family, where I remained the balance of the winter, when not at Superior for treatment. When the ice moved from the lake in the spring I abandoned everything there and returned to La Pointe and was blind or nearly so until the winter of 1861.

Returning a little time to the north shore I wish to relate an incident of the death of one of our Ontonagon Company. Two or three days after I had reached home from La Pointe, finding my eyes constantly growing worse I had the company take me to Superior where I could get treatment. Dr. Marcellus, son of Prof. Marcellus, of an eye infirmary in Philadelphia, who had just then married a beautiful young wife and come west to seek his fortune, was engaged to treat me. I was taken to the boarding house of Henry Wolcott, where I secured rooms for the winter as I expected to remain there until spring. I related to the doctor what had befallen me and he began treatment. At times I felt much better but no permanent relief seemed near. About the middle of February my family required my presence at home, as there was some business to be attended to which they did not understand. My wife sent a note to me by Mr. Melzer, stating that it was necessary for me to return, and as the weather that day was very pleasant she hoped I would come that afternoon. Mr. Melzer delivered me the note, which I request him to read. It was then 11 a.m. and I told him we would start right after dinner, and requested him to tell the doctor that I wished to see him right away, and then return to get his dinner, as it would be ready at noon, to which he replied: "If I am here do not wait for me, but I will be here at the time you are ready for home." Mr. Melzer did return shortly after we had finished our dinner and I requested him to eat, as I would not be ready to start for about a half an hour, but he insisted he was not hungry. We had no conveyance and about 1 p.m. we set out for home. We went down a few steps to the ice, as Mr. Wolcott's house stood close to the shore of the bay, and went straight across Superior Bay to Minnesota Point, and across the point six or eight rods and struck the ice on Lake Superior. A plain, hard beaten road led from here directly to my home. After we proceeded about 150 yards, following this hard beaten road, Melzer at once stopped and requested me to go ahead, as I could follow the beaten road without assistance, the snow being deep on either side. "Now," he says, "go ahead, for I must go back after a drink." I followed the road quite well, and when near the house my folks came out to meet me, their first inquiry being: "Where is Melzer?" I told them the circumstances of his turning back for a drink of water. Reaching the bank on which my house stood some of the folks, looking back over the road I had come, discovered a dark object apparently floundering on the ice. Two or three of our man started for the spot and there found the dead body of poor Melzer. We immediately notified parties in Superior of the circumstances and ordered a post-mortem examination of the body. The doctors found that his stomach was entirely empty and mostly gone from the effects of whiskey and was no thicker than tissue paper and that his heart had burst into three pieces. We gave him a decent burial at Superior and peace to his ashes. His last act of kindness was on my behalf.

In the Old Days

35

Chapter III

———— • ————

THE TIDAL WAVE OF IMMIGRATION – SALE OF ONE HALF OF THE
MILE SQUARE – SHARP PRACTICES – GENERAL DEPRESSION – THE
INDIAN SCARE OF 1862 – SOLDIERS AT BAYFIELD AND SUPERIOR –
AN INDIAN SHOT – A DELEGATION THROUGH THE STATES –
PRESIDENT LINCOLN'S PROMISES

In the year 1855, came the first wave of immigrations.

> Behind the squaw's light birch bark canoe,
> The steamers plow the waves;
> And the village lots are staked for sale
> Above old Indian graves.
> They crossed the lakes as of old
> The pilgrims crossed the sea,
> To make west as they had the east
> A home for trusts and monopoly.

Now for the first time we of the western country realized the meaning of sharp practices. Heretofore a man's word had been his bond and any writing intended to strengthen a man's word was utterly unknown.

Now I must take you to Oak Island, which was my home from the spring of 1855 to the spring of 1862. I was confined to my house during all of his time except such time as I was seeking or receiving medical aid. Being blind and financially embarrassed, the world showed up dark before me. I had exhausted all my ready money in conducting the late treaty and had nothing to fall back upon except a few tracts of land I had secured and the furs I had accumulated the previous winter. I had my furs baled up and they turned out as follows: one of martin skin, one of beaver, one of fisher, and another made of bear and other skins. These I consigned to parties in Cleveland, Ohio, in care of Cash & Spaulding, Ontonagon. They should have brought me $1,200 but I never received one dollar for them. I inquired of Cash & Spaulding concerning the furs and was told that the parties in Cleveland would not receipt for them or receive them until some skins accounted for, claiming they had been broken open in transit on the boat. I requested Mr. Cash that inasmuch as I was sore in need of money he would look the matter up with all possible dispatch. He promised me that he would, but did not think it could be done right away, and the matter rested there the entire season without a settlement.

About the first of July 1856, Mr. Spaulding, of our company, came to my home on Oak Island and told me that my claims against the Indians for old back debts that were arranged for the treaty of 1854 had been allowed by the government and amounted to just $900, and that he was going to Washington in a few days and coming right back and if I would give him and order for the money, and thinking this was the quickest way of obtaining it, I agreed. He wrote out the order himself and I signed it, but being blind, I cannot say whether I signed my name or made my mark. Mr. Spaulding went away, and as far as I am concerned, the money went with him. In the fall when Agent Gilbert came to pay the annuities he told me that Mr. Spaulding had drawn the money in Washington and asked if I had received it. I answered no and neither had I heard from Spaulding. He said he would write so Spaulding about what disposition he had made of the money, but I never saw Gilbert again or heard from the money.

Sometime in the fall of 1856, I met Fredrick Prentice, whom I had known quite a number of years. He called on me at Oak Island as he had heard of my affliction. Mr. Prentice then lived in Toledo, Ohio, and was here at that time on matters of business. Among other things we talked was my "mile square" property, the grant of

Chief Buffalo and said if we could agree on terms he would purchase an interest in the property. At that time I scarcely knew from whence my next sack of flour would come and asked Mr. Prentice what he could afford to give me for an undivided one-half of the property. He told me that he would give me $8,000 and keep up the taxes when it became taxable. We would keep track of my other matters until such time as I could agree to sell all or a portion of the property. If it became necessary to go to Washington to look after it he would do it and should it be necessary to employ counsel while there or at any other time until the title was perfected he would make me a small cash payment. In addition to all the other provisions Mr. Prentice also agreed to furnish lumber and all necessary material for the erection of a house on the property, in which I was to live, and during my residence thereon he was to furnish me with anything I required until we saw fit to sell the property or any portion of it. This was put into a written agreement, duly signed and witnessed, which was afterwards stolen from me with a number of other valuable papers. The cash payment was to be, I think, $250, but also that I might make out a list of goods and provisions that I needed and included a yoke of oxen, and would send me them as soon after his return to Toledo as he could get a steamer to send them by. The balance of the $8,000, after taking out the cost of the things he was to send me and then money then advanced, was to be paid in installments after the patent for the land had been received. The list of the articles he was to send he took along with him and in due time the goods and oxen were received, together with the shipping and purchasing bills showing the total cost of the goods, which amounted to $2,000, to the best of my recollection, including the cash I had received on his visit.

On the day following or conversation, Mr. Prentice returned to my house, bringing with him Doctor Ellis, of Ashland, Wisconsin, and a deed was made for an undivided one-half of the land that was selected by Chief Buffalo for me in the Treaty at La Pointe, September 30, 1854, and in which was to have been patented to me by the stipulations of that instrument. The deed was a warranty but as the patent had not arrived it was impossible to describe the property by metes and bounds. Dr. Ellis drew up the deed and described it as being the land selected by Chief Buffalo and thought the description would be sufficient. The deed was witnessed in the presence of Asaph Whittlesey, but I do not remember whether there was another witness or not. On leaving Mr. Prentice told me he should leave that night on the steamer *North Star* for Toledo, and would go from there to Cleveland and purchase the articles called for in my memorandum and ship them either on the *North Star*, Captain Sweet, or the *Iron City*, Captain Turner, and that they would reach me in about ten days from Cleveland. The goods and oxen I received at Oak Island by the steamer *Iron City*. I next heard from Mr. Prentice from Washington, D.C., whither he had gone on business.

This same fall Daniel S. Cash, of Ontonagon, came to my house, ostensibly to visit me. He sympathized with me greatly and said it was too bad that I should be so afflicted, especially at this time, when the whole northwest, by reason of the late treaty, was to be opened to settlement, and as I was young and active and had a thorough knowledge of the country, there was no reason, if I had my sight, why I should not become the wealthiest man in the whole northwest, and asked, "Why don't you raise the money on that square mile and go below for treatment?" I told him I had already given a deed to an undivided one-half to raise money for my present needs and that it was a hard matter to raise money on that yet patented. He then made me a proposition to let me have the money to go for treatment. He said he would advance $5,000 or so much of it as was necessary if I would give that land as security, and that he would take the chances of the patents and of the land ever becoming valuable and would let me have the money as I required it. I told him that in the sale of the other half I had only received a little money and some provisions to use in carrying on my business and that when my bills were paid my money would be

39

gone. This offer, coming as it did from a man I knew so well, was a tempting one and I told him I would talk the matter over with my wife and let him know on his return from Superior what the decision might be. The boat being ready to leave, he said: "Think it over well. I think it is the best thing you can do. I think too much of you to advise you wrongly. I feel sure that a few months' treatment by a good oculist will bring back your sight, and then you can easily make the money to pay me back what I shall have advanced." I talked the matter over with my family and told my wife I would do what she thought best. She, being well acquainted with Mr. Cash, and believing him to be an upright and good man, advised me to accept his proposition. The day following he returned and I told him his proposition would be accepted, when he produced a contract he had prepared, read it to me and asked me to sign it, saying I could draw the $5,000 if necessary and that I might pay him back the amount I used with and interest at six percent, and failing to do so he would hold the land selected for me by Chief Buffalo at the head of the St. Louis Bay. I signed the contract, saying as I did so that I would only draw such amounts as were necessary and thought I would be ready to start below in about a month. Whether my signature to this contract was witnessed or not, I cannot state but there was no one present who could either read or write the English language and no one but Mr. Cash knew the contents of that instrument.

It was not until the following season that I made ready to go for treatment, when I left Oak Island on the steamer *Iron City*, Captain Turner, who had previously told me that he should stop at Ontonagon to load some copper which would give me time to see Mr. Cash and arrange the money matters according to the agreement. When the boat stopped at Ontonagon I sent a message to Mr. Cash, saying I was aboard and would like to have him come to the boat. He came, and catching me by the hand, said, "I am very glad to see you and am only sorry that you cannot see me," and adds, "I suppose I know your mission. You are going away for treatment and want some money for your expenses." I told him he had guessed it; that I had made arrangements to be gone six months or as long as would be required to be able to see him on my return. Then he told me that money would be out of the question; there had been bank failures throughout the country and that he had not a dollar worth five cents, either to me or anyone else, and that to be able to raise one hundred dollars would be an impossibility. I then told the captain to put me ashore and I would get back home as best I could. "You will not make another trip up this season, but I can get back in a canoe with the help of someone to guide me." The captain replied: "I will do no such thing. Come to Cleveland with me and I will take you to Garlick and Ackley, an eye infirmary, and arrange with them for your treatment." Thankfully I accepted the offer. I then asked Mr. Cash to give me the contract, which I had signed. "Oh!" he said, "that contract is valueless now, as I never paid you any money upon it, and I have not got it here, either, but will mail it to you at Cleveland or any place you direct after you get settled."

I went to Cleveland and my eyes were examined by Garlick & Ackley, oculist, of that place, and they said they could not help me. After two days in Cleveland, Captain Turner drove up to the office and informed me that he should make another trip up the lakes that fall and as the doctors had told him they could not help me, I could return to my home or remain as I preferred. Both doctors having told me that my case was a hopeless one as far as they knew, I returned home with the captain, wholly discouraged and disheartened. I had a few dollars in my pocket with which I tried to buy some provisions to take home with me, but was quickly informed that it was valueless. This was during the great financial panic of 1857. I arrived home safely and found my family well, the first pleasing thing I had met with in a number of months.

I never received the contract back from Mr. Cash, and never saw him but once afterward, and that was aboard a steamboat bound for below, and he was too sick to talk business matters.

Shortly afterward I was told that he was dead. After I had got upon my feet again and was able to look after my business, I found that the supposed contract then in the hands of his heirs turned out to be a warranty deed to Daniel S. Cash and Jas. Kelly, whom I never saw, of an undivided one-half of the mile square before described. I tried to employ council many times to take hold of the matter, but not having money to advance for such services, I failed to obtain help in that direction. It would have been impossible, however, had I then had the property clear of indebtedness to have realized any money upon it or from it sales, because there was a general stagnation in business throughout the northwest for quite a number of years. Many people abandoned their homes and property, leaving behind but few white people, and soon following this the rebellion broke out. This state of lethargy continued for six or seven years.

I had frequent talks with friends who had known me for years, and knew how my business matters stood, as to what I had better do. All were familiar with the fact that I had deeded to Mr. Prentice an undivided one-half of that property and received one or two payments upon it, but none believed I had ever received a penny for the half the heirs of Cash & Kelly claimed to own, and I never saw the James Kelly to whom that deed appears to have been given, nor never heard of him except through this deed. It appeared that he lived in Cleveland. Had I ever received and any considerable amount from Cash on this one-half of that property, my neighbors would have known it, for they well knew my circumstances all these years, and that I had been financially embarrassed.

After trying different occultists without getting any relief I had given up hope of ever seeing again, when by a mere accident my sight was partially restored. It was about the middle of December 1860, when one of my teamsters complained a tree had fallen across his road and he could not or would not, cut it out. Being irritable, cross and morose under my forced restraint, I jumped from my darkened room and told him to lead me to the tree and I would cut the tree from the road, and although I knew I was doing a foolish thing, I took hold of the stakes at the rear of the sleigh and followed to the obstruction. I then told the driver to bring me an axe and lead me to the tree. The first blow I struck the tree – which proved to be a sappy balsam – a bulb of balsam sap flew up under the bandage or shade, which I had over my eyes and struck squarely in my right eye. I yelled with pain and told the teamster to take me back to the house and it was not until I had reached there that I knew what had happened. My wife found spatters of balsam on my cheek and also found that a film, which covered the eye, had been broken. She then began a balsam treatment, which proved to be just the thing to affect a cure of the inflammation I had suffered for so many years. She continued the use of the balsam and in three weeks to be out of doors without assistance, and the next spring my eyes were healthy and strong, though not clear, and never will be, I do not think.

In the spring of 1861 I was appointed by Commissioner Dole, who had charge of Indian Affairs under President Lincoln, to act as special interpreter for General L.E. Webb, the Indian Agent at Bayfield, Wisconsin, and Clark W. Thompson, superintendent of Indian Affairs in the northwest, who was located in St. Paul, Minnesota. I accepted the appointment and preformed the duties of interpreter until the fall of 1864. I moved my family from Oak Island to Bayfield, which was my home while thus engaged.

During the summer of 1862 a scare was started throughout this country to the effect that an uprising of the Indians was quite likely, which resulted in bringing three companies of soldiers to Bayfield and the same number to Superior. When the troops arrived at Superior it was a surprise both to the white people and to the Indians. The soldiers pitched their tents, threw out their pickets, and matters looked quite war-like. It happened that an Indian who had been out hunting a few days came in that night, and at the picket line he was halted. Not knowing that soldiers were there or what the charge meant, he halted, but immediately proceeded forward and was shot down by the soldier. This created quite an excitement for a while, as it was not known what effect it would have on the Indians, but it was thought it might incite them to seek revenge, but nothing of a serious nature resulted from it.

Agent Webb, myself and others had frequent talks over the general outlook for Indian troubles and it was finally decided to take a delegation on a trip through the states and to Washington, as such a trip would give the delegation a rare chance to see the white soldiers and to thus impress upon their minds the futility of any further recourse to arms on their part. Agent Webb arranged the matter and was directed to have me select the delegation. I selected a party of nine chiefs from the different reservations, made up as follows: Ah-moose, or "Little Bee," from Lac du Flambeau Reservation; Kish-ke-taw-ug, or "Cut Ear," Bad River Reservation; Ba-quas, or "He Sews," Lac Courte Oreilles Reservation; Ah-do-ga-zik, or "Last Day," Bad River Reservation; O-be-quot, or "Firm," Fond du Lac reservation Shingquak onse or Little Pine and Ja ge gwa yo or Can't Tell, La Pointe reservation Na gonab or He Sits Ahead, Fond du Lac reservation and O ma shin a way or Messenger, Bad River reservation. We set out about December 1st 1861 going from Bayfield to St Paul, Minn., by trail and from St Paul to La Crosse, Wis., by stage and by rail the balance of the way to Washington. Great crowds of soldiers were seen at all points east of La Crosse besides train loads of them all along the whole route. Reaching Washington I showed them 30,000 or 40 000 soldiers in camp and they witnessed a number of drills and parades which had a salutary effect upon their ideas of comparative strength with their white brothers. Being continually with them I frequently heard remarks passing between them that showed their thoughts respecting the strength of the white race. There is no end to them said one. They are like the trees in our forest said another. I was furnished with a pass to take them to the navy yard and to visit the barracks of the Army of the Potomac at which place one of them remarked that the great father had more soldiers in Washington alone than there were Indians in the northwest including Chippewas and Sioux and that his ammunition and provisions never gave out. We remained in the city about forty days and had interviews with the Indian Commissioner and the President and I was allowed the privilege of a partial examination into the records showing the annuities due the Indians on annuity arrearages but the excitement incident to the war precluded any extended examination which would lead to a settlement of their arrearages at that time. The President made a short speech to the Indians at one of these interviews at which he said:

"My children when you are ready go home and tell your people what the great father said to you tell them that as soon as the trouble with my white children is settled I will call you back and see that you are paid every dollar that is your due provided I am here to attend to it and in case I am not here to attend to it myself, I shall instruct my successor to fulfill the promises I make you here today." The Delegation before President Lincoln, 1862

After visiting all places of interest in Washington, and about a week after the last interview with the President, we set out on our home journey, going by way of New York City, where we stayed two or three days, purchasing goods and presents for the chiefs to take home to their families and relatives; in all amounting to $1,500, which had been placed in my hands by the government for that purpose. This was, in all probability, the most pleasant stop of the trip. We stopped two days at Chicago on our return, from there going to Lacrosse by rail, where we took a boat for St. Paul. We were compelled to take the trail from St. Paul and arrived in Bayfield about the middle of April 1862.

During this season Agent Webb, Samuel S. Vaughn, and one or two others frequently talked with me about my prospects in the "mile square" question, and said it was too bad to lose it all for it was sure to be valuable, and from time to time they would propose what they would do, and one day asked me what I would take for a quit-claim deed of the undivided one-half which I had sold to Mr. Prentice. That if they had it they would take the matter into the courts, and thought that they would have no problem proving the claim of Daniel S. Cash a swindle, because I had never received a cent from him. I told them I could not do it for I had already given a warranty deed to Mr. Prentice. They said they were aware of the fact, and did not expect to make anything out of that part of it, and should not try to do so, but that I could give a quit-claim deed to any property, whether I owned it or not. I told them I would consider it, and I advised with others who told me that I could give a quit-claim deed if I wished to, and as I held no claim to that half I could lose nothing, and one man stated I could give a quit-claim deed to the Mississippi River if a purchaser could be found. The matter was talked over a number of times, but nothing came of it until the following season, when they came to me in a confidential way and thought the best thing that I could do was to give them that deed. Saying at the time, "we must give you something for it, as a deed would not be legal without a consideration. We will give you four or five hundred dollars so as to make the transaction appear a legitimate one." Then they would have a clear foundation to

46

commence suit. I told them I was not posted in law, and did not want to get into any trouble, for I had been led into a good many scrapes already, and came out the loser every time. General Webb said: "We are your friends, not your enemies, and we are not seeking to blind or kill you. If we don't make anything out of it for ourselves we can't for you, but if we can make anything for you we are satisfied we can for ourselves." I finally agreed to do it. The deed was prepared and Mr. Vaughn brought it to me for signature and gave me five hundred dollars.

During the summer of 1862, Clark W. Thompson, Indian Superintendent at St. Paul, came to Bayfield to assist in the distribution of annuities to the Indians of the Lake. We first went to Grand Portage and gave out the annuities, returned to Bad River and gave them out there. While at Bad River Mr. Thompson told me that he thought I would be required to go to St. Paul as there were some matters up the Mississippi relating to Indian Affairs that he wanted investigated. On his return he would find out more about them and let me know. A short time afterward news reached him that the Indians in the vicinity of Red Lake and Leech Lake had captured a mail boat on the Red River and had burned it, and sent word for me to come to St. Paul as soon as I could. He gave me written instructions to go to Red River, or far enough to ascertain if the boat had been burned and try and induce the Indians to come to Leech Lake, for himself and others would be there to meet them. I went and found the boat all right and the story a fabrication. I found the country in a complete uproar, for news had reached the Indians that the great father was going to send soldiers there because he had heard that the Indians had burned his boat that carried papers and they had retreated back into the forest to get out of the way. I had much difficulty in finding them, as everybody seemed to be afraid for their lives. The Chippewas were behaving badly for they had taken the report for granted. The whites saw the Chippewas on one side and the Sioux on the other, and all seemed to think they would unite in one general massacre.

The third day of my search, just before sunset, I found a lake, and looking towards its head I saw smoke rising, probably four miles away in a direct line. Following the shore and picking my way through the brush, I reached the Indian camp at about 9 p.m. When nearby, perhaps a mile distant, I struck into a hard beaten trail, which led me to their wigwams. I made no halt, but proceeded straight to their wigwams, and picking out the wigwam that I judged by its size to be the chief's lodge, I approached it and saw no person, not even a dog to bark at me, until I reached the lodge and raised the caribou skin that hung at the entrance, and entered without being discovered. When inside the wigwam I found a large Indian stretched upon the ground beside the fire smoking his pipe, the balance of the inmates lying around and in sitting positions about the wigwam. Had their eyes been guns I should have feared them and expected a killing at once, but knowing their customs and habits so well, I had to play a little Indian part myself. Taking my pipe I filled and lighted it and smoked a while to show them I felt at home. Profound silence prevailed up to this time. I then seated myself upon the little bundle I was carrying and spoke to the Indian in his own language, by asking him where the chief's wigwam was. He sprang to his feet and reaching out his hand exclaimed:

"How is this! You, white man, speak our language perfectly! I am surprised," He said, "at your getting into our camp without our dogs discovering you."

At the mention of dogs, my hair fairly stood erect for I then remembered that they had Eskimo dogs. The chief said they had forty or fifty of them on guard. They all knew me by reputation when I told them I was the adopted son of Buffalo of the Lake Superior Chippewas. I told them my mission. That the great father had heard that the Indians had burned his boat, which carried papers. I told them that I had been to the river and found the boat all right; that I wanted them to go with me to Leech Lake, as it was their great father's request, that they would meet their great father's agent there who lived in St. Paul, and others, to have a talk over this matter, and that everything would be all right and their St. Paul father would give them presents. "Big Dog," being the head chief of the party, then set a lad to call in his chiefs, and to one of his women he said, "go and see what you can get for our friend's supper," and the other women and children he directed to leave the wigwam. My supper was brought and the chief and men congregated, and while I was eating they had a general conversation, and all expressed their surprise that I could approach their camp without being torn in pieces by the dogs. We talked and joked the whole night and the next day preparations were made for the trip to Leech Lake, and on the morning of the second day we set out with about 20 Indians. Arriving at Leech Lake we found the commissioners there as they had promised. Those present were: Clark W. Thompson, Superintendent of Indian Affairs; Jessie Ramsey, James Thompson, brother of the superintendent, and John Ferron, of St. Paul. I told the party I had found the boat all right, and that she was tied up to trees along the bank of the river, and that the greater portion of the Indians were more frightened than the whites; how I found them huddled together at the head of a lake which was heavily wooded at the north end; that I had been delayed in my search for them as I was a stranger in the locality and could get no guide owing to the excitement through the country.

After I had related my story to the commissioners, Mr. Thompson said: "I would not have taken that risk for the world." The superintendent told the Indians he was very sorry that the story of the burning of the boat had been started as it had given their great father much trouble and the Indians also, and as he knew they could not help these reports and as the reports had proven untrue, he felt it his duty on behalf of the great father, to make them some presents in "provisions and good, which we will turn over to your friend to give you as he chooses." The warehouse was opened and I was told to make the distribution. I loaded each one down and the next day they started for home, thanking me especially by saying: "No other white man would have done this for us, and we hope to see the day when we can do you a kind act." After a general hand shaking the Indians started home. The next morning at daybreak the superintendent and party left for home also. Reaching Crow Wing the next day I was left there to investigate some matters and settle some trouble that had been brewing for some time between the agent at Crow Wing and the Indians. I remained there about 10 days and found matters in bad shape. I reported to the superintendent what I had found and he came up to Crow Wing and had a talk with the agent. Just what the trouble was I never ascertained, but shortly afterward the agent committed suicide and all was kept dark from me. I returned to St. Paul with the superintendent, and on the way he said there was likely to be trouble with the Sioux, as they had been waiting for their annuities a long time and were getting restless and were dissatisfied, and he would like to have me go with him to New Ulm, the Sioux Agency, which I did. We found there was much restlessness among the Indians and equally as much among the white traders. I found parties the first night I was there among the Sioux who spoke the Chippewa tongue, and talked with them. I found out the feeling that prevailed among the people. I talked with Bill Taylor, a half-breed Negro, who made a business of attending Indian payments for the purpose of gambling, and as he spoke the Sioux language. He told me what the Indians and Traders were saying. The traders were continually telling the Indians to receive nothing but coin in payment. I heard at one or two other trading posts the same thing, and knowing that coin was a scarce article just at that time in the United States, I informed the superintendent of what was going on, and gave it as my opinion that unless they were paid right away there would be trouble. The superintendent called the chiefs together and told them that he would give them their goods annuities at once, as they were then on the ground, and then they could their women and children home, as soon as the money came he would notify them and they could come for it. They asked what kind of money it would be, to which he answered, he did not know, but whichever kind it was he would pay it to them. He could not tell what kind of money the great father had on hand, but thought it would be currency. They then demanded coin and said they would not take greenbacks, to which the superintendent replied: "I will go right back to St. Paul and if the great father has not sent the money I will borrow it and return as quickly as I can and pay you." We started at once for St. Paul, but before we arrived there we heard of the terrible uprising of the Sioux and the slaughter of people. This was the awful massacre of New Ulm, with which everybody is so familiar. I attributed the whole trouble then and still do; to the bad advice of the traders. These traders knew that all the money the Sioux drew would, in a short time would be in their hands, and as specie was at a high premium, they allowed their speculative nature to get the better of their judgment, the penalty of which was the forfeiture of their lives. I afterward heard that Bill Taylor was first among the dead.

I now left St. Paul and went to my home in Bayfield and found the Indians in this part of the country peaceable and quiet. After being home a short time I found that Agent Webb and four or five others were bribing boys and children to come in and swear that they were entitled to an eighty acre piece of land that the Treaty of 1854 provided for half-caste and mixed blood people, and were paying them from ten to twenty dollars apiece for their scripts, as circumstance required. I made up my mind that I would be drawn into the rascally scheme by implication, if I remained in the employ of the government under General Webb, so I threw up my position and left Bayfield going to the copper mines of the Bad River, where I remained during that summer, only going to Bayfield two or three times that season. From here I took my family to Lake Portage, Michigan, to keep out of the way, and remained away until the spring of 1870

During the interim I met Mr. Webb at Houghton, Michigan, and asked him what had been done with the quitclaim deed I had given himself and Mr. Vaughn. He told me he had employed attorneys in St. Paul and it would not be long until I should hear from it. I never saw Mr. Webb again and did not know what became of the deed until I went into court in St. Paul, in the year 1884, I think, when I ascertained that the deed had gone to a man by the name of Gilman, whom I had never seen before that time. I spoke to Mr. Vaughn after this and asked him how it was that the deed had passed from his hands. He laughed and said it made no difference who held the deed as he did not consider that it would ever amount to anything as Prentice held a warranty from me for one-half and that Cash would hold the other half under the contract or deed I gave him, and that he had given the matter up. It told him that at some future time I should require him in court, but before my case was reached in which parole testimony was taken, Mr. Vaughn died, and Mr. Webb was dead also, the matter to this day remains unsettled.

Ashland, Wisconsin, businessman, Samuel S. Vaughn (1830 – 1886), engaged in several successful business ventures in Ashland and held numerous mineral claims in the silver mining region near Marengo. Today, in the City of Ashland, one can walk down Vaughn Avenue to see the Vaughn Building across from the Vaughn Public Library.

Chapter IV

———— • ————

First Payment under the 1854 Treaty – Swamp and
Overflowed Lands – Death of Chief Buffalo – An Indian
Tradition – An Axe, a Gun, and a Knife, the First They had
Ever Seen

I will now go back to 1855.

About the middle of September word was sent me at Oak
Island by Agent Gilbert that the annuities had arrived for the first
payment under the Treaty of '54, and if I was able to attend he
should be pleased to have me do so; that he had some talking to do
with the Indians and they as well as himself would like to have me
present to hear it. I arranged matters to leave Oak Island and as I
owned a house at La Pointe move my family there for the fall that I
might have their care. Chief Buffalo had been prescribing for and
treating my eyes and as he was then sick at La Pointe I had parties
take me to his home. I had not talk with him more than an hour
when it became apparent that he was quite feeble. I brought him
articles of food and did all I could for his comfort that night and the
next morning visited the agent and commissioners and told them of
the old chief's illness and said I did not think he would be able to
attend the councils that fall. Col. Manypenny and myself visited the
old man that day. The Colonel gave him his best wishes and told
him that anything he wishes to eat would be brought to him and
hoped in a day or two he would be able to come down and hear
what the agent had to say. But the old man was never able to attend
the councils more.

The Indians were all in from the interior and the councils was
called. The commissioners told the Indians that their last treaty had
been ratified and that their great father had signed it; that the treaty
had not been changed; that all they had asked for had been

conceded, both in regards to the reservations and the script which was to go to the half-breeds and the household goods which were to go to the mixed bloods and to all living in houses he had brought along and would give them out and he hoped they would move onto their reservations and have their young men clear lands and build fences, "for next year great father will cause houses to be built for you and you can rest assured that no white man shall enter your reservation to claim or hold any portion of it, except it be such ones as the chief desires should live there, and that all the land embodied in these several tracts of yours, to be your permanent homes and the sooner you improve our land and open up garden spots the sooner your great father will send you horses, cattle and farming implements to work with and if at any time any white men invades your reservation for the purpose of taking your timber, or minerals, or anything else, you stop them and make them pay you for all damage they may have done.

As I have stated heretofore that misunderstandings have always crept into treaties, and the Treaty of '54 was no exception, I will state what they were. Notwithstanding all the care that was taken and all the precautions used which our foresight could devise, and after everyone understood, and positively too, that the reservations should be and forever remain the home of the Indian alone, it was only a few years after they were set apart that the white man came and claimed to own every sixteenth section of their land under the state school land laws. Following these came men who claimed to have acquired title to all the swamp and overflowed lands on the reservations, depriving the Indians of their rice fields, cranberry marshes and hay meadows. Many times the Indians asked their agents how this was and why it was so, but never received any satisfactory answer. All the troubles with the Indians of the northwest can be traced directly to such misunderstandings, and as is well known the Indian in every case got the worst of it. Still people wonder what makes the Indian so troublesome. Why don't the white people kill them off and be done with it, etc?

Now returning to the annuity payment at La Pointe, where I left the agent giving the Indians advice and making them promises, and from which I left off to speak of treaties not being lived up to on the part of the government. Chief Buffalo not being able to meet the commissioners, I requested them to go with me to see him, stating that I did not think he would last more than two or three days and I should like to have them talk with him on business matters, as he told me himself that he could live but a few days at most. In the afternoon they went with me, taking along their interpreter. I told them I wished they would ask him if he desired to change any of his former devices in the reservations he had made. He only requested that they be carried out as he had formerly directed. After some further talk the commissioners left, but I remained with the old veteran until he died. I gave him a decent burial. Calling all parties together we formed a procession and marched to the Catholic cemetery at La Pointe where we laid the old chief to rest. I ordered and placed in position a tombstone at the head of his grave and also one at the grave of Chief O-sho-ga, which are there today.

The White Men's Cabin

Here I wish to digress again to give an Indian tradition, a legend handed down to buffalo and was one of many, some of which had come down for three hundred years. This one, as near as I can calculate, must be about two hundred and thirty or forty years old and was many times repeated to me by Buffalo, and was about

55

as follows:

"My great, great-grandfather was an important chief in his day, and had a band of about 500 people. They lived in one place a long time, and as the game was getting scarce and wood for the fire hard to obtain, it became necessary to select another place to live, and it was their custom to first send a party to look the country over to see if there was any enemy that would be likely to molest them in moving the band. The old chief told his son, who was my great-grandfather, to take four young men and go and explore the country for a place to remove to. After these five scouts had been out many days they found a good place, plenty of wood, plenty of fish and close to a nice river, but before returning they resolved to explore a little further in the woods from the river. They had only traveled a short distance, however, when they saw a house or shanty made of logs and poles, the first they had ever seen. They dropped to the ground and crawled cautiously along, being sure to keep a tree, a rock or a log between themselves and the cabin, and slowly crept along to discover what it possibly could be, expecting any moment to see it take wings and fly away. Presently they saw a man come out of the house with an axe in his hand, who began chopping into a tree, soon felling it to the ground and afterwards cut it into wood for fire. That was something they had never seen before nor had they ever seen an axe. After he had chopped a while a second man with a pale and hairy face came out and began to carry the wood into the cabin. When this was done and the two men had gone back into the house and closed the door the Indians skulked back to a safe distance, then springing to their feet they ran away as fast as they could, and to their people to tell them of their wonderful discovery. How they had seen a house with two pale-faced Indians with hair all over their faces, and the wonderful instrument they used for making wood for fire. They traveled night and day so as to reach their people as soon as they could. When they had returned the chief notified his headmen the scouting party had returned and to come and hear what they had to say. When they had gathered together the scouts told their wonderful story of what they had seen at the river, which they had selected for their future home. The headmen and their braves held a great war council, but none of them could account for what had been seen by the scouts. The old chief had ever confidence in his son and said: 'My son, I want you to take twenty-five of our best and bravest men and go back and find out whether they are enemies or friends, but be sure you do not harm them except it be to save yourselves from being killed or injured.' Before allowing the party to depart the old chief call on his men to at once prepare a man-e-to-kos-o-wig-e-wam, or religious wigwam, where the medicine man could talk with the great spirit, to find out if there was any danger ahead. The old man spent the whole night in the wigwam and in the morning reported that the way was clear and no danger to be feared. The party started off and feeling they were safe hurried along to the wonderful sight at the river. Arriving there the young chief pointed to the cabin and party saw it as described to them. They resolved to watch for what might happen. Circling themselves as closely about the house as they could without being observed they waited for developments. They had not waited long when a man came out as before and began chopping wood and another came out and carried it in, all of which they watched with the greatest interest. The men returned to the cabin and the Indians continued to lay low.

Soon one of the men came out with a pail in his hand and went to the river, and returned quickly with a pail of water and immediately came with a gun, and placing it to his face fired it and fell a partridge to the ground. The sound of the gun struck terror to their very souls and if they could have done so they would have hidden themselves below the ground. But stand they must, at least until the man should go back into the cabin. The man reloaded his gun and fired again and another partridge fell. The man picked up the birds and went into the shanty carrying the birds in one hand and his gun in the other, closing the door behind him. A signal from the young chief brought the party a safe distance from the cabin where a council was held. Though they were all nearly frightened out of their wits, it would never do to show cowardice by running away, and it was decided that they should walk boldly to the cabin yard and there form a half circle and wait for what might happen. Keeping in mind the old chief's warning to harm no one unless absolutely necessary, they formed their half circle close to the cabin without being observed. Presently a man came out again and found himself standing in the presence of twenty-six full fledge Indians, fully armed and equipped with bows and arrows and spears and was as much frightened as the Indians had been a few moments before, but spoke to them. Presently another man came out and spoke to them and beckoned them to come in to the cabin, but the Indians did not stir or speak until the third man came out, who was old, with white hair and white beard and a red cap on his head and red sash around his waist, which very much attracted the Indians attention, it being so different from any dress they had ever seen that they were completely thunderstruck, but after the old man had spoken to them and showed them signs that they were friends and not enemies, and want them to come into the cabin, they became as tame as pet rabbits. The axe and the gun, together with the gaudy dress of the old man had completely captivated them. Now the traders made them understand that they would exchange with them for their robes and fur clothing, blankets, or trinkets or an axe to chop wood with, or a knife to cut sticks or skin a deer with or a bear, and last of all the gun to shoot with, and after explaining to them as best they could the wonderful gun and how to load and shoot it, and the uses to which the knife and axe could be put, an exchange of articles took place. The young chief determined to exchange his fur clothing for a gun and ammunition and an axe and a knife, as he thought they would be the most useful to his people. The greatest curiosity was the gun and the next greatest was the axe. Now being provided with a loaded gun and many curiosities and much information, they set out for home with light hearts. They ran like wild cattle, for now they had more wonders to relate and

58

the evidence to show for it they carried with them to their people, and they told their whole story of what they had seen and heard and experienced. The axe was the first to exhibit, and it was a great wonder to all. Then the knife, blankets, articles of clothing and trinkets were exhibited, and last of all was the gun, the greatest wonder of all their lives. The young chief them how the man made it speak to a partridge and the bird dropped dead, and then it spoke again and other dropped dead, and he made it speak to a tree and the tree was full of holes, and 'he told me it would speak to a deer and the deer would die, and if we were in battle it would speak to our enemies and they would die.' This was too much for all of them to believe at one time, and many had their doubts about the gun doing all of this, and one old warrior, who had been in many battles and carried many scars from the enemy and wild beasts, and who was no longer of any assistance to his people, and who was sitting near, rose to his feet and said: 'My friends, I do not think that gun will do what they say it will and as I am no longer of any use to you and never can be I will go and stand on that little knoll and you may let it speak to me and we will see what it will do to me.' The old man hobbled out to the knoll and sanding erect said: 'Let it speak.' The young chief took up the gun and did as the trader had told him. First pull back the hammer then place the butt of the gun to the shoulder look along the top and point it to the object you wish it to speak to and pull the trigger and it will speak. Sure enough the gun did speak and the old warrior fell dead to the ground."

How many times Buffalo told me this story I do not know but it was many times and said every word of it was true as handed down in tradition from generation to generation and as he was the only survivor of his family race he wished me to remember it and hand it down The story continues

"The tribe moved to the new home which the scouts had selected and carrying with them the body of the old warrior buried it there with great honors placing the battle flag of the tribe at the head of his grave there to float until the weather should wear it out. The battle flag of the tribe was made of feathers taken from the wings and tail of eagles closely woven together with sinews of basswood bark then taking a pole and splitting the end with a flint put the quill ends in the opening thus made and wrap the pole with sinews and bark and as the pole is charred by fire in securing it for the purpose the flag and staff would stand for many generations. The different bands of the same tribe would designate themselves by attaching to the flag the tail of a wolf, bear, martin, or fox or a feather of a crane, pelican, or other large bird. But in all cases the body of the flag was made purely of eagle feathers and these were hard to get in those times when snares and the bow and arrow were all they had to depend upon. The eagle flag being the national one in those days it was always planted in times of peace at the head of the chief wigwam."

This ends the story of the experience of Buffalo's great grandfather with the first white man he ever saw but I shall have occasion later to refer to a circumstance which came to my own knowledge that very much confirms the tradition.

At or before the conclusion of the payment—which subject I have twice left to tell about something else—the question of hereafter getting their annuities on the several reservations instead of at La Pointe was brought up and discussed, the Indians claiming it was a hardship for them to come so far to get them, and told the agent that they had agreed to ask for the change and hoped their great father at Washington would grant their request. Col Manypenny said: "My children: I assure you that as long as I am in office it shall be done and I will recommend to my successor to do so likewise, until the treaty shall expire which it will do in 1874, at which time your great father is to call all the chiefs together in open council and there settle for and pay all past dues and arrearages. This part of the agreement, however, has never been fulfilled to my certain knowledge. There are now large sums of money still due the Indians under the treaties of 1837, 1842, and 1854. As I had occasion and did look over the records in Washington in 1862, I am justified in making this statement. The Indians have very often since that time inquired of me what I had found, and feeling that I ought not to keep it secret from them by reason of the part I took in the treaty of 1854, I always told them as near as possible what I had found the records to contain. These talks and inquiries continue to the present time and I am asked why it is that the great father's words are not made true. The older Indians have not forgotten what President Lincoln told the delegation in 1862, and the younger ones know it also, which was to "return home and tell your people as soon as the trouble with my white children has been settled I will attend to you and see that every dollar that is your due is paid." I have made several attempts myself to bring this settlement about but have never been able to do so.

Chapter V

———— • ————

EARLY SETTLERS – THE FIRST IMPROVEMENTS – THE BATTLE OF THE
BRULE – COUNTING THE MISSING – THE CHIPPEWAS VICTORIOUS –
THE OBJECT OF THE SCALP LOCK AND THE WAY IT WAS MADE

I now turn back to about 1837 and mention those who were
among the first to make improvements on the St. Croix waters. The
first mill for grinding grain was built on Lake St. Croix by a man
named Boles in 1839; the first settler at Stillwater who made any
improvement was Paul Carley; then followed by John McCusick,
from Maine, who built the first sawmill on those waters in the year
1840. During the same and at the same time Hungerford and others
of St. Louis, Missouri, were building a sawmill at St. Croix Falls.
Also the Marine Company, consisting of Orange Walker, Samuel
Berklow, Asa Parker and Hiram Berkley built the mill known as the
Marine Mill, commencing it in 1841, and completing it in 1842.
This mill was situated twelve miles below St. Croix Falls. These
were the early settlers in this part of the country up to 1843.
Jackson's trading post was the first improvements made on the site
where St. Paul now stands and was established sometime in the
thirties, and it was all there when I came in 1840. The whole
country from this point to Lake Superior was an unbroken forest,
inhabit exclusively by the Chippewa, but their right to this country
was strongly contested by the Dakotas, (Sioux), leading to many
bloody battles, one of which I witnessed at Stillwater on the west
side of the lake. Many were slain on both sides, but it resulted in a
victory of the Chippewas. This, I think, was in 1841. I also
witnessed a battle on the Brule River about October 1st of the
following year, a true version of which I will give you: The Sioux
were headed by Old Crow and Chippewas by Buffalo, each having
a number of sub-chiefs to assist them. The battleground was about

midway from the source of Brule River to its mouth and about fifteen miles from Lake Superior. Buffalo's people at this time were settled over quite an extensive territory, consisting of the Apostle Islands and the whole country surrounding the Chequamegon (Cha-ga-wa-muk) Bay. When Buffalo received the news that they were coming to give him battle and learned how near they were, and knowing the necessity for him to start at once in order to intercept them and choose his position for a battle, he only had time to gather a portion of his warriors. When he started he knew that the force of the enemy far outnumbered his own; that they were coming with the intentions of catching the Chippewas in disconnected parties and thereby be able to annihilate them in detail, as warlike portion of the Chippewas were over near the Mississippi under Hole-in-the-Day. Act quickly he must. He collected two hundred warriors and leaving his women and children he hurried to meet the Sioux the first evening just before sunset at the Brule, the Sioux on the west side and the Chippewas on the east, their pickets eyeing each other until dark, knowing that daylight would find them in mortal combat. The west bank of this river running back quite a distance is level and swampy, while the east side slopes down from the river and it is only about 150 to an almost perpendicular rocky bluff rising from fifty to eighty feet in height, and the slope from the river bank to the bluff gave Buffalo's men a hidden position from the Sioux on the west side. It was not until dark that Buffalo made any show of strength in numbers, for he well knew he was over matched, but as soon as it was dark he had fires built along the river bank for nearly an eighth of a mile, to give the Sioux the impression that his strength was ample to cope with them. These fires were kept briskly burning all night. Just after dark Buffalo came to me in my hidden retreat in the rocks on the bluff where I had gone by his direction, and laid his plans before me, which plans were to divide his force into three parts and at about midnight to send a third of them up the river a safe distance and cross and come own as near the Sioux as they dared without being observed, and there await the opening of the fight in the morning, which he would begin with his center men. The other third were to go down river and cross over, and like the band up the river, move up to a striking distance and then keep quiet until the battle should begin. In those days fire arms were not plenty with the Indians and ammunition scarce and they did not like to use it in battle but kept it for hunting, and the war club and knife were the instruments of death relied upon for this fight. The center position of his men were concealed near the river bank at a point where the Sioux must cross, and as the ground receded back from the river bank to the bluff their position and numbers could not be detected by the enemy. All the maneuvers of Buffalo's men were completed before daylight and at early dawn the fight began with a few gunshots from Buffalo's center, which was to be a signal for his flanking forces to close in. As soon as these shots had been fired, some of his center men, by a prearrangement, began running towards the bluff to show weakness, and the Sioux, quick to discover their apparent fear, dashed into the river in great numbers, expecting to have an easy victory and be able to take what scalps there were between the river and the bluff with the utmost ease an dispatch. The water in the Brule at the east bank was about three feet deep and the bank two or three feet above the water. Whether or not the Sioux had taken this fact into consideration I cannot say, but that the Chippewas depended upon this condition of these things for their victory was certain. The Brule was now filled with a howling, surging mass of Sioux warriors, each trying to gain the lead for the distinction he proposed to get by the addition of numerous scalps to his belt. On they came, clubs and knives aloft, yelling they made and with a dozen or more imaginary Chippewa scalps already in their belt, began to climb the bank. All this time the braves of Buffalo lay hidden and with hurried breath awaited they appearance of the scalp lock above the bank. They were now in sight and if never before had met a foe that was worthy the name they faced them now, for all the Sioux in the river then, not a one set his foot on the east bank. Being in the water they were impelled to scale the bank before their clubs and knives were of any use, and the Chippewas brained them as fast as they came in reach. Of all the thrilling stories I ever read of slaughter and carnage, I now witnessed a greater one than all. The river ran red with blood and the Sioux warriors that had not reached the shore eagerly pressed forward but as fast as they approached their doom was sealed. The flanking forces of Buffalo were now and had been, since the signal

THE BATTLE OF THE BRULE,

gun fired, cutting their way into the Sioux right and left wings, and the war-whoops of the victorious Chippewas could be heard on their right and left and in their rear. The case in front of the Sioux was a hopeless one and they did the only thing that remained for them, to get away and save as many of their scalps as they could and let the Chippewas have the scalps of the dead, which were floating down or lying at the bottom of the Brule.

I witnessed this masterpiece of Indian warfare* from the afternoon previous to the ending of the fight, and from my safe position, having nothing to fear whichever way the battle went, the impression made upon my mind was lasting, and is as vivid today as it was upon that bright October morning, nearly fifty years ago, and I would go a thousand miles to see it repeated if another massacre were pending and could not be avoided. Those Sioux that got away made the best time possible to reach their own country beyond the Mississippi and were followed by the victors to their boundary line. Only a few were overtaken who were wounded and they were dispatched and scalped as soon as found.

Armstrong was most likely the only white witness to the Battle of the Brule, present at the request of his adoptive father and good friend, Great Buffalo. Most academics and historians who have read his account believe it is accurate.

After the pursuers had returned, the Indians were all called to count the dead and ascertain the result of the battle. This was done by counting all the men that were present, and all that were missing that were counted as slain in battle. Their losses being thus accounted for, the scalps that had been taken from the Sioux were counted and their losses thus ascertained. The count in this case was very satisfactory to the Chippewas as it showed their loss thirteen and the loss of the Sioux one hundred and one. This mode of counting up the results of battle has been their custom for hundreds of years, according to their tradition. The scalping practice has been in vogue by all tribes of Indians as far back as tradition goes, and the object of scalping was for a two-fold purpose. First for counting the results of battle, and next to show the personal bravery of individual warriors, as each brave kept his scalps as record of his valor until such time as he delivered them up to his superior in tribal rank, in return for which he received eagle feathers, one for each scalp he turned in, and these he wore in his cap or turban as a mark of distinction.

Prior to the French-Indian War (1754 – 1763,) only a few tribes in the coastal region of the southeast states practiced scalping. However, the French military encouraged scalping during the war, both to create fear among their enemies and to count the dead. Some records show that Native Americans siding with the French received the equivalent of $200 for each enemy scalp. After the war, the practice of scalping spread to Indian nations in the west. Although relatively rare, some Whites also took scalps during hostilities.

Now I will describe a scalp lock, the manner and object of putting it up. All Indians wore their hair as long as it would grow. They first take up three small wisps of hair at the crown of the head and braid them, firmly braid about midway the length of the hair, after which they then wrapped this braid with moosewood, basswood or other strong bark so that the braid would stand erect on the head from about six to eight inches. Then the hair above the braid was allowed to fall over, giving the lock a parasol appearance. After cloth came to their knowledge they preferred it to bark for winding the braid, and always took red flannel when they could get it, because it was more showy. A genuine brave thought as much of his scalp lock as he did of his war club and desired to make it look as conspicuous as possible. The scalp lock was invariably put up before going upon the war path if they had time to do so, and if any man in the tribe refused to do this he was drummed out of service and sent home to do camp duty with the squaws; his pipe was taken from him and his using it was prohibited and in many cases they were compelled to wear the costume of a squaw as a mark of cowardice. The amount of hair used in a scalp lock would be the amount of growing on a space about the size of a silver half dollar. All bands on the war path, when going into battle know that the enemies scalp lock is ready for them if they can get it, and the enemy expects the same thing of them, and the only question is which gets it. The scalping always takes place as soon as the victim falls to the ground, if the fighting is with clubs and if with guns as soon as they can get to the fallen man. They always go into battle with a club in one hand and a knife in the other, and do not wait till the fight is over to collect the scalps but take them immediately. If they should wait until the fight has ended some brave might not get the share that properly belonged to him, and thus be deprived of the eagle feather, and I believe that the expression in common use, "That's a feather in his cap," had its origin from this custom. The custom of scalping thus quickly accounts for the many cases where persons are living who have been scalped, of whom I know quite a few. It so happens that the person was only stunned by the blow from the club, and consciousness returned after the scalping had been taken.

The Battle of the Brule was the last great battle fought between the Chippewas and the Sioux in this part of the country, though there were others afterward, of less importance, one at the St. Croix River in 1846, where but few were killed, though many hundred were engaged.

Chapter VI

---•---

THE AMERICAN FUR COMPANY – AN INDIAN LAW – MAKING A
CHOICE OF A WIFE – AN INDIAN MAIDENS WAY – INDIAN COURTSHIP
AND MARRIAGE – THE TREACHERY OF THE SIOUX – THE MASSACRE
OF THE CHIPPEWAS BY THE SIOUX

Until 1842 about all the white people living in this section of the country were Canadian voyagers and adventurers, mostly connect with the American Fur Company. This company consisted of John Jacob Aster, Ramsey Crooks, Doctor Borup and David Oakes. The universal custom here before 1842 was that all white men who came among the Indians to trade were compelled to take Indian wives. This custom was encouraged by the Indians for two reasons. Wars had depleted the male portion of the tribes, and as the female portion greatly predominated, the Indians were desirous of providing as many of this surplus with homes as they could. In the second place the American Fur Company had almost complete control of the Indian trade and were not giving them fair bargains in the estimation of the Indians, and they were anxious to have individual traders come among them, and by getting them into a relationship by marriage they thought they would secure fair dealing in future. How well the Indians' ideas were confirmed in the practice may be judged by what followed. The American Fur Company lost their hold upon the business through this agency (La Pointe) and removed their company in 1847 to the Mississippi River. As soon as they were established there they caused the agitation, which resulted in the order for the Indians to remove from this country to the Mississippi. This order did not come until 1849 and was countermanded by President Fillmore in 1852, on my visit to Washington with the Indian delegation.

The plan which the Indians used to get these white son-in-laws was this: When a man came among them to establish himself in the trading business they would at first have nothing to do with him, except in a very small way, and thus gain time to try his honesty and to make inquiries about his general character. If satisfied on these points the chiefs would together take their marriageable girls to his trading house and he was given his choice of the lot. They would sometimes take as many as a dozen girls at one time for the trader to choose from. If the choice was made the balance of the group returned and no hard feelings were ever engendered by the choice. If the trader refused or neglected to make a choice the first visit they would return again in the same manner a few days later, then if no choice were made they would come only once more. In the meantime they would not trade with him a single cents worth, nor would they trade with him unless he took one of their women for his wife. If he had three times failed to choose a wife, and afterwards repented because he had no trade, he became a suitor and often had much difficulty in securing one.

One time when girls were brought to a trader to select a wife from, I saw a trait in human nature whereby a person, by a certain boldness or assurance in their disposition can gain advantages over others without creating any enmity on the part of those over whom the advantage is gained, nicely exemplified. The chiefs had assembled with a dozen eligible maidens before the trading house, but before the trader had made any sign or shown any disposition to make a choice, one of the girls darted into the cabin and began arranging the furniture, sweeping out the place and making herself perfectly at home. The balance of the party looked on with astonishment, and still their wonder was mingled with a sort of admiration for the bravery and assurance the girl displayed. The chiefs and other maidens returned to their homes without a word and waited to see what turn the affair would take. The trader at first seemed bewildered. The audacity of the girl as he at first thought was inexcusable. Still he could not help by admire the manner in which she had installed herself as mistress of his household and the more he thought the matter over the more he admired her style. The match was consummated and the brave little woman ruled the roost. In Indian marriages the proceedings differ from those of any other nationality. A young man believing he can maintain a family will pick out, usually from an adjoining band, a maiden that suits his fancy. He speaks no word to the maiden but takes himself to the forest to capture and kill an animal which is recognized as the symbol of love. This differs from time to time and in different places and depends largely upon the kind of game most numerous in the locality, but it is generally a moose, a deer, a bear or a caribou. Having secured one he proceeds with it to the wigwam of his girl. Leaving it outside he enters the wigwam, saying nothing, but lights his pipe and makes himself at home. Should there be more than one girl in the lodge, he has a sign by which his choice is made known. If the girl does not like his appearance she remains where she is, but if he is agreeable to her fancy she takes a knife and proceeds to skin the animal and take charge of the meat, after which her suitor takes his leave. The parents of the girl, being advised of what is going on by the presence of meat not of their killing, commence systematic proceedings to ascertain the young man's habits, his ability as a hunter, warrior, etc., and if satisfied with them they proceed to the young man's parents, who are now for the first time made aware of the youth's aspirations and they in turn make inquiry as to the character, etc., of their prospective daughter-in-law. If all is satisfactory the young man is given permission by the girl's parents to visit her, but all she and he may say must be said in the common wigwam and before all who happen to be present. If they become satisfied with each other and he has been able to convince her parents that he is an expert at hunting and fishing and is considered a good warrior, and is able to comfortably support a home, the chiefs of the two bands are notified and a wedding is arranged, with the two chiefs as headmen, and it is always the most elaborate of any doings of the tribe.

Before concluding this chapter I wish to relate a piece treachery on the part of the Sioux Indians towards their Chippewa brothers, which well shows the deceptive character of the Sioux. I think it was in 1844 that the Sioux sent messengers to the Chippewas inviting them to a peace council, to be held in the Sioux west of the Mississippi. As was the custom they brought tobacco to present the party who were to smoke with them in case the invitation was accepted, but in case the proposition to consider is not entertained the tobacco is not received. In this case they accepted the tobacco and smoked with their visitors. The messenger stated their proposition to the Chippewas by saying: "All the trouble between us in the past has grown out of a difference of opinion as to our respective territory, and now, as we can see the white people will soon be the owners over all of this country and we will have nothing to fight over, therefore let us meet as brothers and friends and smoke the pipe of peace and bury the war club and scalping knife forever. Our chiefs request you to meet our people just west of Sauk Rapids, near the Mississippi River. As your country is better to hunt in during the winter on account of your forests and ours better in the summer on account of our prairies, we will try and agree that we may hunt here in winter and you hunt there in summer, and we are instructed to say to you that we will allow you one moon to consider the matter and at the expiration of that time or before you can send a messenger to us with your decision."

This arrangement was agreed to. The Chippewas held councils from time to time and finally agreed that they would meet the Sioux as proposed. A messenger was sent to notify them of their decision. The Chippewa messenger was told upon arrival there that they would be ready to meet them after ten days, and that the first hunt would be in the Sioux country for buffalo. In accordance with this arrangement, to hunt first in the Sioux territory, the delegation to the peace council was made up of from fifty to sixty of the choicest hunters and braves among the Chippewas, and with two or three chiefs they met the Sioux at the appointed time and were received with every mark of attention and utmost cordiality.

All joined in a feast and dance that lasted two nights and a day, when it was proposed that the Chippewas return to their country and get more hunters with the understanding that they were to be back in five days, when the march to the hunting grounds would be commenced. As a mark of friendship and good faith towards each other exchanges were made of clothing, pipes, locks of hair and other things, cementing the good faith of the truce that had been concluded and the next morning the Chippewas started for home, highly pleased with the settlement of all former troubles and happy in the belief that thereafter nothing but peace and good will would enter the tribes. But alas for the Chippewas the battle of two years before at the Brule had not been forgotten by the Sioux, and never having been able to best the Chippewas in an open fight; that had drawn them into a trap to get a revenge that they could not otherwise obtain, for the Chippewas had only proceeded about four miles when they were surprised by a large body of Sioux in ambush, volley after volley of rifle shots poured in on them. Before they could recover themselves for resistance the major portion of them lay dead upon the trail. The few who escaped returned to their homes but the fire of hatred kindled in the hearts of the Chippewas by that act of treachery on the part of the Sioux will never be quenched, and it would be quite as easy to mix oil and water as to patch up any kind of truce between them. This was the first and only time the Sioux ever got the best of the Chippewas in combat. The Sioux call it revenge but the Chippewa cannot see it in that light.

Chapter VII

————— • —————

The Indians in the Old Days – How They Managed to Build
Boats, Make Pails, Pots, Kettles and Pans – Birch Bark and
Its Uses – The Flint Rock – How They Obtained It and
Worked It Into Knives, Axes and Arrowheads – The Building
of a Wigwam – The Queen of Pocagemah

Now I wish to give the Indian manner of living before the white race was known to them and how they managed before they ever saw an axe, a knife, gun, a pail, or a kettle, etc. The greatest hardship they had was in getting along without an instrument for cutting. This was especially hard in preparing firewood and they were obliged to pick up and break small limbs of fallen trees and gather old bark, etc., for their fires, which compelled them after quite a stay in one place to go a long way for it, but for most other things they provided themselves with substitutes that did very well. I have seen bows that with only the strength of an average man put to them would throw an arrow through an inch pine board. It must have been a tedious task to make them without axe or knife, but it was accomplished by the use of wedge, flint and fire. Then they took certain bones from animals, especially the horns of buffalo, and by heating them they could peel them in layers. These strips were fastened to the back of the bow with a glue which they made from the heads of sturgeon, and to assist the glue they wrapped the bow with tendons from the loins of animals. The article they used for cutting was flint, and from this they also made their arrowheads. Where this particular kind of flint was procured I have never been able to find out, but I judge from the length of time it took a party to get it, as told in tradition, and from the descriptions of the lakes and rivers they saw and the distance they were said to have gone, that it is somewhere in Ohio. They describe the flint beds as being on a mountainside and as being from one to four feet under the surface of the ground, and with only their hands and sticks to remove the earth, the task of getting to it must have been difficult. After this was accomplished the next thing was to build a fire upon the rock. The fire they started by friction, always carrying with them a thoroughly dried black-ash stick with a groove worked into one side of it and a dry piece of white cedar to match the groove. When they wanted to start a fire they would lay a piece of dry rotten wood or punk on top of the black-ash stick holding it there with one hand, and with the other would rub the cedar stick in the groove of the ash block with all the rapidity they were capable of until it created sparks, which would ignite the punk and from this a fire was soon kindled. After the fire was built upon the rocks and it had been heated to a proper heat, the fire was cleared away and water thrown on the rock, which cracked it in all different sizes and shapes. This process was repeated until they had the desired amount they wished to carry home. From these pieces they would select the ones nearest to a cutting edge, and taking another piece of flint or hard rock they would chip off little by little, eventually getting down to nearly an edge, and then with sand and water and a flint stone rub the rough surface until they got as good an edge as possible. Some of these they used in skinning animals, and the larger ones they make into tools for heavier work such as cutting bark, small stick and poles for different uses. Upon the larger ones they fasten a handle, which was done by working a groove on each side of the flint and splitting a hard piece of wood, ash or hickory, they would insert the flint between the prongs made by the split and bind them close to the flint on both sides. This is both knife and cleaver, and when one is obtained it is carefully preserved, and when in use much caution is used lest it be broken. Their arrowheads are also made of this material, and their every spare moment was utilized in their manufacture, that a supply might be in readiness in a time of need.

Are you wondering what they carried the water to throw upon the heated flint? They carried it in pails made of birch bark taken from the White Birch tree. Pots and kettles were also made from this bark. Canoes are made from this same bark, which they obtain by climbing the tree or sometimes by building a rude staging of sticks and logs. They cut the bark around the whole tree at the height sufficient for the length of the boat; then again around the bottom. They then cut the bark lengthwise; it is then worked lose from the tree, and at the proper time of year it peels off easily, and if properly managed, can be taken off in one unbroken sheet, and as the bark of the birch is very tough, the danger of spoiling the sheet is very slight. When this bark is fresh from the tree and exposed to the rays of the sun, it will warp and nearly close itself with the outer side in. The bark is straightened out upon the smooth surface of the ground, the inner surface downward, as this side is want for the waterside of the boat. Three poles are now put in lengthwise along the middle of the sheet, upon which are placed three stones, the larger on in the middle and the smaller at either end, then the bark is turned up and sew together at each end with black spruce roots which are very tough and pliable, procured from twenty to forty feet long, in diameter being from one-sixteenth to one-eighth of an inch. The needle used is a splint found in the deer's foreleg, near the hoof, and attached to the lower end to the dewclaw joint. Cedar poles are put along the edges of the bark inside and out and firmly sewed in place. From the pole in the bottom to the pole inside at the top they spring split cedar about one eighth of an inch thick the whole length of the boat making a solid lining inside the bark. Then they put in thwarts or braces across from rail to rail probably three or four in its length which gives it stability as well as shape. Sticks are then fitted in at the ends and sewed in place and if any rents are made in the bark in building they are sewed up and pitch from the black spruce tree is then melted into and around all seams and rents by holding a fire brand to the crude pitch which is daubed on a stick for the purpose. The boat is then complete as it was made in primitive days but since tools have been in use the bark is cut and rounded at the ends and better symmetry is observed and they are made much nicer in every way and more durable but the material used in their construction is substantially the same.

The pails the Indians used for carrying water and sap were made water tight by spruce pitch the same as the canoes as were the pots they made for cooking meat and making sugar. A kettle made of birch bark will not burn as long as it is filled with water and not until it is nearly empty. In boiling sap for sugar the Indians always boil a pail of sap until it is reduced to about one third the quantity first put over the fire. They then keep adding and boiling until the kettle is full of syrup; they then turned this syrup into another vessel continuing this until they had enough for a sugaring. A different vessel was then used, but of the same material and was made tray shape. It hung suspended over the fire by cords of basswood bark at each of the four corners, and when the boiling commenced the stirring was constant to prevent scorching until the signs of graining appeared. It was then removed from the fire to a bowl made of rock and there stirred and cooled until the graining of the sugar was complete The rock bowls are made as follows: Securing a sand stone as near flat as possible and from twenty to thirty inches square, the hollowing process is begun by taking a stone or boulder harder than the bowl stone and as pointed as they could find. They would commence and continue the picking process until the center of the stone had been crumbled away to a proper depth and circumference, then it was rubbed with a stone, sand and water until the inner surface was perfectly smoothed and polished. It was a long and tedious undertaking, but when one was completed it was highly prized, and they were heirlooms for many generations.

Birch bark is also used in building wigwams and being wind and waterproof, it makes their lodges warm and comfortable. Building a wigwam is begun by setting poles into the ground in a circle and cone shape, leaving an opening at the top of six inches to two feet, according to the circumference of the structures at the bottom. The poles are woven together with strings of basswood bark, thus completing the frame, a doorway being made by leaving out poles upon the side where they wish the entrance and when the lodge is complete the skin of an animal is hung over to keep out the cold. In this country the skin of the caribou was most generally used. They then take birch bark and after tearing into strips the width they desire for making a tight covering for this cone shaped frame, they sew the ends of the bark together until the length is sufficient to go around the bottom of the structure, then another strip is made to go above the first one and is sewed to it, and so on until the top is reached, which is left open for smoke to escape. Birch bark cannot be torn lengthwise of the tree but clockwise it tears almost like cloth. This bark is of a very peculiar nature and fitted for a great many uses. The Indians used it as a torch when fishing at night. It was used to light the wigwam when needed and burns brightly and equal to an oil and waste torch and is almost proof against decay. I have found birch trees which had been buried a long time, some two and four feet under the surface, that had been covered by changing sands and channels, which were so decayed that when the trunk was removed all the inside would run out like mush, but the bark would be in a perfect state of preservation and it seems to me to been a provision of the Almighty for the Indians' good, for without it I cannot see how they could have managed to get along.

Dogs were the only domesticated animal known to the Indians until the white people settled among them, and they were never known to have had any other pet or tame any animal of any kind. The Esquimaux dog they had when I first came among them and which, according to their tradition, they had never been without, were different from the dogs of today that are so called, they were large and their make up was almost that of a lion, only smaller. Their heads were large and their bodies tapering from their shoulders back, their hinder parts being much lower than their shoulders. Their neck was covered with long hair and they had a mane or long bristly hair running from the neck along the back to

78

the root of the tail, the tail being bushy only at the end. They were very savage animals and were kept for their watchfulness, although they were submissive and kind to their masters. The other dogs of which they had great numbers, were of all sizes, breeds, shape and color, from a cur to a dog that would weigh from fifty to sixty pounds, and all were of a snappish disposition. These they used for hunting different animals and more especially those species that burrow in trees or in the ground. The smaller ones were the best for treeing bears, for they were quicker than a bear and their constant worrying would soon cause a bruin to take to a tree, where they would keep him at bay until the hunter arrived. The larger dogs they used for sledging. These dogs were also quick to give warning of the approach of strangers.

There is another tool the Indians used before the advent of the white men. It was used for knocking off bark for firewood, driving stakes and at any work were pounding was necessary. They would find a stone of wedge shape and work a groove around it and tie a handle to one side of the stone with a groove worked in sufficiently deep to protect the string. This served quite a purpose. This with the awl which they used for sewing taken from the foreleg of a deer or elk, and a pointed horn that they sharpened by the use of stone and sand made up the tools used by the ancient Indians.

I forgot to mention that the poles and sticks used in canoe building were brought to a proper length by the use of fire and line used for measuring was the black spruce root.

In the winter of 1846 I was trading at a place between the Snake River and Pocagemah Lake in Minnesota and on the bank of the Snake River near its entry into Cross Lake, I built my trading house. The name of the lake was derived from the name the Indians gave it, which was Pem-ma-che-go-ming, and means to cross or go through. In the Potawatomie language the word would be Kosh-ko-ming, a name they gave to a lake through which the Rock River runs in Jefferson County, Wisconsin.

After the treaty of 1837, lumbermen were in the habit of

cutting choice pine timber wherever it was handy to get a market, without owning the land or getting permission to cut the timber. In other words they were stealing it from the government. The Snake River was the outlet for much of this timber, or so much of it as was cut as far up as Knife Lake, on the Knife River, Rice and Tamarack Rivers, and Colonel Sims, of New Orleans, Louisiana, was the man whom the government sent to look after the trespassing. He had been in the Mexican War and had lost one arm. He arrived at my trading post in the spring of 1847. After informing me of his mission he asked to make his home with me for a while, as it was central in the country in which he wished to make his investigations and would also like to have my assistance in locating points where trespassing had been done. I took the colonel in and made him as comfortable as circumstances would permit. I found him a pleasant companion. He would relate his adventures in Mexico, in turn, for which I would recite matters about this country that were interesting to him. As he was an army officer I told him of the Indian soldiers, how they had their war dances, drills and parades, as well as white soldiers. This interested him very much and he was quite anxious to witness one of them where he could see a genuine medicine dance and feast and listen to the speeches of the braves, telling of their miraculous adventures and many hair-breath escapes.

At this time there live a missionary near Pocagemah Lake by the name of Boutwell, which lake was about four miles from my place by trail. Boutwell's wife was a half-caste Chippewa and a daughter of a member of the American Fur Co. She had been east and was educated and spoke both languages quite fluently. There also lived on the bank of this lake an Indian chieftain by the name of Bic-a-jek, who had a band numbering about 150 souls. His own family consisted of a wife, one son and a daughter. This daughter had lived close to the mission some time and became a favorite of Mrs. Boutwell on account of her naturally good manners and her Indian beauty. She had, with the assistance of Mrs. Boutwell, taken up the white women's mode of dress and was as neat and tasty as could be. She was the idol of the old chief and her brother, and for my part I must say she was the prettiest Indian maiden I ever met. She was pretty in feature, and in manners she was feminine to a degree not often overmatched by her white sisters. Mrs. Boutwell often told her she was pronounced handsome and that she must set her cap for a white husband. These teachings had their effect and caused her to appear at her best on all occasions, and especially when white people were present, consequently she became faultless in her attire.

The Colonel was telling me one day of the beautiful Creole women in New Orleans, and I told him there was an Indian beauty in the neighborhood, who, in features and form, could not be beaten in the whole south. Just them it happened that the chief and his wife and daughter were in sight coming to my place to trade. I told the Colonel that they were coming and he rushed for his uniform, which he always did when parties came, to whom he wished to show his rank. When the chief and party arrived at the post he was at his best in military attire and awaited an introduction, which I interpreted between them. The chief said he was glad to meet a white officer, as he was an officer among soldiers himself. The Colonel related his experience in war, the hard times he had seen, and how he had lost an arm in the bargain, to which the old chief replied: "He who strikes must expect to get struck," which was equivalent to saying, in the Indian understanding, "That's all right, don't grumble." The Colonel, turning to me said: "Your description of the daughter is correct. She is as pretty as a pink." He told me to cut her off a couple of calico dresses and to give the chief some tobacco also on his account, and urged me to arrange with the chief to have us present at their next war or medicine dance, and to tell the chief that he should be much pleased to see it, and perhaps he could give them some pointers in military matters that they would like to know. I interpreted the request to the chief, who said he was not then prepared for such an entertainment, but would have one as soon as the necessary arrangements could be made. I knew what that meant, for they never have one of these dances until a surplus of meat ahead to last from two to six days, so they can be spared from the chase, and these councils always last while the stock of meat holds out.

It was only a few days after that I heard that the hunters had been very successful, having killed a couple of bear and several deer, and knew the council would soon be called. The Colonel was in high glee. The next morning, and but a little after sunrise, I saw two Indians hurrying up the river in a canoe, and guessed they were messengers to invite us to the feast. I told the colonel of their coming and he was soon inside his uniform. And with the eagles upon his shoulders, he looked the veteran he really was. Along came the braves, and taking positions on either side of the doorway, said the chief had sent them to invite us to a drill and feast, and pointing to the sky where the sun would be at about ten o'clock, said that was the time for us to be there. One of them told me that the chief's daughter had told them to bring some salt and pepper for the meats of the visitors, which I gave them with a plug of tobacco to be smoked at the dance, and they hurried away. The Colonel was delighted, and said he could tell by the warlike looks of the chief and the beauty of the daughter that we would have a good time.

When we arrived at the Indian camp we were met at the shore by about twenty braves in war paint, clubs and knives in hand and scalp locks up, all ready to commence their drills and exercises. The war-whoop was given and a circle formed with the chief and drummer-boy inside, the chief acting the part of drum major and drillmaster. The dancing began; "round and "round went the circle, the chief going through the manual of the arms and being imitated by all the braves in the circle. This opened the Colonel's eyes as he saw the braves were no novices in handling the club and knife. The changing of club to knife hand and vice versa was gone through with for quite a time and was most beautifully done, when one luckless brave made a mistake. At a signal from the chief the drum

82

was sounded and everything was stopped, when the unlucky man was taken aside by the chief and drilled in an awkward squad of one until he became perfect, when the dance went on by giving the emergency war whoop. It was continued some time longer when speeches by the braves were in order, telling of their experiences since the last council, with varying effects. The feast came next in order, but first I will tell you how a war whoop is given. There are two kinds, the general and the emergency whoop. The first is given by a yell loud and long enough to allow the maker to slap his hand over his mouth three times, and then repeat and once again, which agrees with the white man's three cheers. The emergency one is given in the same way but only one is given in the same way but only one yell and signifies that there is no time to lose, but hasten quickly, and corresponds with the long roll in white military service. Dinner was now cooked and ready, the chief's daughter being the leader in that department. She brought and spread upon the ground in the long wigwam, which had been prepared for the occasion, new rugs and mats made of rushes woven together with bark. She placed the nicest one where she intended her white visitors to be seated. She appeared more neat than ever; with a nice fitting dress and sailor collar of white with beads in braids in great profusion about her neck and of many colors, her collar lapping at the throat in an artistic manner and fastened with the claw of an eagle; her fine black hair braided and coiled at the back of her head in the finest style, her beau catcher locks at the temple in shape, she was a perfect picture of health and beauty combined, and she was the chief waiter at the table on the ground. She first brought to each a piece of roasted meat that had been done at the fire on a stick. It was served on a plate made in tray shape of birch bark. This comprised the first course. The Colonel having but one arm, I had provided myself with a sharpened stick to use as a fork in cutting his meat with my pocket knife, which I did after excusing myself to the chief and his daughter for this lack of etiquette at an Indian dinner, where knives and forks, cups and saucers are considered unnecessary. The Colonel spoke in the highest terms of the cut of meat and the good taste in which it had been served and inquired of me what kind of game it was, but could not tell him as I only knew of their killing bear and deer. This course being over the daughter proceeded to take the orders for the next, inquiring of each their preference for boiled or roasted meat. The Colonel ordered both kinds, remarking that the bear meat was a choice meat to him, but venison rather beat them all. During this course the colonel said that it was nice, but could not compare it favorable with the first dish, and said he

must have the hide of that animal to take home with him to show to his people and tell them that it was from that animal that he had feasted at an Indian dinner, upon the choicest morsel he had ever eaten, not excepting that prepared by the French cooks of New Orleans. Taking from his pocket a five dollar gold coin wished me to tell the daughter it was for that particular skin. The old chief smiled at the sight of the "shiner," and more so as it was aimed at the hand of his idolized daughter, though he knew not for what it was being given, for I had not yet told him. The daughter was not at first inclined to take the gold, fearing it might be a breach of good behavior, but I assured her it was all right, and the coin was dropped into the hand of the dusky maiden, who, by the way, the Colonel had named "Queen of Pocagemah." The meal having been finished and the braves were preparing to continue their dancing and festivities, the Colonel requested that I call the maiden and go with them to see the skin of the animal that he might give orders to have it properly tanned and ready for him when he should start for home. I called the girl and we proceeded to the place where the hides were kept. The Queen of Pocagemah pointed it out, and there, stretched between two poles, hung the hide of a very large black dog. At the sight of it the Colonel's anger got the best of him, notwithstanding the presence of his charmer, and he arraigned me before the bar of his judgment in terms much more forcible than complimentary, and had he been provided with a gun he would no doubt have slain me, so great was his anger. But with only one arm he was convinced that he would be obliged to wait till another time to get even with me. The Indians became alarmed, thinking the man was crazy, as they knew not a word he was saying, and it was some time before I could get in a word of explanation. I quieted the Indians' fears by telling them it was a way he had, but that it was nothing against their treatment of him. But nothing would do the Colonel but to take our canoe and go home. On the way he became cooler and finally declared he had made an unnecessary show himself, without a cause, and after my explanation that I knew nothing of what kind of meat we were eating, and that it was no joke played by me, he became perfectly cool, and after a week or so sent for the hide, which had been neatly tanned, and took it home with him, as he said, a reminder of the war dance and his display of foolish anger. He returned to New Orleans after a few weeks and I heard from him several times in relations to trespassing matters, and in all his communications would mention the medicine dance, and was particular to enquire after the health of his "Queen of Pocagemah." About this time Mrs. Boutwell left Pocagemah and joined a mission up the Mississippi, but the chief's daughter continued her pursuit of a white husband, in which she was successful before the summer had passed.

In August 1847, a man by the name of John Drake came to Pocagemah. He was a fine looking man and although his business was a whiskey peddler, he won the smiles of Colonel Sim's queen and married her. He started a whiskey shop near Knife Lake where he traded in steel traps and trinkets with the Indians. A man named

Henry Rusk, who could talk some Chippewa, went into partnership with him so they would be able to trade. Quarrels and fights became frequent at their place and one or two shooting affairs. When Chief Bi-a-jek heard how matters were going at Drake's place, took his wife and went there to make them a visit. As is the Indian custom in such cases they took along their wigwam and pitched a short distance from Drake's house. They then went and called on the daughter and invited her to call upon them at their lodge. At this he objected and said she should never put foot in their wigwam. He also said, through Rusk, that if the chief was not away from there before morning he would shoot him, for he did not propose to have any interference in his family affairs. The girl was offended at this remark and watching an opportunity, she stole away and went to the lodge of her parents. Drake soon discovered her absence and found out where she had gone and became so angry that he took his rifle and fired a shot through the wigwam. It was now dark and Rusk prevailed upon Drake to desist as he had threatened to kill the whole family. Rusk now had the gun and told Drake if he would be quiet and stay in the house he would go to the wigwam and fix up matters with the chief. When the shot was fired by Drake the three occupants of the lodge had skulked away to the brush and the chief had taken a position behind a tree with his rifle to defend himself from any further attack, and as Rusk came out of the door gun in hand, so that Drake could not use it during his absence, the chief espied him by the light of the house and believing it to be Drake he fired at him, inflicting a mortal wound. As Drake now saw trouble ahead he quietly slipped away from the house, leaving everything behind him and reached my place just at daylight. He told me what had happened and wanted me to go and see to Rusk. I did so, taking with me three men. We found him just breathing his last. Drake took to the woods and I heard from him a month or so afterwards at Wood Lake here he had a quarrel over some steel traps. He afterwards went to a wigwam of the party with whom he had the quarrel, and not finding them drove the family from it and set it on fire. The Indian coming from the woods just then, where he had been hunting, saw what Drake had done, hunted him up and shot him. A sort of investigation was had over the affair, which resulted in the sending to the authorities at St. Croix Falls a report of justifiable homicide, but nothing more was done about it.

Chapter VIII

———— • ————

I wish now to go back to the subject relating to the difference in the Indians' condition before and after the white man's appearance among them, for it is a subject that I am sure will be eagerly sought for and studied before many years have passed, and that when it has been studied and fairly understood, the feeling that is now a general one among the people – which is if the Indians have been ill-used it is nothing more than they deserved, will be removed, and the blame for all the troubles made by the Indians placed where it properly belongs; the unbiased judgment of the future will be that the Indians were found good and were made bad by white people, and that the conditions of things has not been one whit improved by white associates, but, on the contrary, has been degraded.

Before their forced association with white people, the standard of their morality, for generations at least, and by tradition, had been most perfect and complete, as to the female portion of their tribes, but now it is assailed. The deadly firewater (whiskey) was brought among them and virtue fell. Fathers and brothers saw that the example of the white people was far from the teaching of the missionaries, far from the truth and the pretensions of the traders and far from justice and right, if their early teaching had been correct. Thus the naturally quiet and peaceable mind of the Indian men were disturbed and they were further agitated by the up braidings of their wives and families for having sold their lands and encouraging white people to come among them. Soon they realized

88

the error they had made, and with them, as with all people, the feeling created by having made a bad bargain, would not easily (*settle*)down. Promises of better times, or better clothing and better fed were not fulfilled. Annuity payments were delayed or missed altogether, and the father who heretofore had been a ceaseless toiler for his home and his family had become indolent, selfish and morose, and the few families who by reason of their connection with the traders though their daughters were better clothed from the trader's goods or better fed from his larder, become the objects of envy of those less fortunate. From bad to worse matters went until the once peaceable and industrious race of a few years before had developed into an indolent, vicious and beggarly mob. But this was not all that was in store for them. When a trader had finished his stay among them, which he was sure to do when his trading from any cause became unprofitable or his riches sufficient we would abandon his Indian wife and children and leave them for the Indians for support. I have known several instances where and Indian girl was the second time abandoned by these inhuman wretches and left to the care of her relatives, with additions to her first family.

There is now scarcely a day that I do not meet and have occasion to converse with some of these same children, in many cases where their fathers are or have been prominent men, wealthy and respected.

When I see a son or daughter of wealthy and respectable men, living as they do with the Indians, the finger of scorn pointed at them, with no one to care for them on account of their Indian blood, or to protect them for their father's sake, it is far from a pleasant sight for me, and I feel called upon to relate at least one incident which happened by recently and in which one of these daughters, now a woman of perhaps thirty-five or thirty-six years of age, and the child of a man once a member of the cabinet of our country, was a central figure. She had once been married to a respectable half-breed, who died shortly after their marriage, leaving her in poor circumstances. A certain class of hoodlum white men – whose presence has ever been a curse to the Indian – gained entrance to her home against her wishes, and with whiskey and unbecoming conduct caused reports to be circulated which ended in her being arrested for keeping a house of bad repute, all because her Indian blood made impossible for her to be heard or considered by her white neighbors. She was placed in jail and remained there for thirty days without trial. About the time of her arrest or a short time previous, there had been several white women arrested in the city for the same offense, but they were prosecuted under city ordinance, making the offense a finable or jailable one, while the charges in her case was brought under state statutes, which made to offense punishable in the state prison. There were then a fair number of half-caste people in the community who could read fairly well. They saw the discrimination and had seen it before, and they believed the disposition of the officers was not to give them fair play, and from the fact that I had been identified with the Indian for fifty-four years and from the further fact that I spoke their language, it was natural for them to come to me to be informed in this as well as other matters, and they asked me why this discrimination existed. Knowing they were aware of its existence, I told them the truth: "It is because you are Indians." In the case of the young woman I went to the judge and district attorney and pleaded for her. I told them I knew the woman well and had since her birth, and also knew her father; that he had many times sent me presents and kept it up until he died, but at his death as far as I knew, he had made no provision for his daughter of the forest. I told them I did not think she should have any greater punishment than the others, who had been arrested and prosecuted for a like offense, and thought the punishment she had already received was sufficient, and that she had no money and no one to defend her. I asked that she be allowed to go upon her promise to sin no more, and when the prosecuting witness refused to testify against her if her punishment was to be greater than her white sisters' had been, the judge and district attorney agreed to and did release her on her promise never again to give them occasion to arrest her. The result is the woman is now living on the reservation and as far as I know has never given cause for another arrest.

I have done all I could in the past to keep the Indians quiet, peaceable and satisfied, hoping that the government would someday take hold of the matter and right their wrongs, and wish to say without any desire to flatter myself in anyway, that I have in the past had the good fortune to keep in check the number of uprisings among the Indians, which, without the counsel I gave them, would have resulted in butchery. I always gave them counsel when they were in the proper mood and sober of senses, and never when they were excited or intoxicated. I never sold an Indian a drop of liquor or helped them in any way procure it. I always dealt fairly with them and gave them as good bargains as I would a white man.

From my earliest recollection I have been more or less among the Indians, in fact the principle part of my life has been spent among them, first the Cherokees, Choctaws, and Creek nations in Tennessee and Georgia, and at the age of ten years I spoke the Cherokee language better than English. Leaving that part of the country at ten years of age, I never saw much more of those tribes. When fifteen I came north and have been with the Sauk and Foxes – Black Hawk's people – the Sioux, Winnebagos, Potawatomies, Ottawas, Menominies, and Chippewas, but since 1840 with the Chippewas most all the time and have been brought up as might be said with their habits and customs. I readily learned the Chippewa tongue by being familiar with the language and signs of other tribes with whom I early associated and within two years. I had their language almost perfect and from my earliest contact with Indians, I learned that the best to adopt was truthfulness and fair dealing a "do as you would be done by" policy as it was the true and only one that found favor with them. I never promised an Indian anything until I was positive I could fulfill it. In this way I soon had their confidence and friendship and I must say I have ever found them the truest of friends and the most implacable enemies.

A once prominent citizen of Ashland and a resident of Bayfield at a time when a plan was being matured by which a number of white men through a deal they were contemplating with the Indians, could make a quantity of money, and after I had been informed of the plan and offered an interest in it, which I refused because I thought it was an unfair deal for the Indians, made a remark after I had left the room, which was: "I believe Armstrong would steal from a white man to give to an Indian." Afterward in conversation with this gentleman, I told him that his words had been given to me by one of the party and that I took no offense at the remark, but in very forcible language told him I would under no circumstances "steal from an Indian to give to a white man."

The Indians are a very quick-sighted people and have a memory that is traditional for its volume and they were not long in discovering that they were being unfairly treated by the traders and others, and they reasoned in this way: These men are now our relatives by marriage to our sisters and we must make the best of it for the sake of this relationship. Under this way of looking at things, matters continued for a number of years and was borne by the Indians as the best way of getting along.

But the climax came when the traders quit the country and left their families to the Indians' care. This led to family troubles. The abandoned woman would go back to her family where there were probably several children and dependent persons to support and only one or two men to hunt for their living. The addition to the perhaps already heavy burden was hard to bear. The white race were cursed, family talks resulted in aggravating troubles that were already heavy enough. Division of sentiment in many cases led to bitter quarrels and bloodshed and in some cases separation between man and wife, a thing unheard of until recent years. The abandoned women have in many cases lived to see their former husband married to white women and too proud even to speak to their wife or child of a few years before. I do not wish to reflect on any one or more persons to whom this may be personal but give it for history only. I give no man credit for marrying an Indian woman and claim he gains no honors by so doing, but I do claim that once he has married her he puts himself upon a level with her and really is no better than she and certainly the children are of his blood and he should at least see that they are cared for and educated instead of leaving them to grow up in ignorance with a race he had voluntarily left as unfit for his association. Go upon the reservations and one can see that of those people there now, not one fourth remain that have no white blood in their veins, and two thirds of this amalgamation is traceable to those persons who located themselves among the Indians for the purpose of trading exclusively, Indian agents and government employes.

It has always seemed to the Indians that the disposition of traders was purely selfish and now they know that their only object in coming among them was to profit by and through their unskillfulness, and never had any intention of dealing fairly and being honorable with them, myself also included with the victims, for certainly I have been wronged and swindled by this same class of men, who betrayed me after my confidence was gained.

Annuity Payment at La Pointe, 1852

I wish now to say something of the conduct of the Indian Agents and the manner in which they have dealt with the Indians and to state fact that have come under my personal observation, and I wish to say in beginning this subject that but one agent, whose distribution I attended dealt fairly with and used no deception in his transactions with the Indians, and that was Agent Hayes, who was appointed by President Tyler. When he arrived with the annuities and after they had been placed in the warehouse, he sent for the chiefs and asked them to take their interpreter and the way bills and go through the warehouse and satisfy themselves that all packages called for by the bill were there all there, and all boxes, barrels, bales and bundles were checked before they were opened. A few packages where short and Mr. Hayes told the chiefs that when he came next time they should be added to their goods for another year. The packages were opened and the Indians were satisfied that all was there before anything further was done. The Indians were then enrolled and the goods were divided among them. First, goods were put in packages dividing them equally – the packages for families and packages for single persons were all put up and labeled with the name of the owner. Then the Indians were notified that the annuities were ready to be distributed, and would be on a certain day. One man at a time was let into the payment house, and he came as his name was called by the interpreter. When he entered he was asked to touch that pen and his goods and money were given to him. This payment was conducted without a jar or any trouble and after the distribution was completed the chiefs were sent for and all the boxes, burlaps, and even the cordage was given to them, and quite a handful of money which was left over, for where even change could not be made in all cases was given to the chiefs also, and they were told to divide it as they saw fit. The acts of Mr. Hayes all through the distribution were praiseworthy. He would explain, through the interpreter, the amount that was due, and count the Indian's money before him.

The custom practice before Mr. Hayes and after him was to allow the traders places by the pay table, especially the American Fur Company, with an open sack in which to take the money claimed to be due them from the Indians and as soon as an Indian had touched the pen the bill against this Indian was handed to the agent and the money poured into the trader's sack, the bill was generally enough to cover the Indian's dues. But at this payment the scheme did not work, the agent told the traders beforehand that he was not there to pay traders, but to pay Indians, and if they had bills to collect they must do so outside the payment house door, as he would not be a party to a division of the Indians' money. He also had the interpreter explain to the Indians that the great father had sent him to pay them and that he hoped if he owed these traders any honest debts they would pay them, but he should not allow the traders to impose upon them and take money that was not their due.

Had the manner of doing business that was adopted by Mr. Hayes been commenced and carried out in making payments a great deal of trouble would have been avoided and the strongest point of Indian objection to the traders would not have existed. But Mr. Hayes never came back to make another payment and the old ways were again adopted.

James P. Hayes served as Indian Agent at La Pointe on Madeline Island prior to the Sandy Lake incident. La Pointe was both the center of regional trade and the political seat of the tribe at the time. Armstrong tells us Hayes was concerned for the Natives and urged for a sense of fair play regarding their treatment. Although Hayes recommended their removal from Wisconsin to lands west of the Mississippi, it is likely his inspiration for this came from his superiors. Still, some say it calls his concern for the Ojibwe into question.

His way of doing business did not suit the traders and charges were preferred against him, one of which he drank too much. The charges were made so strong, whether truthfully or not the public can conjecture, that he was removed from the position and Dr. Livermore appointed in his place, who seemed to satisfy the American Fur Company much better, although the Indians were much displeased. Following Livermore came John S. Waters,* of whom I have spoken previously, then H.C. Gilbert was appointed and still not improvement. The next to follow was Silas Drew of Indiana, the L.E. Webb of La Crosse; after him Asaph Whittlesey, who took charge of the office for a few months but was not confirmed by the Senate. Col. John H. Knight superseded him but his appointment was not confirmed and he too served only a few months. After him came Major Clark of the army; then Dr. Mahan, and it was during his administration that the treaty of 1854 expired and since that time I do not care to say what agents have or have not done, as it is of recent date and within the reach of any who care to look it up.

*Representing the Chiefs of the Great Lakes tribes, Chief Great Buffalo formally accused Indian Affairs Agent, J. S. Watrous, of the grave neglect at Sandy Lake that killed many of their people. In Buffalo's eyes as well as the other chiefs', Watrous was the government official primarily responsible for their removal to Sandy Lake. They claimed he knew full-well that the allotments would never arrive and the long journey would be disastrous. The five tribal chiefs felt it was his doing that they were denied their money and supplies, fed spoiled food, and deprived of reasonable shelter — all resulting in the illness and death of hundreds of their people. However, the root of the removal of the Ojibwe and the appalling, outrageous treatment they received at Sandy Lake originated not in Wisconsin, but in the highest government offices in Washington, DC.

I will now refer to the Modoc troubles* a little, as I had a friend, Col. Ben. Green, a cousin of mine, there at the time, who sent me full particulars of the affair, diagrams of the county and other matter pertaining thereto. I do not care to enter into details as to the orders of General Canby to the Modocs as they are already in history, but will say that he was informed beforehand that if the orders issued were attempted to be carried out without first giving the Indians a chance to be heard, there would be serious trouble, as the Indians had good reason for not wishing to remove to the reservation which had been set apart for them. It seems Canby did not take kindly to this advice but took steps to carry out the orders he had issued, and the Indians, who knew of his coming with troops to eject them, ambushed the troops, General Canby being killed and the Lava Bed campaign began. The death of General Canby in history may differ from this as to the place and the manner in which he was killed, but I got this account from a disinterested eyewitness. I have no doubt, but that the Indians in that campaign were misled by Capt. Jack (*Kintpuash*) and others for the notoriety and gain there was in it they not thinking or perhaps not caring for the consequences such an affair might produce. As a rule but one side of Indian war stories get to the public and that is the side that comes from and through the parties most interested, and this accounts for the deep-seated hatred which everywhere exists for the red man, but it is my fixed opinion that before many years have passed a great change in public opinion will take place; the Indians will be credited with having had an abundance of honor in their primitive days and a heap of abuse since.

In 1872, U.S. Army troops engaged the Modoc people who refused to leave their homeland for a neighboring Klamath, Oregon, reservation. Around 150 Modocs resisted, 55 of them able-bodied warriors. They secluded themselves in caves within an ancient lava bed in the lands they knew so well. In battle, Captain Jack (Chief Kintpuash) killed General Edward Canby, the highest ranking American officer ever slain in combat with Native Americans. Eastern newspapers called for vengeance. Unable to penetrate the Modocs' natural fortress, the Army increased their numbers to more than 1,000 soldiers and volunteers.

In June 1873, the Modoc warriors were captured. Captain Jack and five others were prosecuted for war crimes in what is now regarded as an illegal trial. The defendants, who had no counsel, could not speak English. And the jurors included soldiers who fought in the conflict. Captain Jack and three others were hanged in a public execution with much fanfare, bringing the Modoc's losses to thirteen. The military losses numbered over 200 dead and 55 wounded. Two Modoc warriors were given life sentences in Alcatraz. The remaining resisters were transported by train to a reservation in Oklahoma, their women wailing in grief the entire way.

I will now give space to a clipping from "The Minneapolis Journal" of February 4th, 1891, entitled "Some Indian History:"

"I see the people are making a great fuss over Gen Miles," said a prominent Dakota man to a Journal reporter recently. "When he returned to the 'World's Fair City' the bands greeted him playing "See the Conquering Hero Comes"; he was banquetted and nearly all the prominent citizens made speeches landing his masterly conduct of the Indian campaign. It is possible that there is something of a political nature in all this buncombe, but it is to be hoped that the country will not allow itself to be deceived with regard to the recent Indian uprising. General Miles is praised for his sagacity in averting one of the bloodiest Indian wars ever known to the history of this country. This statement is absurd and a calm and impartial investigation of the facts will prove my assertion. Without entering into the fact that the government has shamefully treated the Sioux Indians and that they were half starved and illy-clothed, the fact remains that there was no uprising whatever. The "ghost dance," so called, was nothing more

98

than a half-crazy religious excitement, and had the Indian bureau placed a brave and competent man in charge of the Pine Ridge agency, there would have been no need of calling out the military whatsoever. Even after Gen Miles' army arrived there, if we may take the word of the most noted Indian scouts, notably that of Maj. J. M. Burke, who is a sort of a white chief among the Oglala Sioux, the trouble might have been averted. Burke says emphatically that Col. Cody (Buffalo Bill) could easily have succeeded in inducing Sitting Bull to go with him peaceably, and that had he been allowed to carry out his program there would have been no Wounded Knee fight and no bloodshed. You must have noticed that Gen. Miles or the Indian department gave strict orders against allowing the chiefs who were taken to Washington to talk to anybody. Inasmuch however, as they have gone to the capitol to hold a powwow with the government, I do not care to talk about the matter or to have my name mentioned, but if you want to hear the other side of the story you should interview some person who is connected with the Indians and who knows their grievances. Hunt up Gus Beaulieu, of your own state. He had charge of all the treaties here and has represented the Chippewas in all their land deals. He may have an interesting story to tell you."

Gus Beaulieu* who is a resident of St Paul and who is widely known among all the Indian tribes of the northwest when found said:

"The whole truth of this sad business will come out some day and when it does some of the events that preceded the Custer massacre and led up to that bloody butchery will startle the country. I think it was in April, 1876, and something like two months previous to the annihilation of Custer's command, that Miles and his soldiers rushed in one day upon an Indian village in Montana and killed every man woman and child in it. Bucks, squaws, and pappooses were shot down without mercy. There were between 200 and 300 Indians killed. The village was far from the railroads and the telegraph, and information of the horrible affair did not reach the government and the people until after the Custer massacre, and then, of course, the public mind was so occupied with that butchery that no attention was paid to the previous massacre of the Indians. When the Sioux met Custer they expected no quarter and gave none. Even had the whole truth about the outrage committed by Miles and his soldiers been known at the time no action would have been taken, such was the excitement and prejudice against the red men. Here in Minnesota when the Mille Lac Reservation was opened to settlement, Indian Commissioner Marty, Rice, and Whiting made a treaty with the Chippewas in which each Indian was promised land in severalty. Bishop Marty, one of the commissioners, gave me the treaty to interpret. I then told the Indians that in my opinion they were transferring all their rights to these lands. Bishop Marty and Commissioners Rice and Whiting were asked to hold up their hands and swear that if the Indians filed on these lands for homesteads their rights would be observed the same as white men. This the commissioners swore to. Afterwards white men filed on the lands that had been taken by members of the Chippewa tribe and when the matter was referred to the Secretary of the Interior that officials decided that the Indians had no rights whatsoever."

"Why is it that you or some person for the Indians have not made complaints to the President?"

"That is precisely what is now being arranged for. The Indians through the entire northwest have agreed to send representatives to some point not as yet designated, to collect the data and fact regarding Miles' outrage in Montana, the starvation at Pine Ridge, Cheyenne and Rose Bud Agencies, and the failure of

100

the government everywhere to keep treaties. This council will be held as soon as practicable and certain chiefs will be designated to go on to Washington to present all the facts, their wrongs and grievances, and more especially to expose the whole truth in regard to the outrage committed before the Custer massacre."

After this interview with Beaulieu I got a letter from him in relation to other matters as well as this interview, and he says he was misquoted as far as to the name of the commanding officer at the massacre in Montana. He said his was hearsay to a great extent, and that the officer commanding at the massacre of the Indians was General Baker.

*Augustus "Gus" Beaulieu, born the son of an Ojibwe woman and a French fur trader in 1852, devoted himself to improving life for his people. Among his successes was The Tomahawk, a Minnesota newspaper. In it, his editorials often corrected statements and stories about Native American issues found in eastern papers. Gus testified in Washington on behalf of Natives, much to the chagrin of Bureau of Indian Affairs agents, often the subject of his complaints. The motto of his paper, "Justice and Fair Dealing For Every Indian Who Desires to Become a Good Citizen," reflected its purpose to act "in behalf of and to secure the welfare of the Indians of the United States." Gus gained the highest respect from his fellow Minnesota tribesmen. Other Ojibwe also benefitted from his good will. One of his final editorials exposed wrongs done to individuals in Wisconsin. Gus died in 1917.

When the Modoc hostilities began I saw the opportunity for which I has long been watching, of taking a band of Indians east to show them the great white nation and what civilization really was, and at the same time be engaged in a paying pursuit. Under an assumed name, to cover the nationality of the Indians I had with

101

me, which I represented as Modoc, I made the trip. I collected a party of six of the most intelligent of any Indian people in this section, five of them young and active men and one and old and experience chief.

We left Lake Superior in the early part of November, 1874, and went on foot to Eau Claire, Wisconsin, there took the train for Boston, only stopping one day at Niagara Falls, showing them the sights. The old chief had been there before however when he was a boy. While in Boston I had and offer from a theatrical manager of $5,000 for a three month's engagement at a theatre there, but as that would have prevented me from showing my people what I set out to show them, I declined and took a train to Manchester, New Hampshire, intending to go as far east possible and then work my way west, stopping at all the principle cities. When we arrived in Manchester I met the manager of a large show named E.S. Washburn, whose show was named "Washburn's Last Sensation," and was constantly traveling over the eastern states and was then going through Maine, Vermont, New Hampshire, Massachusetts, Connecticut, Rhode Island, New York and Pennsylvania. I thought this the best opportunity of showing my people the great wonders of the east and at the same time keeping up expenses and accepted the offer from him. The combination then consisted of forty-four persons and we traveled with him for eight months. I showed the Indians all the manufactories possible and with them examined all objects of interest that came our way. Whenever we stopped overnight and especially over Sunday we were visited by a great number of people and the conversation naturally turned upon the subject of the Modoc War. I avoided it as much as possible to assign reasons or the probable cause of the uprising, more especially because I found a great prejudice existed everywhere in the east and against the Modoc people and against all Indians in general, and it would not be policy for to speak in their favor, or even to infer that they possibly might have in the right in that uprising.

At one meeting where a goodly number of people were gathered, a gentleman whom his companions called "Captain," related to me briefly his experience in an overland trip to California. Before making his start he said he was particular to provide himself with a particular rifle, as it was possible he might want to practice his marksmanship on Indians before he got through. On a certain morning while on his journey, somewhere in Utah, himself and one other started ahead of the caravan to look for antelope or other game, and after traveling a few miles he espied a squaw with a back-load of wood, which she laid down, as he supposed to rest and sat upon it. Thinking this was a good opportunity to try his marksmanship, he leveled his trusty rifle and fired. The girl dropped from the pile of wood and he remarked to his companion that her posterity would never scalp white people. An old gentleman in the party then asked: "Captain, did they follow you, or what happened next?" The Captain answered: "No, they did not follow us and we saw no more of them," but, said he, "I heard, after getting to California, that the caravan that was following in our wake and a few days in our rear, were attacked near that place and the whole party slain," and then he added: "Gentlemen, you see what a savage nature and brutal instinct those Indians had, to

surround that caravan and kill the party." I could hold myself no longer, whether it was policy or not, and said, 'suppose a band of Indians were passing through your country here and one of them should deliberately and without cause shoot one of the women in your neighborhood, is there a man in this house or in this city that would not jump for his gun to avenge that murder?" Turning to the Captain, I said: "Your language shows, whether your story be true or not, that your natural disposition is to commit such an atrocity as you have mentioned, whenever an opportunity should present itself, and you can resent these words of mine or not as you please." But he did not resent it and I stated then that this very act of this self-confessed murderer, and similar acts of others had always been, and still were the cause of all the troubles with Indian tribes. Here is a fair example of many others where the real murderer escaped, but the consequences of his act was visited in a ten-fold manner upon the heads of innocent and defenseless parties. This dastardly and unprovoked assault upon an innocent and harmless woman had caused a wail o woe to go up from many a broken home, and the Indian must bear the stigma of a people, when by right it belongs at this man's door. There was considerable agitation in the meeting at my remarks but it broke up without any open rupture. One more incident that occurred upon this trip, which is in connection with a tradition given in a former chapter, I wish to mention. We stopped one Sunday in Springfield Mass., and I took the Indians out for an airing, as we usually took tramps on Sundays. We went six or eight miles up the Chicopee River to Chicopee Falls, where the old chief fell behind the party and when I first noticed him he was intently surveying the surrounding country. I asked him at what he was looking and he replied: "I have many times heard Buffalo tell you of the experience his great-grandfather had with the first white man he ever saw, and I believe from the description that this is about the place. If I could get over to the other side I could satisfy myself in an hour or two." We crossed over and the old man made a thorough survey of the whole locality and when he returned, said to me:

"This is the place." He told me that he had found signs of a burying ground and that here had someday been a hard battle fought there, either between whites and Indians or between two tribes of Indians, and was quite sure from the signs that one of the burying grounds was that of the Algonquin tribe, but could find no monument to indicate any particular persons that were buried there.

After we had returned home the talk for the next six months was concerning the sights they had seen in the east and one incident connected with these talks, was when the old chief was asked how may white people he saw on the trip. After a short hesitation replied: "Go down along this fence to that tree," pointing it out, "then to such another point; thence to such a rock and back here," – I judged there was six acres in the tract, – "and then count the blades of grass growing there and that number of will give you some idea of the number of white people I saw."

Chapter IX

———— • ————

THE MOUND BUILDERS AND THE GROUND HOUSE PEOPLE – THE
ORIGINS OF THE CHIPPEWAS – EARLY MISSIONARIES – EARLY
ASSOCIATIONS AND INCIDENTS – WATERMELONS – AN INDIAN
EXECUTION – BLACKHAWK'S CAPTURE

Among the most interesting matters to which I have listened
while with the Indians is their tradition and belief regarding the
earliest inhabitants that lived in this country, the trend of which is
that two distinct races of people were upon the earth before the
Indians were,—the Mound Builders and the Ground House
People,—though many of the most intelligent believe that the two
races were on the earth at the same time. Their opinion and belief,
however, is founded upon tradition, and what they what they can
see on the face of the earth. The mounds that are familiar to many
of us, are supposed by most people to be of many years standing.
The Indians have no tradition concerning their origin and are as
much in the dark as we are as to whom or by what race they were
built.

I am aware that this does not agree with many eminent
historians and there are many educated people who have made deep
researches, who believe they were of Indian construction, but I
have talked scores of times with old Indians upon this pint and am
satisfied that they knew nothing of them, nor have they any
tradition that the people who did build them were like themselves
in any particular, but believe whoever they were that they were
destroyed by a pestilence. Nor have they any idea of the origin but
do believe that it has been many thousand years since their race
began.

The race or tribe from which Buffalo descended were the
Algonquins. He had tradition covering that point. The first mention
I can find of this tribe in history is in 1615, on the River St.

Lawrence, and no Indian could ever tell me anything of tradition that I could make out to be farther back than that date. A few years subsequent to this I find them at Sault Ste. Marie and Father Marquette with them as a missionary, and at this time they are mentioned as the Northern Algonquins, from which I infer that more of the same tribe were found south. In 1641, according to Sadlier, "We find the Jesuits among the Chippewas at Sault Ste. Marie, Fathers Ryambault and Joques in charge," and in this account he says: "Father Ryambault was well versed in the Algonquin customs and language and Father Joques was an adept in the Huron tongue. It was at this time that the Jesuits that the far famed Sioux dwelt only eighteen days further west – warlike tribes with fixed abodes – cultivators of maize and tobacco and of an unknown race and language." Again Sadlier says: "On the death of Father Joques, the war broke out anew, the fierce Iroquois desolated the lands of the Huron drove the Northern Algonquin from the shores of the lake and slew the French and their allies under the wall of Quebec," and again he says: "in 1656 a projected mission to Michigan was frustrated through the cruelty of some pagan Iroquois. Thither, however, in 1660, at the entreaty of the Algonquins, was sent Father Menard, a survivor of the Huron Mission, and the companion of Joques and Breboruf and four years after Father Allouez found the mission at the further extremity of Lake Superior, and in 1668 Father Allouez with Fathers Marquette and Dablon founded the mission at St. Mary, the oldest European settlement within the present limits of the state of Michigan."

These are the last accounts I find of the Algonquins from whom Buffalo descended and it must have been about this time that the Algonquins were merged into and became a part of the Chippewa people – almost 230 years ago.

As to the tradition of the Indians in regard to the Mound Builders I quote from Gerard Fowke: "The chroniclers of DeSoto's Expedition mentioned many villages of Schellakees (Cherokees) in which the houses stand on the mounds erected by those people and describe the methods of their formation. The French accounts of the Natchez Indians tells us that the king's house stood on a high mound with the dwelling of the chiefs on smaller mounds about it – when a king died this successor did not occupy the house of the deceased but a new was erected on which he fixed his abode." It is conceded by a majority of students that many, if not most of the earthworks of western New York and adjacent portions of Pennsylvania were built by the Iroquois and allied tribes. Even Squire admitted this towards the last. At the foot of Torch Lake near Traverse Bay, Michigan, are two mounds which an old Indian told me were erected, one by the Chippewas and the other by the Sioux over their respective warriors slain in a fight near there, about a century back. Near the north line of Ogemaw County, in the same state, are some small mounds built over their dead by the Indians, who lived there until a few years since. Some lumbermen opened one of them some years ago and taking two skeletons ran a pole through the chest of each, to which they fastened the bones and then tied them to a tree with a piece of bread between the teeth of one and an old pipe in the fleshless jaws of the other. The Indians soon discovered what had been done and hunted several days for the despoilers of their kinsmen's graves, swearing to take their lives if they should find them. A few other mounds in this section of the country are said to have been put up by the Sioux and the Chippewas and one, at least, by the Iroquois.

Great stress is laid on the fact that in the same mound may be found "mica from North Carolina, copper from Lake Superior, shell from the Gulf of Mexico and obsidian from the Rocky Mountains," and this is supposed to indicate, in some undefined manner, superior powers and intelligence. Cameron says the Chippewas informed him they formerly carried copper to the south and east to exchange for such small articles as other Indians had in those directions for barter, going sometimes as far as the coast of Virginia. On inquiring of them whether the old Chippewas, that is those of previous generations, had worked the ancient mines, he was told they had not. That the mines were there before the Chippewas came into the country and latter obtained their supplies by gathering up fragments where they could find them, or by chopping off pieces with their hatchets from nuggets or boulders that were to be found in various places.

Here the writer of this work will give a few points in his experience in Wisconsin in quite an early day. I came to Jefferson County, Wisconsin in June 1847, with my father's family from Madison County, New York, had a lad of seven years of age, and well I remember the Indians of that time in that part of the country. The tribe was Potawatomies, and the name of their chief was Ke-was-kum. They were peaceable and friendly and lived at this time on the eastern shore of Lake Koshkonong. Within three days after our settlement on the farm four Indians came to the house, and seeing some bread that mother had just taken from the oven, gave father signs that they wanted some. He gave them a loaf. The next morning before the sun was up, the family was awaken by a rapping on the window – all were frightened and the first thing we thought of was bad Indians. Father went out and found two Indians with a pickerel on a pole between them on their shoulders, the tail of which touched the ground. They soon made father understand that the fish was in payment for the bread he had given them the day before, and their manners showed they were thankful besides. On another occasion a few years later, a few came to our house one day in autumn, and my brother and self gave them some watermelon to eat. They saw the patch from which we got them; that it was large and that there were plenty of melons there, and made father understand that they wanted more, to which he assented, and they soon went away. The next day about noon Ke-wash-kum and about 40 of his people, men, women and children, with twenty ponies, came down the land and made known their errand. They wanted melons. Father motioned them ahead and the patch was soon covered with Indians and with sacks to carry on their ponies like saddlebags, made of rushes woven with together with bark, they were soon well supplied, having as many melons as their sacks would hold, and they had not forgotten to bring saddle bags for each pony. The patch was stripped, but their joy over their good luck was very much appreciated by us children, and ten times more than the melons worth. They were the happiest forty people I ever saw at one time. It was only a few days after our arrival on the farm that I heard a man say to my father, "You ought to have been here about a month earlier. We had and Indian execution down to the river." He then went on to tell how it was done and what it was for. It seems that one Indian had killed another by shooting him from the opposite side of the river. Court martial was held and the culprit sentenced on the eye for an eye plan. He was sent to the spot where his victim had stood, and at a signal from the chief, the executioner, who was a brother of the deceased, raised his rifle and at the same time, said the relator, the Indian to be shot held open his blanket and like a martyr, stood and took the shot that quickly sent him to the happy hunting grounds. I have many times been upon these banks, which are about one-half a mile above where the Rock River enters Lake Koshkonong. The right bank of the river is the identical place where General Atkinson cornered Blackhawk in the campaign against him and from where he escaped in the night, not until he had reached the point of his capture near Prairie du Chien. This is Blackhawk Island, so-called, although not an island, but peninsula between the river and set back of the lake on the west called "Stinker Bay."

On both sides of Lake Koshkonong are many mounds built in different shapes – two I remember, one shaped like a turtle and one representing a man lying on the ground with his arms out stretched. These two mounds are on the east shore of the lake and the highest portion of them not more than five feet above the level of the ground around them. The Indians made this made this lake their spring and autumn home for a number of years after I knew the place coming regularly in the fall to gather wild rice which abounded there. I have seen them often gathering this rice which they do in a canoe, on squaw paddling the boat and the squaw in the bow bends over the plants and with a stick whips out the kernels into the canoe. Many have tried time and again to get from the Indians some knowledge by tradition of the mounds surrounding this lake, but as far as I ever heard in the twelve years I lived there it never could be done. They claimed to know nothing about them. I used to think they did and would not reveal it, but in the late years I have come to the conclusion that like ourselves, they found them when they came and know no more of their origins than we do. On the banks of this lake in 1847 and until the plow had obliterated were plainly to be seen the cornrows and hills of the aborigines. The Indians of whom I speak did not till the soil. They lived on lived on meat, wild rice and fish. I have picked many arrowheads on my father's farm near a little lake there was upon it and the surroundings in that part of the country plainly show that for many years it had been the home of a prehistoric race."

As there has been much history written in regards to mounds having been built by ancient Indians and some by more modern tribes, I wish to add the knowledge I have gained by association with the Chippewa tribe, and to say that during my long experience with them I have become satisfied that neither the present Chippewas nor their predecessors as far back as their tradition goes, knew anything whatever of their origin or how they came to exist. I know their mode of burial for many years back and if it had changed from any other mode for a number of generations, I should have found it out. They have always claimed simply to know nothing about them. I have met many people who think the Indians know all about them, but by reason of their great love for their dead, and fearing the graves would be desecrated if they should divulge the secret, they will not tell, and some claim that the secrets of the mounds are religious and therefore sacred.

Chapter X

———— • ————

EXCITEMENT AMONG THE WHITES AND INDIANS OF LAKE SUPERIOR – ORIGINS OF THE FAR-FAMED GHOST DANCE – WAS A HALF CRAZY RELIGIOUS TEACHING

I will now relate some circumstances, which connect themselves, in an indirect way, with the interview with Gus Beaulieu, printed in the "Minneapolis Journal" of February 4th, 1891, given in the previous chapter.

It was the spring of 1878, I think, that considerable excitement was caused in and around Ashland, Wisconsin, over a report in circulation that Indians were dancing and having powwows further west and were working their way toward the reservations in this part of the country. Settlers came to me at different times to inquire if I knew or could tell the cause of it knowing that I was familiar with the language and could give the information if anyone could. All I could tell them was that I had heard of something of the kind going on in Minnesota and they were moving toward this state. The next I heard of them they were within one hundred miles of Ashland; that the party were performing and teaching a new kind of dance. I resolved to meet them and did so when they were about 20 miles from Ashland, at a place where the Courte Oreilles Trail crosses the White River. When I arrived they were preparing their camp for night. There were between sixty and seventy in the party, which consisted of a young Sioux girl and her interpreter, the balance being made up of Chippewas from the immediate vicinity. Before I had a chance to talk with any of them their camp was complete and the dance began, which I watched with much interest, it being the first of kind I had ever seen and to see it had been my object in meeting them. About the time the dance had been completed I got an opportunity to talk with an Indian I knew and he pointed out the Sioux girl and said there would soon be an opportunity for me to talk with her. As soon as the ceremonies were ended I had a talk with her, through her interpreter, who was a half-breed Chippewa. She represented herself to be of the Sioux tribe and a member of a band of the tribe that were massacred by Custer's Army on the Little Big Horn, about May 1876, in which all her people were killed except herself; that she saved herself by jumping into the water on the approach of the soldiers and hiding herself by clinging on to the roots the bushes of an overhanging tree or upturned root until the slaughter was over and she could make her escape; that she was in the water about twenty hours; that she reached a band of her tribe and told them the story.

Whether the girl was crazed by the events and her mind shattered by awful trial and exposure she endured, I do not know but she said that spirits had told her she must teach a new dance and to teach it to all the Indian tribes and she had come to this reservation to teach. She taught that the Indians must put away the small drum they had always used and make a larger one and stop their war and pipe dances and practice only the one she was teaching. She said the small drum was no longer large enough to keep away the bad spirit and the larger one must be used on all occasions. Her nation, the Sioux, she said, had given up all other dances since the massacre of her own little band. We can all readily imagine under those circumstances and the excitement of those times how readily the Sioux took up this new dance. They were ready to accept anything of a spiritual nature at that time and took to the teachings of this girl as readily as they would to a manifestation from the sky. Knowing the Indians disposition so well I saw how quickly they would fly to this new idea.

All Indians believe in a hereafter, not a single infidel was ever known among them, and the sooner they get to the happy hunting grounds the better it will suit them. With these ideas they prepared for war. The recent slaughter of all the people in that village led them to believe that the white soldiers intended to exterminate them as soon as possible, and they were in daily expectation of another raid, and were well prepared for their coming on so that when Custer's command came in their sight and went into camp they watched their every move, and when their pickets were thrown out the Indians fell back enough to allow them to post, and when it was dark they crawled upon the pickets and soon dispatched them with clubs and hatchets and then proceeded to the camp where the man body of Custer's men were and put them to their final sleep. This I give as it was related to me by a mixed blood of the Sioux's own people.* From the date the girl gave in telling of the slaughter of her band and until the massacre of Custer, the Sioux had been gathering all small parties together and in one army awaited and expected another attack from the white soldiers and when Custer's command came within their reach they were well organized, and as my informant told me, had a great many warriors.

*This nighttime attack conflicts with most historians' accounts of the Battle of Little Big Horn.

I have since met from time to time since the Custer horror, a number of persons who at the time lived among the Sioux, some of whom were white men whom I always believed were renegade confederates of the rebellion that went there for the purpose of stirring up strife if they could. One man in particular, whose name I did not learn, but was a southern man, which I could readily detect by his speech, corroborated in every particular the manner in which the Custer command was annihilated as related to me by the eyewitness.

The girl who represented herself to me as the sole survivor of that village massacre, remained here among the Chippewas some days and the last I heard of her she was going further west among the Crow and other tribes, teaching as she claimed, by the advice and direction of spirits, what is now known as the "ghost dance."

Armstrong's memory fails him here. Either he has the wrong decade in mind, or the girl mentioned may have been teaching something other than the Ghost Dance, credited to Wovoka (Jack Wilson), a Northern Paiute spiritual leader. In a January, 1889 solar eclipse, Wovoka experienced a vision. In it, he saw all Whites leaving the west while Natives danced the new dance.

Seeking a new form of spiritualism and hoping to return to their former ways of life, many Indian Nations adopted the new dance, adding their own variations. Concerned that it gave new courage to Native warriors and might lead to uprisings, the War Department outlawed the Ghost Dance, yet some Natives still danced it. When practiced later at Wounded Knee, tensions mounted and the Ghost Dance contributed to in the U S Army massacre of 150 - 200 Lakota. Most were women and children. Twenty-five soldiers died, almost all by friendly fire, as the Lakota were unarmed.

Chapter XI

—————— • ——————

During the winter of 1841, an uncle of mine, who was a resident of St. Louis, made a proposition to start me in the trading business, provided I could locate a place outside of the Hudson Bay and American Fur Company territory, to which there would be some means of getting supplies to, and also of shipping furs from, and for this purpose I made a trip up the Mississippi. I picked two of the best guides I could find to accompany me during my trip.

Our little party, which consisted solely of myself and guides, left Pocagemah Lake, Minnesota about the first of May in the spring of 1841 taking very little provisions of any kind. When we started, we had only enough to last two or three days, with the exception of salt, and pepper, which I took for my own meats and had a sufficient quantity for the trip. We depended wholly on our guns, with which I had provided the Indians; they carrying shot guns and myself a rifle, each carrying his own ammunition, of which we had plenty. We were continually on the look-out for game, for we were careful to keep our larder supplied with at least one day's provisions, which was an easy matter as game was plentiful and one need go but a short distance for want of a shot at a deer or any smaller game, while traces of elk, moose, caribou and bear were frequently met with.

The route we traversed going up I cannot describe, there being no surveys of any kind, but we went up on the east side of the Mississippi the whole distance only seeing the river twice on the trip, keeping into the wood for several miles, my guides telling me it was far the best part of the country to travel through to avoid lakes, rivers, marshes, etc., which we would otherwise be obliged to cross. The whole country was then inhabited by Indians, who we met frequently on the route, who were then dressed in their native ways.

The guides I took from Pocagemah Lake led me somewhat astray, taking me considerably to the northwest of my destination, and we arrived at the Lake of the Woods about twenty-eight days after starting. Here we found that we were out of our course and not, as I supposed, anywhere near the Mississippi. At this information I determined to procure a new guide which I did, who went through with me to Lake Itasca, and told me that this was as far up as any white man had ever been. The guide was a man of about thirty-five or forty-years of age, and was born and brought up between Lake of the Woods and the head of the Mississippi, and had trapped and hunted over the entire country.

Just before arriving at Lake Itasca we came upon an Indian camp, of five or six lodges or families, and stopped there with them over night. Here I found another Indian pretty well along in years, who must have been upwards of fifty, and who was more familiar with the country around the head of the Mississippi than the former guide claimed to be. In listening to the conversation in the lodges that night, between the guide who brought me through from Lake of the Woods and our host, who was the old gentleman spoken of before, I found him giving my former guide many directions, and concluded he was thoroughly acquainted with the country. He described a river as coming into another small lake just above Itasca, the source of which was the dividing ridge between the waters flowing east and west, the outcome of which was that I employed the old man to go along with me, and also to furnish a canoe, leaving the first two guides behind to remain and hunt for the folks in the camp till we should have returned.

Soon after leaving the camp with the old gentleman he told me he could take me to the headwaters of the Mississippi if I cared to go there. This was not my object in making the trip, but when I found it would be impracticable to start a trading post, there being

117

no means of transportation, I determined to get acquainted with the whole country, hence my visit to the headwaters of the Mississippi.

After exploring the river thoroughly as we proceeded up stream, which took considerable time, we at last launched our canoes on the waters of Lake Itasca, which had for more than a century been considered the headwaters of the Mississippi River. The Indians from that country disputed the long standing supposition that Itasca was its headwaters, and said that there was another lake and another stream further up, the steam being entirely fed entirely by springs, of crystal like appearance, and they were positive that the stream at the head of this little lake was the headwaters of the Mississippi, to confirm which I explored the whole country thoroughly. After going through Lake Itasca we were compelled to abandon our canoes, and proceed on foot. This we were obliged to do, the stream being so filled up with driftwood as to make it slow work to get a canoe ahead. In going up this stream we made it a point to explore on both sides. The distance traveled after leaving Lake Itasca I cannot give accurately, it being so long ago, but it must have been considerable, it having occupied quite a time, and can only estimate it. It was probably between twenty and twenty-five miles.

Just after leaving Lake Itasca we came to a widening of the river, which my guide told me was something called a lake. This was not more than three or four miles above Itasca. About twenty miles beyond this we beheld one of the most beautiful little lakes in the whole country, it being surrounded by hundreds of small springs, in fact it is almost entirely fed by springs, having a stream at the further end which has its source in these crystal-like springs at the foot of and up the sides of the hill, I concluded that the Indians were right in saying that this was the true source of the Mississippi. All of these small lakes were filled with finest speckled trout I ever had the good fortune to see.

From the top of the hill to which the Indians took me at the head of the small, which runs into this little lake above Itasca, the sight was the most grand of anything I ever witnessed. The surface of the earth descending as far as the eye could reach and the landscape was beautiful.

For some time afterward I intended making another visit there for the purpose of taking notes and getting maps to present to my uncle for writing it up, but before another opportunity offered my uncle died and I was blinded and the trip I had intended for the interest of myself and others had to be abandoned.

This trip to a country where moose were then plentiful brings to mind a short story of the attempted capture of one of these animals on Chequamegon Bay.

Quite early in the forties, I think it was in '43, there lived on the banks of Fish Creek, a small stream which empties into the head of Chequamegon Bay, near the present city of Ashland, Wisconsin, an Indian named Da-cose and his wife. They were childless and lived apart from the Chippewa tribe, to which he belonged, by reason of his eccentric nature. He was a lazy, indolent and selfish man and at Fish Creek game was as plentiful and in greater quantity and greater variety and could be more easily obtained than in any other section of country that he knew of.

In case of an invasion by the warlike Sioux he would temporarily move his abode and join the tribe and would remain among them until the battle had been fought or the scare was over when he would invariably return to Fish Creek which for many years had been their permanent home.

I knew this family well. The old man was lazy and improvident throughout his whole disposition and was one of that class of people whom we often meet that seem to think the world owes them a living whether they strive for it or not. His wife, on the contrary, was directly the opposite nature. She was a hard worker, always busy and industrious. She tended the fish nets, set and attended the snares and traps for larger game and fur bearing animals, and in fact was a whole family in herself, and as is the nature of such people she often complained to the old man of his

119

selfish nature and reminded him that only for her care and watchfulness for their welfare they would have nothing to eat or wear, and as the old man believed his ways were right and that it was folly and useless to fret about the future, and from the fact that a wife among the Indians was only expected to be seen and not heard, he never took kindly to her advisory way of making remarks to him and these differences in their general makeup led frequently to hot words and petty quarrels, though I never knew that the old man ever allowed himself to chastise his wife for her interference with his superior position in the family, but it was an almost daily occurrence for him to chide her for her fretfulness and to him her uncongenial disposition. He was always satisfied with his lot and what they had to eat, be it little or much, and as a matter of course thought she ought to be. He would shoot what ducks, geese, and other game came handy or providentially his way and trust to luck or the old lady to do the rest.

One morning as the old lady was passing out of the creek to her nets she espied a moose plunging into the water from the southeast shore of the bay, closely followed by a pack of wolves and she knew the moose only had one way to escape from his howling pursuers, which was to swim to the opposite shore, some three miles away, as he could not land in the swampy ground around Fish Creek. The point where he entered the water was not far from the Keystone Lumber Company's sawmill. As she would have plenty of time she hastened back to inform her liege-lord of the circumstances and request that he make ready and accompany her and assist in capturing the moose while he was yet in deep water and unable to defend himself against their attack from the canoe, and she quite forcibly insisted that he waste no time in making his preparations to start and remarked: "If you move as slow as you generally do the moose will be across the bay before we are ready to go."

This ruffled the old man's equipoise somewhat and he retorted: "There it is again! Always fretting about something. How many times I have told you to take it easy. Don't you see that the moose is coming our way, as things generally do?"

She said something about his enterprise, having had little to do with the discovery of Mr. Moose but desisted from further relieving her mind on this point with true womanly tact, knowing the old man would rather argue than go after the moose. He made inquiries as to the size of the moose and whether in her opinion he was in good condition and the probable chances of her being able to overtake him, until she became too vexed to make further replies. This he took to be a cooling down of her irritable temper, and he followed along to the bank of the creek and actually only stopped once on the way, and that was to sharpen his knife on his gun barrel remarking to the old lady as he did so: "It takes a sharp knife to skin a moose." But as he was about to step into the canoe he stopped and shouted "Te-wah! I forgot my pipe," and back to the wigwam he goes for it.

The old woman's patience was about as nearly exhausted now as it well should be, she paced up and down the creek in rage and her Indian vocabulary had about ran out when the old chap returned and seating himself in the bow of the boat with his little flint-lock shotgun, he says "I am ready" but refused to take up his paddle and assist the old lady in moving the boat saying: "You paddle along, I want to talk to you. I know you can catch that moose before he can get half way across the bay and I want to tell you what you have got to do."

The old woman retorted: "Take up your paddle and help me, there will be plenty of time to talk after we have got the moose."

But the old man could not see that his duty ran in that direction and just then catching a glimpse of the moose he says: "I will now take a smoke for after we have got that meat to take care of there will be plenty of work to do and no time to smoke," and he deliberately takes his pipe from his kinnikinnik sack and with his flint, steel and punk he starts a light and began to smoke.

The moose was now quite well along over the distance he had

121

to swim and the old lady was and had been from the start using her paddle as for dear life and was fearful that she would not be able to overtake it him before he should reach low water and again she tried to induce the old man to take his paddle and help her, to which the old hero replied: "I will now tell you what I started to a while ago and then I will help you paddle. You see, as soon as we get this meat, your relations will come and want some of it, but don't you give them a particle. We will carefully cut all the meat from the bones and dry it and lay it away. It will last you and me a long time and when your friends come you may make some soup from the bones and that is good enough for them. Of course I will be there and be busy telling them what a hard time we had in getting the moose and how we got it to shore and will show them the moccasins we will make from the hide, which we will ornament so nicely with porcupine quills. I will manage to keep them busy and you be sure and not give them a bit of that meat.

The old woman had now given up all hopes of getting any help from the old man's paddle and she kept brushing away satisfied that she could overtake him without help, for the moose was now getting tired as well as herself. The old man now faced about and saw the moose but a little ways off and shouted: "Bo-shoo! Moose, you are always afraid of an Indian. Don't hurry we want to get acquainted with you."

In a few moments more the canoe was alongside of the moose and the old lady said: "Take your knife and cut his hamstrings and cut his throat, too, he may get away from us yet."

"Yes," the old man said, "there it is again, always in a hurry. Lay down your paddle and rest. I will take a hold of the moose and he will pull us along," and laying down his pipe he took hold of the moose, and patting him on the back says: "How nice and fat you are. I say, old woman, what nice eating he will be."

The old girl now made a rush for the knife to disable the animal, but the old warrior fought her away, saying; "Don't be in so much of a hurry. Give the poor fellow all the time to live you can. His meat will soon be boiling in the pot." But the old woman's fever was not going down a bit. She saw they were nearing the shore and knew the sand bars could not be far away and she again entreated the old man to kill the animal. She took the pole that she carried in the canoe for use in shoal water and sounded and found she could touch bottom with it, and with a shriek of despair she shouted, "Be quick or he will get away." Just then the moose caught his hind feet on a sand bar and darted ahead and broke the old man's hold on him. The old lady made the best use of the pole and kept as well up to the animal as she could, and the old man really began to realize that something must be done pretty soon, and raising to his feet brought his gun to his shoulder to shoot, but snap went the old flint lock again and again. The moose could now use all four feet, as the water was getting shallow. The old lady was doing her best but the moose was gaining on her. Snap and snap again went the gun, and the old girl saw that the jig was up. Her anger had reached it bounds, and reversing the pole she set it firmly on the bottom of the bay ahead of her and shouted "Mar-chi-an-

iem" which means (the "old devil's dog" and was the only word used among the Indians as a substitute for stronger language until the appearance

Don't Eat Moose until You Catch Him

of the white man among them) The canoe paused and Mr. Indian and his flintlock went head long into the bay. The old woman turned her canoe around and paddled homeward; leaving the old man to get out of the water the best he could and foot it around the head of the bay home, a distance of about two miles.

I hailed the old woman from the shore, a short distance from Fish Creek, where I had been standing during the chase, and she took me in the canoe and paddled me around to their wigwam, there relating the whole story to me. I did not wait to hear the friendly chat between the couple on the old man's return, but started on my journey into the woods. On my return I made it a point to reach the lodge in the evening and stay overnight with them, and laughed and joked with the old lady and gentleman over the mishap of the day.

CHAPTER XII

———— • ————

Two Languages among the Indians – Their Religious Beliefs
– A Secret Order Similar to Those of the Civilized World –
The Happy Hunting Grounds – The Mysterious River

During my early associations with the Indians I discovered that, at times when the head men and chiefs were congregated and discussing some private subjects, they used a language that I could not understand, and I inquired of others what they were saying who like myself could not understand them, and all the reply I could get from such people was: "That is Chief talk."

From that time forward I interested myself in the matter and persevered until Buffalo told me there were many secrets in the Indian nation known only to the initiated, and that it was connected with their religious belief. I continued to persevere and interceded with Buffalo until finally he told me he would take my case before the council and it was possible that I might be allowed to receive a part of the secrets but said no white man had ever been admitted that he knew of and thought my case a hopeless one. This was after I had been adopted as the son of Chief Buffalo, and through his intercession I was at last admitted to the order, and what I have seen of the world leads me to think it resembles very much the secret orders of white men, and I claim that it is impossible for anyone not a member to be able to give any sign correctly though some may claim their ability to do so. In many cases applicants are admitted but few get through. I also claim to be the only white man on earth ever to gain that distinction. This may seem the argument of a braggadocio, but I will give any man in the world all the opportunity he may desire of showing me any knowledge of the ceremonies and signs belonging to the order and if he is able to Show it aright I will admit that he is possessed of the knowledge that I claim belongs only to myself among the white race.

125

There is much that I could say upon this subject that would be interesting reading but to say much more would be the commencement of an exposition which under no circumstances would I divulge. The oaths and pledges that I gave in gaining entrance to and elevation in the order were made in the presence of Almighty God and are as sacred to me as though they had been made in any temple of the Most High and there can be no order in existence where any member could feel the weight of his obligations more keenly or absolutely than I do. There are some things that were secrets in the order that I may mention. For instance, show me a wigwam that has been built by direction of a chief who was a member of this order or an old framework of one, and I will tell you the number of the party that inhabited it, the number of males and the number of females, the direction from which they came, and the direction they had taken on their departure. This was done for the information of these who might follow or to assist the chief in hunting up his people in case he needed them in council or to repel an invasion, and his posted men who were following up the roving portion of his people could quickly tell if any were missing—and whether male or female—from a previous count.

Old, very old tradition with the Indians is that all are created equal—that the earth is given them for a temporary purpose and that they are to have the use of all they see, but are not to dig or delve into the Great Spirit's treasures that lie hidden in the earth, except for such as are absolutely necessary for their existence and comfort. They had a belief that there could not or should not be such a thing as individual or tribal ownership of lands or to search in the Great Spirit's possessions to find what He had hidden there for his own use and benefit. That to search for such hidden treasures would provoke the Great Spirit and greatly jeopardize their chances of ever reaching the "happy hunting grounds," and when the white men came among them to make treaties they had no idea that whites thought for a moment that Indians owned the lands or their hidden treasures, but supposed they look upon their occupancy of the earth the same as the Indians did – which was tenants at will, of the Almighty. You therefore see that the theory that the ancient Indians worked the mines of the country for profit must be abandoned.

The Indians, as shown by tradition, did and still do believe that the "happy hunting grounds" lie just beyond a mighty and beautiful river, over which they cross immediately after death, provided their whole life here had been such as to entitle them to pass without a prohibition on the banks on this side, and those who had lived a life beyond redemption were washed away in a mighty river, while those whose lives had not been perfect were held to await the final judgment. They also believe that the conduct of the friends they had left behind had much to do with a favorable or unfavorable decision at the river. Another firm belief they had was that should one of their number, who was at the river awaiting judgment, attempt to evade the judgment by crossing the river before the sentence, he would be washed away and that would be his eternal ending. The later believe is in accordance with Indian belief from first to last, to never attempt to evade a duty, however slight or great, but like a man, to stand for the right thing and fear not. In this they believe that no matter how upright a man had been through his whole life, if after death he should seek to evade the judgment, his entire future was lost. When once across the river he was beyond all tribulations and in a land of perpetual sunshine and with all friends that had gone before him.

Now to show you the attention they paid to the graves of their dead and the consistency of their remembrances of their deceased friends, which in their belief, was necessary to a favorable consideration of their friend's case at the river, they would divide whatever they were possessed of and place a portion of it on the graves, until such time as they felt that their sacrifices had resulted in a favorable decision of their friend's case at the river. The period of this sacrifice would be kept up depended on the collective

127

opinions of the friends that were left behind as to the probable time it would take to compass a favorable decision, and if, in the opinion of the friends of the dead, he would not promptly pass the final tribunal, the ceremony would be kept up at the grave indefinitely with the firm belief that at the last of this intercession would avail and result in the passage of their friend to the "happy hunting grounds," where their forefathers were.

It is a universal practice with the Chippewa to sit with a sick person incessantly till the breath had left his body, keeping up a constant beating on a drum to keep the bad spirit away and to let the spirit of the dying go in peace and in the possession of the good spirit. This practice has always been condemned by the missionaries and teachers as being the Me-de-wa religion, the real meaning of which neither missionaries nor teachers ever understood. The Indian belief is that both the good and the bad spirits constantly hover around a sick bed and that the sound of the drum kept the bad spirit away; that the good spirit cannot be offended; that if they can only keep the bad spirit away until death takes place the good spirit immediately takes charge of the soul and carries it to the river, where it pleads with the Great Spirit for its immediate transportation to the good land.

Now in regard to the custom of Indians carrying game and eatables and distributing them at the graves of their dead as a token of their remembrance and as a mode they had adopted for pleading to the Great Spirit. Everybody knows that the chief subsistence of Indians in olden times, and even yet, is game, no great stock of which can be laid away for future use, which made the procurement of food a daily struggle for existence, and no Indian, from all I could ever learn was well fed. They had feasts as well as others, but food was a scarcity, and from this fact all will admit that to part with a portion of their food was the greatest sacrifice they could endure, and it was for this reason and none other than this system was adopted. To think for a moment that the Indians were so devoid of expedients as not to be able to adopt any other plan of remembering their dead is bosh and nonsense.

The Indian people were in all essentials a band of brothers and aside from family relations they nationality extended. As an example, one hunter who by reason of his better sense and ability to devise new and improved methods for capturing game had succeeded in bringing to camp a large moose or other animal, such as is not frequently secured by the average hunter, a feast upon this animal would always follow, as was the custom, the only reward the hunter got was the distinction he had won by his marvelous prowess. Everybody was invited to this feast and was expected to be present, and all who had buried friends not gone a sufficient length of time to have secured their passage across the river were expected to take a small portion of this meat as an offering of sacrifice to their graves. The bond of unity was never lost sight of, a favor to one was a favor to all and an insult upon one was an insult upon all, and in either cases the act was never forgotten or allowed to become rusty in their minds.

As I have mentioned of the secret order among the Indians in early days, and that they had signs by which they were enabled to hunt up the different bands and families of the tribe, I will say that they also had other signs, one of which was a sign of recognition that called for protection the same as a flag of truce, and I will mention a case where it was used to good advantage. There is now a man living at Ironwood, Michigan, to whom this incident may be referred to for its correctness. His name is William Whitesides, a photographer at that place. In the fall of the year 1865 Indian Agent Webb left Bayfield, Wisconsin for Grand Portage, Minnesota, near the mouth of the Pigeon River, to make an annuity payment to the Chippewa Indians on the north shore of Lake Superior. Mr. Whitesides and myself embarked with him on this voyage as passengers, not being in any way connected with the business of Mr. Webb. When the boat was anchored, about 4 pm, in the bay just inside the island a messenger came from the Indian village in a canoe and inquired of General Webb if he had brought specie* for the money payment, and if not they did not wish to have him and intimated that it would not to be safe to do so.

Specie refers to money in the form of gold or silver, rather than paper notes which could lose value if the market collapsed.

Mr. Webb replied, through his interpreter, that he had not brought specie but had brought all the goods that had been promised them and paper money. The messenger said they would not accept greenbacks; consequently they did not desire him to land at all and then went back to the shore. This led to a long talk between General Web and the men aboard the schooner as to what had better be done, and it was decided as the weather just then was unfavorable to lift anchor, they would depart the next morning, as there was not a man on board who thought it would be advisable to attempt a landing. I told General Webb that if he would have his men lower a yawl I would scull it ashore and find out what the trouble was if I could. All pronounced me crazy and Agent Webb said I would be foolish to attempt it, but the boat was lowered and I got into it feeling satisfied that there was some Indian on the shore that would recognize the sign I intended giving them, as soon as I was clear of the schooner and sufficiently near the shore to be distinctly seen by the Indians I gave the sign and immediately saw that it had been recognized, for the Indians began to move up to the shore and seat themselves upon the beach. This was an assurance to me that I would be protected and when the yawl had reached the bank the Indians assisted in pulling it up on the beach where it would be safe from washing away. After getting on shore a few Indians recognized me as the interpreter who had previously been with Mr. Webb. They shook hands with me, saying: "We heard that you were no longer with Mr. Webb." I told him I was no longer in his employ now, but was only a passenger. I then began to inquire what the trouble was, and quickly discovered that they had been getting bad advice from the traders, the same as given to the Sioux previous to the massacre at New Ulm, and for the same reason—

they wished to profit by the difference in value then existing between specie and greenbacks and had advised the Indians to accept nothing but specie in payment of their annuities. I told them the agent was not to blame for not having gold and silver to pay them. He had brought what the great father had sent him to give them and if they refused to received it he would be compelled to take it away and store it in some warehouse and await orders as to what he should do with it, as it was not at all likely that he would attempt to come back again before spring and that my advice would be to accept it under protest or the promise of the agent that he would see that the difference in value between gold and greenbacks was made good to them at the next payment. This resulted in three chiefs getting into a canoe and going back to the boat with me and they told the agent that they would accept what he had brought upon his promise to make up the difference on his next trip.

Making the Landing at Grand Portage

The next morning the goods and money were distributed, and a more peaceable and orderly payment I never witnessed. It was all brought about by my knowledge of the secret sign, for as soon as the chiefs discovered I was a member of their secret society my word and advice went almost the same as law. I mentioned this one case only as there is a living witness to the statement, but I have often found it useful in my intercourse with the Indians.

I will now undertake to show with what love superstitious awe, reverence or by such term as you may see fit to call it, the Indians hold the Great Spirit and to what extent they will go in keeping secret a matter, the revelation of which might, in their estimation, provoke the Great Spirit. The custom of holding religious councils, which is as old as tradition goes, is begun by assembling in a wigwam where someone, generally a chief, calls the attention of his hearers to the main matter under consideration. Then each person present in turn is expected to add remarks upon the subject, which is being considered, giving information of any experiences he may have had personally since the last council. Back in the 1840's and when one of these councils was being held at La Pointe, about twenty miles from Ashland, an old man who had, by the help and guidance of the Great Spirit, as the Indians imagined, discovered a place where pure silver could be obtained which the Indians in those days used for ornaments. An especial use they put it to was mounting pipes that were to be used on special occasions, such as a visit to the great father, and whenever silver was wanted this particular old man was asked to provide it as he alone knew the secret location. For years he had obtained it whenever wanted. He would start out alone and unobserved and return with the silver, but no one knew where he went or by what route. Neither did they consider it a matter of their concern. In fact they considered it would be greatly wronging the Great Spirit them to inquire after the secret that He had vouchsafed to the old man, with much agitation, arose to make his speech, and I saw there was something coming from him that was not expected. He told his people that as they knew he had for many years been the possessor of the secret where the silver was found, it was with much regret that he must tell them that the Great Spirit was angry with him for he could no longer find the place where the silver was. He then described the outlook of the place, but did not give its geographical location. He described it as being a narrow passage at first through which his body would only pass with much exertion, gradually

132

growing larger until he could proceed on his hands and knees, and finally large enough to stand erect. He reported that it was a huge cave where he could pick up or chip off such pieces as he required, and I will add that the Indians believe it was not right, in cases of this kind, where they were getting rare specimens, to take of such but sparingly and under no circumstances to search for what was hidden, but would take only such parts or pieces as the Great Spirit had left in sight for their use and benefit. Another example is where an Indian had found a silver bar, from which he cut with his hatchet a piece that weighed a pound, and never to his dying day, a good many years afterwards, would he reveal the place he found it. I have many times seen this piece of silver and weighed it, in fact it was in my possession a number of years, and this Indian three times started with me to the place where he had found it, and as many times backed out and each time after going, as I afterward learned, to go just one-half mile towards the setting sun from the moss covered log where he had turned back from his first visit with me and I would find it, but between the time he had gone to show me, I lost my eye-sight and although I have tried, since my eye-sight has been partially restored, to find the place, I have never been able to do so, but where he found it is still a mystery, for if anyone had ever found the place they probably would have seen the piece from which the Indian cut the specimen he brought in which plainly showed the marks of his hatchet at each stroke made in securing it from the piece he had found.

The circumstances connected with this case I often think over; How the old man started with me on three occasions, and each time would begin to falter about the same distance from home, but he would keep on until his conscience would no longer allow him to proceed, the reproach he felt by reason of his belief caused him to turn back, the fear the Great Spirit would be offended, was too much for his untutored mind. He feared should show me the spot it would result in digging and taking away from the Great Spirit the treasure that He had hidden for his own benefit, and all

133

the glitter of prospective wealth, should the mine prove valuable, could not drive out this fear.

In my novels about the life and times of Chief Namakagon, I explain that he traded silver for supplies in the busy Lake Superior port city of Ashland, Wisconsin, during the early 1880s.

I also mention he was very secretive about the location of his mine. Namakagon chose to show only one person the way to the mine. As the story goes, on the way they came upon a black bear. The bear stood upon its hind quarters,

Chief Namakagon, also known as Mikwam-mi-migwan or Ice Feathers, is a legendary figure who lived in Bayfield County in northwest Wisconsin from 1846 until his death in 1886. Prior to living in Wisconsin, he was known as Shaw-shawa nay-baysay or Swift Swallow and also known as John Falcon Tanner, an adventurer, war hero, and author from Canada, northern Minnesota, and Sault Ste. Marie, Michigan

raising both front paws. The chief took this as a bad omen—a warning to turn back for fear he would offend the Great Spirit. Although specific details are scarce, local historians agree this event most likely did take place. Armstrong's memoir somewhat supports the claim, though there's no mention of a bear.

It's said Namakagon never again offered to take anyone to the mine. He was found dead in the same vicinity a year later. The circumstances of his 1886 death remain suspicious. But that's another story.

My investigation into this brief episode in the rich life of Chief Namakagon turned up several intriguing points. Late in life, Benjamin Armstrong, while in Ashland (a city frequented by

Namakagon), was quite likely acquainted with the chief. They held much in common. Both men were fluent in English and Ojibwe. Both were Caucasian. Both married Chippewa women. Armstrong spent decades learning the customs and traditions of the Ojibwe people. Namakagon, raised as an Ojibwe, lived according to those customs and traditions. Was Chief Namakagon confident that sharing information about his mine would result in the Ojibwe people one day benefitting from its riches? Indeed, long after Namakagon's 1886 demise, Armstrong kept a large chunk of raw silver on his desk, purportedly given him by Namakagon.

Was Armstrong the sole friend chosen by the chief to visit his silver mine? Armstrong relates a tale of not one, but three journeys to see a secret silver mine, led by the old man. Though there's no mention of a bear, they turn back prematurely all three times, hoping to not offend the Great Spirit, according to Armstrong. Was he speaking of Chief Namakagon when he mentioned these trips? Did he deliberately omit his friend's name? Keeping Namakagon's identity secret, even after his death? Did Tanner, once wanted for murder, ask that he never be named? Or could Armstrong have had another reason to omit the old man's name? The answer may remain forever lost along with the truth behind the suspicious death of Chief Namakagon and the location of his legendary silver mine.

The American Fur Company knew of [another] find and tried all the persuasion and strategy of which they were capable to extract the secret from the Indian without avail. When a man found the silver his brother was in company with him. They had stopped by a creek to rest, as they were carrying home a deer they had killed. He often told me the circumstances of the find. He said they had stopped to rest and get a drink from the creek and while seated there had smoked, and after he finished he pounded out the ashes from his tomahawk pipe on a stone near him and then in a sort of pastime way he began tapping his pipe on different stones near, when he discovered that the sound of one was different from the rest, and that a little moss had gathered over it, which he brushed off and discovered the point of a silver bar. At first he thought it lead and said to his brother: "We have something to make bullets from."

Another story in connection, which I will not vouch for entirely, is that the American Fur Company devised a plan by which they would decoy his brother with whiskey to the spot. They first gave him a few drinks, and promised him more as they went along to the place they wished him to point out and told him that in case he succeeded in showing them the bar from which the piece had been cut, he should receive a heap of presents. Some say he was promised a house to live in. At any rate they got him into a canoe with another Indian to help him paddle across the water to the main land, over which he was to proceed to the place where the silver was found. The company men were to go in another boat, but just as this brother was to start the idea flashed across his mind that his canoe was the proper place to carry the bottle of whiskey, and he would not budge another step until the men gave him the whiskey. Although the men were almost certain the scheme would miscarry if they let him have the bottle, it was their only show, for he would not go without it, and after a consultation it was decide to let him have it. The chance they took proved a slim one, for the Indians were wildly drunk before they had proceeded half way across the water, when they both fell to fighting over the bottle and were drowned.

Although some parts of this is true, I will not guarantee that all of it would have borne investigation, but enough of it was true to carry to the living brother the conviction that the Great Spirit was displeased by the actions of his brother in attempting to reveal the secret and he was drowned by the will of the Great Spirit.

I give these incidents, which look more like stories than history, for I firmly believe the two places I have mentioned will be discovered, and should this occur, some may be living who can connect the stories with the find and thus establish the fact that the poor Indians knew of them, but by reason of religious zeal, would not disclose it lest those hidden treasures of the Great Spirit should be appropriated to the use of man, and their hidden recess be desecrated. There were parties living on the Apostle Islands, and in the surrounding country, subsequent to the advent of the American Fur Company, who have seen this piece of silver. One is still living at Bayfield, Wisconsin; his name is Ervin Leihy, who, until he, was a member of the firm of Leihy & Garnich, of Ashland, Wisconsin, who established a hardware business there in 1872.

For years after it became known that I had more knowledge of the whereabouts of the silver bar than anyone else except the old Indian, I was watched if I undertook to go to the woods by parties in the hire of men I could mention, which prevented me from making any extensive search for the deposit until after I had lost my eyesight.

I know of silver and native gold also being found in the vicinity of Ashland by different men from time to time. One man in particular who claimed to hail from Missouri, found two or three specimens of gold, which I saw. I am well acquainted with the locality where he had his camp, where he left when he went away a rude map, which, although indefinite, would give a person acquainted with the locality an idea of the country he wished to describe by his map, and later on, in company with Col. Whittlesey, of Cleveland, Ohio, a geological expert, I spent several days in the vicinity indicated by this map, but we failed in our attempt to locate the particular place where he may have found the specimens. At the time the Missourian left he said he would go below and form a company and return. He said he had been offered a big sum by the American Fur Company to explore the location on their account, but had refused it, and proposed to explore on his own account, but

137

he never returned, to my knowledge. Col. Whittlesey told me that the formation of rock he found at this time led him to believe gold was located in the vicinity, but said: "I have studied geology for forty years, more or less of the time, but I find when I get into this country I am entirely at sea, but I believe gold or silver, or both, will be found at the junction of the trap rock and granite, and think in all cases that the gold, silver and copper is north of the iron, first coming the copper, which may be found anywhere in the trap and conglomerate therewith, and that silver will be found with it also, and that silver-lead exists somewhere in that section of country."

The Indians have always told me that there was no doubt of there being large deposits of precious metals in and around Lake Superior, particularly on the south and west sides. I have also met and talked with Indians who thought such deposits existed on the north shore particularly in the region of Pigeon River, and back in the interior thirty or forty miles and I have seen fine specimens brought in by them to Grand Portage, one which was purchased by Clark W. Thompson, Superintendent of Indian Affairs of the Northwest, then stationed at St. Paul, and in talking with the party who brought in the specimens, I should judge by what little he would say, that the silver was found in a cave or crevice of rock, and as I was anxious to find out where it might be, I took every occasion that presented itself to ply the Indians with questions that might lead to its immediate location, but I was unsuccessful, only learning that the place was not likely to be discovered by any casual observer, even though he might happen near it. I have talked with many men who do not like to give Indians credit for their claims of finding these things as they were wholly ignorant of geology or any other information that would lead them to search in right places for such metals, but I account for their finds in this way, for I know they did find them as a matter of fact, and as there was no mining going on in any of this country at the time, they must have found the specimens native and without searching in the earth for them. The Indian in those days often lived in one locality for from ten days to six weeks, and made their stay always the longest in sugar making time, and as hunting was their only occupation, they had occasion to become familiar with every locality in their vicinity, and as they moved frequently, the whole country came under their explorations. The Indians' nature was to closely search for dens of animals, and no matter how dangerous looking a cave or cavern was, the Indian was in his elements until the last nook and niche was visited, and as many of the most valuable fur bearing animals were found in such places, they were especially looked after, and as the women's duty in those days was to do all the labor in moving camps, pitching them in new places, and doing all work attached to camp duty, the men's time was all taken up outside of camp. Indians in those days lived to a good age, from 100 to 125 years was not at all uncommon. You readily see what a thorough knowledge of the whole country they must have had. There would probably not be a rock, tree, stream or lake that they could not speak of by reason of some peculiarity he had noticed. I never knew of one Indian divulging to another any discovery he had made, the nature of which would lead to his being considered and acknowledged as a child of the Good Spirit, and any Indian was considered as a favorite with the Great Spirit who could bring the proof, by specimen or otherwise, of anything that was not a common knowledge or theory. Each Indian had his own exclusive hunting ground, which was pointed out to him and described by the chief, whenever a new location was settled, and none encroached upon the hunting domain of another. Thus each man had an opportunity of becoming a favorite with the Great Spirit if by his researches he could find or discover any new thing or theory that was not commonly known, and although an Indian received no distinction of title or other advantage by reason of his discoveries, except the distinction of being favored by the Great Spirit, the natural sequence was that each man thoroughly search his own domain.

The Indians believe that thunder is the voice of an immense

invisible bird that comes at times to warn them that the Great Spirit is displeased with something they have done, and that it always comes when the county is already storm-vexed, as the time is then opportune to add its voice to the naturally saddened feelings of the people, thereby making its presence more effective. The lightning they believe to be flashes from the eyes of this enormous bird, and when the storm is fierce and the flashes vivid it is taken as a warning that their bad deeds are many and that their retribution must be great. When one is killed by the fluid they believe it is a judgment sent by the Great Spirit through the agency of this mysterious bird. They call this bird Che-ne-me-ke. When they see distant flashes of lightning and do not hear the voice, as they believe, of this great bird, they know it is at a distance, but still believe it is teaching a lesson to distant people and will soon be with them. But should a storm pass by without the voice and flashes coming near them they are happy again, for they feel relieve, believing that the bird is not angry with them. They firmly believe this bird to be an agency of the Almighty, which is kept moving about to keep an eye on the wrong doings of the people. When a tree is stricken and set on fire, the lesson it wishes to impart has been given and the rain is sent to prevent the fire from destroying the country.

There is a point of land in this part of the country that the Indians call Pa-qua-a-wong – meaning a forest destroyed by the great thunderbird. I have visited this place. It is now almost barren. The timber which was once upon it having been destroyed by lightning and the Indians believe that the storm bird destroyed this forest to show its wrath, that they might profit by the lesson. A hunting party of Indians was once caught on this barren in a thunderstorm and took refuge under the trunk of a fallen tree, which had been burnt sufficiently on the underside to give them shelter. One of the party, in his hurry to get out of the rain, left his gun standing against the log. The lightning struck it, running down the barrel and twisting it into many shapes and destroying it and the owner of this gun was thereafter pointed out by the whole band as the person upon whom the storm bird desired to bestow its frowns. So deep seated are their convictions upon this point that there is not enough language in the Indian tongue or words enough in the English vocabulary to convince them of their error. The quotation is a truthful one, which says:

"They saw God in the clouds and heard Him in the winds."

Since white men came among them the Indians they have not been slow to learn. I have often heard them remark

"The earth is the white man's heaven and money is his god."

The true Indian belief as regards the earth is that it is the mother of all things, vegetable, animal and human. They place the sun as the father and the air as life. The reason they put forth in support of this belief is that if air is taken from anything, either human, animal or vegetable it will immediately die, and that the sun is the father, for to cover up or shut out from the rays of the sun any plant, grass, or vegetable, it will wither and droop; but let the rays of the sun strike it and it will immediately spring to new life. They also believe there is a temporary mother who guards all things in their youth, when nature's further development is left to the sun.

You will see that the Indian pronunciation of sun is as near our pronunciation of Jesus as two human tongues can speak it, they pronouncing sun as "geses". They believed in what they saw; they read the signs in the heavens as manifestations from the Great Spirit and they looked upon them for their guidance the same as white people look upon the bible to get an understanding of what our creator would have us see and understand. Take from the white race their bible and their science and the Indian religion is as orthodox as any now extant. One thing is certain; they believed in their religion and practiced what they preached. No hypocrite was ever known among them.

CHAPTER XIII

———— • ————

THREE PROMINENT CHIPPEWA CHIEFS – BUFFALO, HOLE-IN-THE-
DAY, AND ES-KE-BUG-A-KUSH – THE MOST NOBEL OF THE TRIO –
HOLE-IN-THE-DAY AS A WARRIOR – A CHIEF'S DAUGHTER

I see by the history of T. E. Randall entitled "A History of the Chippewa Valley," and written by him in 1875 at Eau Claire, Wis., that Chief Hole-in-the-day of the upper Mississippi Chippewas, was in his estimation the greatest chief of the Chippewa tribe. The facts are that Hole-in-the-day was a great warrior but was far from being a peaceable Indian. I also find in Warren's history that he seemed to think that Chief Flat Mouth (Es-ke-bug-a-kush) was a great chief which I admit. He was a good warrior but did not set the good example that Chief Buffalo did.

Of course it is probable that a long acquaintance with different Indians leads men to form a very fixed opinion. I was well acquainted with all three of these chiefs. Hole-in-the-day and Flat Mouth were continually on the warpath, committing bloody butcheries upon their enemy, the Sioux, whenever there was an opportunity, and if no good opportunity presented itself they would make one, while Buffalo, on the contrary, never went on the warpath and would only agree to fight when it became actually necessary to repel an invasion, and his battle at the Brule river was one of these very cases. Hole-in-the-day and Es-ke-bug-a-kush were stirring up strife about the Mississippi river, and a party of Sioux started for the peaceable portion of the Chippewas expecting to catch them napping and wreak upon them the revenge they had failed to get from the fighting Chippewas that were with Hole-in-the-day and Flat Mouth. "Sherman-like to the sea" they had cut around the warlike portion of the Chippewas and would have annihilated the peaceables had not Buffalo got word of their coming in time to meet them at the Brule.

The general character of Buffalo was as different from that of Hole-in-the-day and Es-ke-bug-a-kush as daylight is from darkness. Buffalo always set a good example was a very temperate man in all things and was very industrious a man of immense frame and an iron constitution. I have heard many stories related of him when he was young and related by people of his own tribe They claimed he was a great hunter and the best bow and arrow shot of his time. It was said that in his prime he shot the swiftest arrow of any man then known. His practice was to frequently give his people good advice more like a father to them than a domineering chief.

After the treaty of peace at Prairie Du Chien and the Chippewa country had been set apart for them, war parties and peace parties were the only thing upon which they were not perfectly agreed. Hole-in-the-day headed the contingent while Buffalo was the leader of those inclined to perpetual peace. The peace party were in the ascendency in numbers all the time from that treaty forward.

Mr. Randall, who had short experience with Hole-in-the-day, was doubtless honest in the opinion he had of him as a wise chief and peaceably inclined but that was not his general character. Mr. Warren, whose history of the northwest I claim to be the best of any that has come to my observation, was born at La Pointe, Madeline Island, Lake Superior and up to the time he was ten years old saw more or less of Buffalo, but the next ten years of his life were spent at school in the east and on his return to the country of his nativity he associated himself principally with Chief Es-ke-bug-a-kush and it appears that this individual dictated a great part of the history which his book contains.

As to myself, from 1840 to the death of Buffalo, I was almost his constant companion and it would be natural for me to know more of Buffalo than Warren could have known of Flat Mouth and I could write a good deal about the bloody battles of the Sioux and Chippewas that Indians have told me but do not care to do so as Warren has entered upon that subject quite exhaustively and as he

143

learned it from a fighting chief. I claim to know the Indian character as well as any man now living. Mr. Warren was a good man intellectually and otherwise and every word he wrote he believed to be true. He died before the completion of his work.

While writing about chiefs and their character it may not be amiss to give the reader a short story of a chief's daughter in battle, where she proved as good a warrior as many of the sterner sex.

In the '50's there lived in the vicinity of Rice Lake, Wisconsin, a band of Indians numbering about 200. They were headed by a chief named Na-nong-ga-bee. This chief, with about seventy of his people came to La Pointe to attend the treaty of 1854. After the treaty was concluded he started home with his people, the route being through heavy forests and the trail one which was little used. When they had reached a spot a few miles south of the Namekagon River* and near a place called Beck-qua-ah-wong they were surprised by a band of Sioux who were on the warpath and then in ambush, where a few Chippewas were killed, including the old chief and his oldest son, the trail being a narrow one only one could pass at a time, true Indian file. This made their line quite long as they were not trying to keep bunched, not expecting or having any thought of being attacked by their life long enemy. The chief, his son and daughter were in the lead and the old man and his son were the first to fall, as the Sioux had of course picked them out for slaughter and they were killed before they dropped their packs or were ready for war. The old chief had just brought the gun to his face to shoot when a ball struck him square in the forehead. As he fell, his daughter fell beside him and feigned death.

At the firing Na-nong-ga-bee's Band swung out of the trail to strike the flanks of the Sioux and get behind them to cut off their retreat, should they press forward or make a retreat, but that was not the Sioux intention. There was not a great number of them and their tactic was to surprise the band, get as many scalps as they could and get out of the way, knowing that it would be but the work of a few moments, when they would be encircled by the Chippewas. The girl lay motionless until she perceived that the Sioux would not come down on them en-masse, when she raised her father's loaded gun and killed a warrior who was running to get her father's scalp, thus knowing she had killed the slayer of her father, as no Indian would come for a scalp he had not earned himself. The Sioux were now on the retreat and their flank and rear were being threatened, the girl picked up her father's ammunition pouch, loaded the rifle, and started in pursuit. Stopping at the body of her dead Sioux she lifted the scalp and tucked it under her belt. She continued the chase with the men of her band, and it was two days before they returned to the women and children, whom they had left on the trail, and when the brave little heroine returned she had added two scalps to the one she started with.

The Chief's Daughter

She is now living, or was, but a few years ago, near Rice Lake, Wisconsin, the wife of Edward Dingley, who served in the war of rebellion from the time of the first draft of soldiers to the end of the war. She became his wife in 1857, and lived with him until he went into the service, and at this time had one child, a boy.

A short time after he went to the war news came that all the party that had left Bayfield at the time he did as substitutes had been killed in battle, and a year or so after, his wife, hearing nothing from him, and believing him dead, married again. At the end of the war Dingley came back and I saw him at Bayfield and told him everyone had supposed him dead and that his wife had married another man. He was very sorry to hear this news and said he would go and see her, and if she preferred the second man she could stay with him, but that he should take the boy. A few years ago I had occasion to stop over night with them and had a long talk over the two marriages. She told me the circumstances that had led her to the second marriage. She thought Dingley dead, and her father and brother being dead, she had no one to look after her support, or otherwise she would not have done so. She related the pursuit of the Sioux at the time of her father's death with much tribal pride, and the satisfaction she felt at revenging herself upon the murder of her father and kinsmen. She gave me the particulars of getting the last two scalps that she secured in the eventful chase. The first she raised only a short distance from her place of starting; a warrior she espied skulking behind a tree presumably watching for some one other of her friends that was approaching. The other she did not get until the second day out when she discovered a Sioux crossing a river. She said: "The good luck that had followed me since I raised my father's rifle did not now desert me," for her shot had proved a good one and she soon had his dripping scalp at her belt although she had to wade the river after it.

In his text, Wentworth uses two spellings for the same word: Namekagon and Namakagon. Coincidentally, two different cartographers did the same. The result today is that the lake that forms the headwaters of the river is spelled Namakagon, while the river below is spelled Namekagon. Oddly, the Ashland Weekly Press used a different spelling in the late 1800s, Nameh-Kagon.

146

Chapter XIV

———— • ————

FATHER BARAGA AND THE CHIPPEWA LANGUAGE AND RELIGION – SOURCE OF THE RELIGION – HEAD OF THE CHIPPEWA CHURCH

Father Baraga was probably the best-posted man in the Chippewa Language who ever attempted to explain it and write up their customs and religious beliefs, but he fell into error. I had frequent talks with him about his works and he explained them to me as he understood them and gave the source of the greater part of his information. I did not tell him the source of my information and never attempted to disabuse his mind of the error. The facts are that the source from which my information was derived was the head of the Chippewa Church, while his was obtained at the foot of it. For me to say that the true Indian religion was a secret from the majority would be equivalent in the minds of most people saying that the majority of Indians did not profess religion. While this statement would be true in part, taken as a whole it would be untrue. All Indians practiced the true Indian religion, but the greater portion of them were ignorant of true understanding of the belief they practiced. The more wise Indian tribes, as well as the greatest thinkers of any people, knew that the majority are more easily governed and ruled through a belief of the hereafter than in any other way, and anything that was told to this majority by the chiefs and headmen as coming from traditions affecting their hereafter was eagerly sought after and reverently cherished. It may as well be said that these headmen had too much wisdom to venture the whole truth to the majority, lest they should depart from their teachings, for it is as true as anything can be that had the more ignorant, which is the majority of any people, been made aware of the fact as to what the true belief was, that the gun and all the belongings of the deceased where not needed by him on the trail to the happy hunting grounds, they would no longer have put such things in the grave and would have ceased their devotion in taking from a scanty supply of provisions a part to the grave of such deceased. Their desire for the possessions of the articles they buried and the real want they suffered in doing without them would have been too strong a temptation for them to resist after they once knew that keeping and using them and eating the food they carried there would not imperil the hereafter of their dead.

Although it is not well known nor a subject of much reflection upon by white people, yet it is a fact that Indian tribes were never well fed and their contrivances wherewith to capture game along were always inadequate to their needs. Their food was game, no great quantities of which could be preserved. They had a way of drying meat and could thus keep it for quite a time, but it was unwholesome and they practiced it but little. They would rather take their chances of procuring it daily than to eat what might prove unhealthy. The best fed Indians were never as well provided for in any respect as the poorest family of white workmen. This knowledge is the result of the great many years spent among them. The Indians lived a hard life with but little sunshine in it.

To return to their religion, when an Indian has shown himself capable of a thorough understanding of that part of the religion that he has been entrusted with, and shows a sense sufficient to overcome his natural earthly greed to enable him to keep the faith, he is allowed to go a notch higher in the secret councils and as headmen become satisfied that he is possessed of the true belief to a degree that he would discountenance any deviation from it by others he is taken along to the top of the ladder of secrets. This is true Indian religion and the manner in which it is practiced, and Father Baraga's version of it is in so far as it disagrees with this is erroneous. Nothing is put in the grave of the dead to assist them but is put there as a sacrifice on the part of the living and for no other purpose.

I will now trespass on the good nature and patience of the reader for the purpose of giving a brief history of one of the islands belonging to the Apostle group, called "Hermit's" Island, and sometimes called Wilson's Island, which received its name from the following circumstances:

In the year 1845 there came and settled upon this island a man by the name of Wilson – his first name I have forgotten. He lived there alone, neither family nor neighbor and would not allow anyone to land, using his gun to enforce his orders when necessary. He wounded several people, but he never killed anyone that I ever heard of. He had a few friends he had made through dealings with them, whom he would allow on his island, but they were few and such as he had learned to like and considered his friends. He told me stories of his adventures and claimed that he embarked with the Hudson Bay Company when a boy and was transferred from place to place, even to the Rocky Mountains, but the route he took he could not or would not explain, but thought for many years he was a life prisoner with them as he could see no way to escape out of the company. Finally he found his way to Lake Superior but by what route he was unable to say but said his sufferings and hardships before reaching the lake were terrible.

When I first met him I should judge he was about sixty years old and I have often wished I had jotted down his stories for reference for some of them were wonderful, but as it is I can only give a few points that I best remember. At any rate he was monarch of the island and all he surveyed. He had no pets except chickens and a rat and would allow no other animal about him. He kept liquor by the barrel though I never saw him under its influence and never knew him to offer a drink to anybody. He ordered on barrel of whiskey through me. During some of these years I lived at Oak Island, probably about two and a half miles from the hermit's house by the route we took with our boats. He sometimes came to my place for a visit but would never stay more than an hour at a time. For two or three years I bought what hay grew in a little meadow back of his house – a spot of ground he had cleared up in previous years and used for crops but allowed to grow up to grass and this

149

patch afforded about two tons of hay a year. Through this dealing with him and his visits to my house there grew up an acquaintance, which in him amounted to a friendship and he appeared to look upon me as the best friend he had. At the time the barrel of liquor came that ordered for him he came to the landing at my place with his boat for it and after it was loaded into the boat he insisted on my going with him to help get it out of the boat, saying: "The men you have ordered to send along I don't want, and continued: "I will pay you for the liquor at my house and bring you back as soon as we have finished our business." I went along with him and assisted in the unloading of the barrel and getting ashore when he requested me to come into his house and he would pay me for the whiskey. He brought out either three or four bags of coin in buckskin and one stocking leg filled with coin, and laid them out on the table. From one he counted out the money for me and when he had finished asked: "Is that enough?" I told him it was a little too much and gave him back some change, when he remarked: "You must count those sovereigns at five dollars apiece;" to which I replied: "Yes, they pass for that in this part of the country, but not be banked for that." He then requested me to count his money and tell him how much there was of it, that he might know how he was getting along at his business, which was barrel maker for fish companies. As he said this he barred the door and came back to the table where the money laid and told me to go ahead. I put the money he had paid me in my pocket and preceded to count his. I put each $100 in piles, there being about $1,300. The money consisted of gold, silver, English sovereigns and a few Mexican dollars. After the count had been finished and the money returned to the bags, he unbarred the door and said: "We will now go back to the boat" and as I passed out continued, "you bail out the boat and I will be out shortly." He then re-barred the door inside. I went down to the boat and got the water out and waited a full ten minutes before he came. He rowed me to my home but did not remain for any visit this time, but returned immediately.

During 1861 my folks told me they had seen no smoke from the old man's chimney for a few days, which had been a common sight for years, and it was missed in that country where neighbors were not plenty. A few days after this it was again reported that there was no smoke from the old hermit's chimney. The circumstances led me to believe something had befallen the old man, for he was not in the habit of going away from home, and I took a boat and a couple of men and rowed over to La Pointe to get someone to go with me and find out what the trouble was. I found Judge Bell and asked him if he had seen Wilson lately. He answered that he had not seen him in a couple of months. Then I told him of the circumstance of no smoke from his house for the past week or more and feared the old man was sick or in some way disabled. The judge got a boat and some men and we went to the old man's island and found him dead upon the floor of his cabin and appearances indicated that he had been murdered. I then revealed to the judge what I had seen and done some years before at his request and thought the money must be hidden somewhere in the house. The judge and his men instituted a search for the treasure but only found about sixty dollars, which was in a box behind the clock and was entirely hidden from sight when the clock was in place. This money, together with some trinkets and effects that he had, the judge took charge of, saying he would give him a decent burial and pay for it with the money and the remainder he would keep until called for by his relatives. Mr. Wilson once told me that he had been married and the loss of his wife was what had driven him to the life he was leading, but he did not tell me any particulars. No one ever appeared to claim a relationship and nothing more is known by the people of Lake Superior of this strange man or from whence he came except what he told himself.

Chapter XV

———— • ————

I cannot close this work without mentioning the names of some of the men who braved the dangers of the new west in the early days and who are entitled to the good opinion of all who write of the early days in this country.

John W. Bell, whom I met at La Pointe, the first time in 1842, was a remarkable man. It was just previous to the treaty of that year that he related some of his past history. He told me he left Montreal at the age of twelve years and engaged with the Hudson Bay Company to stay until he was twenty-one and about the year 1841 came to Lake Superior but how he came I do not remember that he told me. He first located at Iron River about 12 miles west of Ontonagon, and there, as was the usual custom, he married a Chippewa woman and engaged in the coppering business in the employ of the American Fur Company, but did not remain there a great while, but one season, making barrels for salting fish. When I saw him in 1842 I think he had moved to La Pointe with his family and was then engaged in a bakery, making bread for the Indians from flour the government had sent for distribution. He remained at La Pointe until he died, in 1889, during which time he educated himself, and for many years was lawyer, judge and jury for the county of La Pointe, which when first organized was a very large territory, and his title "King of the Apostle Islands" was accepted by everybody. No one ventured or desired to dispute his title or authority. He virtually conducted the whole business of the county up to 1872, at which time the name of the county was changed to

Ashland, and the town of Ashland was organized and made the county seat.

The first town meeting held in Ashland was in the spring of 1872, electing a town board of supervisors, clerk, treasurer, assessor, etc. Hon. Sam S. Fifield was chosen chairman; A.S. Perinier and myself were chosen for side supervisors. At this time there was there was $45,000 in the hands of Mr. Bell as county treasurer, which was to be apportioned to the different towns in the new county as fast as they were organized and the proportion of each was ascertained. But as the new town of Ashland was much in need of funds to carry on improvements it became necessary to go to Judge Bell for relief. He saw the situation but had no authority to divide the money without orders to do so according to law, but finally said, "Go on with your improvements and I will honor your orders to the extent of $10,000," and gave us $1,000 for a school house and $1,000 for a bridge, saying as he did so: "I am overstepping my authority in this matter but will try and keep the accounts straight until the apportionment is made and then deduct the amount that you receive from the total that shall be apportioned to be your due."

In a few years thereafter it was thought advisable to investigate the books and accounts of Mr. Bell, over which he had exclusive control for many years. Experts were appointed and this work completed without finding any considerable discrepancies in them. The number of men in any community is not legion that would for more than twenty years and with a check of any kind upon them leave to their posterity the record of Mr. Bell.

A case in 1852 where he played the part of complaining witness, warrant issuer, warrant server and judge on the bench is worth of note. In that year a man by the name of Wright came to the island on business and was there several days waiting for a boat to take him to the head of the lake.

During the subject of his stay he became the object of an interference of the law and the judge complained to himself and issued the warrant, which he served himself, bringing the prisoner before his tribunal, where he sentenced him to pay four hundred dollars or serve six months in jail. He would not pay the fine and the judge put him in jail, but it was not properly provided with locks and the prisoner escaped. It was not long before he had heard where he had gone. He followed him to Douglas County, where he seized him and returned him to the jail that he now had provided with proper fastenings where the prisoner remained until a boat arrived at the dock, when the judge discovered that the opening at the jail that had been left for the chimney had not been closed and Mr. Wright was the first man to arrive at the dock. But the judge was not to be thus outwitted and again seized his man on board the boat, where happened to be a lawyer to whom the prisoner had told his story, and as the lawyer saw a loophole through which he thought his client could escape prevailed on the judge to reopen the case and give the man the benefit of legal counsel, to which Mr. Bell assented and all three marched to the hall of justice where the judge, good to his word reopened the case upon his books and told the attorney to proceed – giving the lawyer the full use of his stock of law books and precedents. But the lawyer ignored them all and relied upon the one point to clear his client. He pointed to the statutes upon the point he had chosen and had the case boiled down to his own satisfaction and sprung his point. "Your honor! You far exceeded your jurisdiction when you went into the county of Douglas and arrested this man," and straightening himself up to his full height continued, "You cannot go into another county and take a man on your warrant;" to which the judge listened and then replied, "Can't eh! But I did and the man is now in my jurisdiction and will take the consequences of my sentence, which I now re-affirm. [Exit the lawyer just in time to catch the boat.]

In the summer of 1886 the writer of this work went to the home of Judge Bell of La Pointe with the intention of taking notes from his conversation from which to weave a sketch of his life, but found him a sufferer from an injured limb and unable to physically by reason of this and his advanced years to submit to any extended interview and took from him a few sentences which are here repeated; "I came here from Montreal in 1835 with the American Fur Company as a cooper. Great quantities of fur were then brought to this place from all parts of the western country and shipped to Montreal. I came here in the brig *John Jacob Astor*, Captain Standard (or Stanard.) She was built this side of the River Sioux. Her frame was built in Canada and put up at the River Sioux. I went to Washington from here with a delegation of eighteen Lake Superior Chippewa Chiefs. We had two or three audiences with President Lincoln. We were in the theatre when Lincoln was assassinated. I put in at Washington a claim in favor of the Chippewa Indians of seventy-three thousand and six hundred dollars, one-third of which belonged to the Mississippi Chippewas and two thirds belonged to the Lake Superior Chippewas. These arrearages are still held back by the government. I have an arrangement with the Chippewa Indians, which is to allow me two thousand dollars of this money for my trouble and expenses on this trip to Washington. When we started on this trip to Washington we walked from hereto Eau Claire, Wisconsin, on snowshoes. We went first to Bad River then to Leihy's farm at Lac Courte Oreilles, from there to Chippewa Falls, thence to Eau Claire at which place we got three teams to take us to Sparta. One Gurneux was interpreter on this trip. He is now at Lac Courte Oreilles, which name means "Short Ear" and is a Chippewa name. The land around the old church here was once tilled. A man by the name of Austrian owns about five-sixth of it. We once polled between four and five hundred votes here and as long ago as 1856, but there are not now thirty votes on this island. We use to build boats here. This house I now live in was built in 1853 by David Oakes. Dr. Borup's youngest daughter, now living in St. Paul, was born upon this island."

This was all the writer got from Mr. Bell as he was it was

fatiguing to him. He was a man of very powerful frame and in his prime must have been almost a giant.

The town of Bayfield was located, surveyed and platted in the spring of '55. Major McAvoy, who was the agent of the town site company, remained about two years. A man named Day was another early settler in Bayfield. Sage & Mathews were early carpenters here. The first married a daughter of Major McAvoy and Mathews married a Mrs. Jeffrey. Jacob Schafer was an early settler there and married Ann Steel. Andrew Tate came about a year later. James Chapman, who recently died in Bayfield, came there quite early. Asaph Whittlesey was there and remained there until he died. Samuel S. Vaughn was one of the first settlers in Bayfield and moved to Ashland in 1872. Ashland's first settlers were Martin Beaser from Ontonagon. It had been claimed that Asaph Whittlesey mad the first clearing in Ashland, but only for a building. George Kilbourne was here about the same time and Conrad and Adam Goeltz and Martin Roehm came here about 1854. Katie Goeltz, now Mrs. Ellis, of Calumet, Michigan, was the first white child born in Ashland and she was presented with a building lot by Martin Beaser, in remembrance of this distinction and she still owns the lot. About this time Edwin Ellis came and located at a place called Bay City, which is now a part of Ashland. His son Edwin was the first white boy born here. The mission was built at Bad River about 1842 by Leonard Wheeler, who continued there until 1864 or 65. Erwin Leihy settled at the Falls of the Bad River bargained with and bought out a man named Woods who claimed to own the falls property. He moved from there to Bayfield about 1870. Elisha Pike settled about two and one-half miles south of Bayfield at what is now called Pike's Creek in 1853 and bought the mill property there that was owned by Julius Austrian. Mr. Pike built a house on it where he lived until his death about two years ago, leaving a wife, son and daughter. His son R. D. Pike now lives in Bayfield and his daughter is Mrs. Bicksler, of Ashland.

While this mill property was in the possession of Julius

156

Austrian and quite out of repair he bargained with me one day to fix it up and run it, he to furnish all supplies for logging and sawing for half the lumber I could make. I was to do all repairing and furnish the help for logging and sawing for the other half. At this time Julius Austrian had a brother in his employ about fifteen years old who was kept busy at any odd jobs that he was large enough to do. One day he was sent from La Pointe to our mill with a load of supplies. He had quite a load for his one horse and it was his first trip over this road and he could not lose his way; to keep to the bay until he reached the ridge and to follow it until he came to the mill. The boy's name was "Joe" and he did as he was told and in due time found himself at the top of a hill near the mill. The mill set quite low down in the ravine on the creek bottom, the hill was quite steep and the slipping nice. Joe saw the hill was steep but others had been down and he anticipated no trouble in getting safely to the mill. His sled was made entirely of wood and with much more regard for strength and durability than beauty and was a load of itself, the thills being made of iron wood poles that were at least four inches in diameter and turned out at the end trill fashion so as not to injure the shoulder of the horse. Joe started; the horse began to move slowly, its own instinct telling it that the chances were not even for getting to the bottom of the hill without a mishap. The load soon proved too heavy for the horse to hold back and Joe pulled and tugged away on the rope lines to assist the horse in holding the sled. In doing so he reined the horse a little to one side of the track where stood a tree leaning at an angle of about 45° away from the road. One thill point hit the tree but glancing off brought the horse upon the tree roots, the load kept pushing and the horse at last was full length up the tree and entirely off the ground. Joe who had jumped off the load inflated his lungs and whoop after whoop escaped him until the mill stopped and all hands proceeded to the spot where the mishap had occurred and there Joe took shaking from head to foot, a perfect picture of despair. The sled was got away and the horse rolled off the tree but little worse for the

157

accident, but Joe, I dare say, has not forgotten it and never will.

Joseph Austrian is now a resident of Chicago, Illinois, and has been for several years past. He has accumulated a considerable

 fortune, now being principally interested in the Austrian-Leopold line of steamers plying on the Great Lakes.

Joseph Austrian Up a Tree

There was another incident at this mill that will interest a few still living. Henry Smitz, an old comrade of mine, was acting as tail sawyer for me and Joseph Hole, an Indian, was taking the lumber from the saw. One day as the saw was nearing the iron dog that held the log in place Smitz having forgotten to get it out of the way, and just as the Indian was leaning over to take the slab the saw struck the dog and flew in a dozen pieces that went screeching in many directions. The floor of the mill upon which we were was twenty-five *(feet)* above the creekbed beneath us and the whizzing of the broken saw so frightened the Indian that he ran and jumped headlong into the creek below. He was not seriously injured and picking himself up lit out for Bayfield. Henry Smitz afterward lived upon a copper claim northeast of Duluth and had an interest in a shingle mill at La Pointe but removed his family to Hancock, Michigan, leaving his shingle business in the hands of his partner, occasionally returning to see it. He was in business in Hancock at the time the village was nearly destroyed by fire and his property went with the rest. He rebuilt and was nicely started again when he came to La Pointe to see to his business interests, but just as he reached the mill the boiler exploded, killing him and several others who were working about the place. His remains were taken to Hancock and buried.

In the spring of 1855 M.H. Mandlebaum, formerly of New York, but then from Cleveland came to La Pointe to take charge of the local business of Julius Austrian. He was certainly one of the most pleasant men I ever met, honest and square in all his dealings. From the start he ingratiated himself into the highest regard and esteem of all with whom he had dealings. He was a whole-souled, live and let live man whom everyone respected, but as his motto was to give to give dollar for dollar and strict weights and measures, his way of doing business was not in conformity with the manner of doing things that had obtained for the past few years in this country and his place was filled by another. He was induced to go to Bayfield by his friends and became a candidate for clerk of the court. He accepted the nomination and was elected, serving his term, after which he was urged to run again but declined, as there was not sufficient salary to the position to suit his ambition. While in the capacity of clerk a dispute arose between the judge and himself in regard to some point in his duties and Mr. Mandlebaum was compelled to travel in the dead of winter and on foot to Superior and get an attorney to defend him. He got and attorney, however, his case was tried and his position vindicated. Soon after this he went below, bought a stock of goods and established himself in business in Hancock, Michigan. In his business career here as at La Pointe and Bayfield he was fully up to the standard of an honest man. Sickness and death overtook him while he was in the prime of life and his untimely taking off was mourned by all who knew him. I do not think he had an enemy in the world. At his death he left a wife and two or three children. A son bears his father's name, whom I met in the winter of 1891.

During the stay of Mr. Mandlebaum at La Pointe he was a

great favorite with the Indians, always ready with tricks and jokes to keep them in high glee – was greatly missed by them and was often inquired after by them when he had gone to Hancock. An example of his happy turn of mind and general disposition to be merry on festive occasions was exhibited on an occasion when a dancing party was in progress in Bayfield. Unknown to anyone he succeeded in changing the clothing of the babies, several in number, that had been brought there by their mothers and were sleeping away from the noise of the dance, and so completely disguising them that an hour was spent before every mother could tell her own and the merriment indulged in over this freak of his imagination can be pleasantly recalled by a number of persons still living.

At Ontonagon, the first settler after the government had abandoned the fort at that place was Lathrop Johnson, who purchased the buildings formerly used by the government, and settled there about 1844. About 1847 James Paul come there and claimed to own the town site, and between him and Johnson there were bitter feuds and disturbances, which culminated in the shooting of Paul, the shot coming from a rear window of Johnson's house. Paul's breast was punctured with many shot, which only went through the flesh, but a more frightened man would be hard to imagine. Johnson was put on trial charged with the crime, but the only witness who saw the shooting was a Cornishman who was boarded with Johnson and it was evident that he did not care to see Johnson convicted, for all the evidence he would give was "I saw the shot fired but faith I cannot say whether he or she did it." The first firm to locate at Portage Lake, Michigan, was the firm of Douglas and Sheldon and the first at Marquette, in the iron district, was Bob Graverot about 1844.

Chapter XVI

───────── • ─────────

Early Settlers in the Chippewa Valley – The First
Lumberman at Hudson, Wisconsin – West Superior's Earliest
Settlers – Sailor Jack and His Partner – an Early Execution

Of my first acquaintances in the Chippewa Valley, in 1840, I wish to mention James Page, a man much noted for his feminine voice. He was the first lumberman on the Willow River at Hudson, Wisconsin. James Perrington was another of the first. Blake & Greely also came there about the same time. Asa Parker, of the Marine Mill Company, was another early settler. Taylor and Furber were there early. Joshua Taylor, of this firm is still living, and the winter of 1890 and 91 he spent with his niece, Mrs. D.G. Sampson, at Ashland, Wisconsin. He is now seventy-five years old.

Elam Greely, of the firm Blake and Greely, continued in the lumber business until his death about two years ago at Stillwater, Minnesota.

Moore & Loomis were there also, the firm consisting of Martin Moore and Burton Loomis, the former from the state of Maine and the later from Alton, Illinois. I was personally acquainted with Mr. Moore and his three brothers and his sister, who is now Mrs. R.W. French of Ashland, Wisconsin. The names of the brothers were Horace, William, and John. The former of these two I found the summer of 1844, sick in a hay meadow on the Snake River, suffering from cholera or cholera morbus. I did what I could for him and started to take him below, but he died before we reached Stillwater. Captain William Moore, another of the brothers, died in Bayfield. I was acquainted with him and it was at Bayfield that I first met his sister, now Mrs. R.W. French. Martin Moore, after severing his connections with the firm of Moore & Lormis, built what was known as the Arcola Mill, about six miles down the river from the Marine Mill. He operated it until his death, and was also heavily interested in the boom company. He lived to be fully seventy years old and was unmarried. He left a fortune of about $100,000. John Moore died about six or eight years ago in Stillwater, Minnesota, leaving a wife and four or five children. Mrs. R.W. French is not the only living member of that family that I know of.

William Colby was an early settler. He came to St. Croix in 1840 or 1841 and as remained there ever since. He married a daughter of Mr. DeAtley, and I had the pleasure of attending his wedding, one occurrence at which I will mention: "A serenading party undertook to force their way into the house during the ceremony and Mr. Colby hurled a table at the leader which broke his arm and otherwise injured him, but it put a stop to their further uninvited ceremonies."

The company that built the Osceola mills in 1844 at Osceola, Wisconsin, was composed of William Kent and William Mahoney, under the firm name Kent and Mahoney. They also had a silent partner by the name of Walker, who was a brother of Orange Walker, of the mill firm of Walker, Berklow, Parker & Berkey.

A Mr. Hungerford was the first settler and rightfully owned the property know as St. Croix Falls, on the Wisconsin side but as I understand was since beaten out of it by Caleb Cushing of Boston.

Mr. James Perrington was drowned in what is now called Apple River Falls. He had formerly been the agent at the St. Croix Falls Company, but was relieved of his duty by the appointment of a man named Perkins, who was also drowned while engaged in repairing the dam at St. Croix Falls.

The McCusick's were also early settlers, coming in about 1840 or 41. John, Jonathan, William and Jott, who perhaps may now all be living except Jott.

Jessie Taylor was an early settler and located at a place now known as Taylor's Falls, where he began the foundation for a mill at the head of the dells, but abandoned it and the property went into the hands of Joshua Taylor, who is still living at that place.

A man by the name of Tuttle settled early at the first falls above the big falls on the St. Croix River, and the village there derived its name from his getting upset in a boat in an eddy below the falls where he came near being drowned.

William Vincent, was also a pioneer in that country and married a daughter of a Mr. North.

Mr. Patridge was an early bird and the village of Quailville was named after him, It is near Tuttle's Falls and it was called by that name rather than call it Patridgeville.

John and Orin Weymouth were there also.

B.T. Otice died here, as did also William Holmes, Thomas Bishop and Doane Porter. Some of relatives of the latter I met afterwards in Quincy, Illinois.

Joseph Bowron was an early settler at St. Croix Fall, and an acquaintance of mine, and was a man of high esteem for his many good qualities.

I recall no more who were among the settlers prior to 1845, those coming after that were not called early or old settlers. From 1840 to 1844 my time was spent more or less roving around the country from St. Croix Falls to Lake Superior and beyond, to the source of the Mississippi and was located in Minnesota when Ramsey was elected governor.

At West Superior Captain Holcomb and the Newton's and Washington Ashton were among the first. Mr. Ashton edited the first newspaper published there. Captain Markland, of Kentucky and George Perry were also located early in West Superior.

One fall when I was trading at Namakagon, a messenger came to me from St. Croix Falls and said I was wanted to interpret and ferret out a murder that had taken place on the trail between St. Croix Falls and Balsam Lake. When I arrived there I was told that Sailor Jack and his partner, two traders, had been murdered but whether by white men or Indians was the question to be solved. Blood had been found in their yard and upon their doorstep and the bodies subsequently found in a lake not far from the cabin. These

163

two men were known by the names given here and no other and had established themselves as traders.

The man acting as Justice of the Peace at St. Croix Falls at this time, whose name I cannot recall, desired me to look up the Indian side of the question as I could talk their language. I told him I would try it as far as the Indians might be concerned in the matter, but if it should appear that white men had done the deed it belonged to the white officers to look up. The justice directed me to a trader who had some dealings with these two men and I found that he had sold to Sailor Jack a pair of pants with his own name on the waist band; that these men used a gun quite different from any other then known in that vicinity. I began my search in the Indian camp nearby and worked back without any success until I had reached Balsam Lake. Here was located about twenty wigwams around the trading house of Fred Miller. I pretended to be buying furs and skins thus got easy access to the lodges. My first discovery was the breech of a gun sticking out from under some bedding, which, upon examination, proved to be the one I was looking for, and I had the good luck to find the pants, with the trader's name still on the waistband, in the same lodge. This was evidence enough and I went to the chief and inquired if he knew who killed Sailor Jack and his partner. He hesitated but finally said the man did not properly belong to his band. If he did he would give him up; that he had come to him from the Hudson Bay country. I told him I was there in the interest of the Indians and as their custom had always been to give up murderers I thought it was best for his people to give this man up also. All this he acknowledged, knowing who the man was, and said I had better get help before trying to take him as he was a desperate man. His name was Belcore. He said the Indians should not interfere in either way, although this man's squaw was one of their people. I went back to St. Croix Falls and got assistance. George Aikens and Walter Carrier went back to Balsam Lake and that night walked into Belcore's lodge and found our man rolled up in his blanket. I pounced upon him, telling the two other men to

164

look out for the squaw, as she was likely to use her club or knife upon us. She fought hard for her man but we succeeded in tying him with cords and stayed in camp until daylight. We charged him with murder and told him what we were going to do with him, and asked him what he had to say. He denied it all. I then asked where he had got the gun and pants and he said he had bought them. He frequently told his wife to get the Indians to come and liberate him but no Indians came. We would not allow the squaw to leave the lodge during the night, not for fear she would get help, but for fear that she might arm herself and make an attempt to liberate the man.

Justice Under
Indian Law

We started with the prisoner at daylight for the falls, followed by Indians. At time he would refuse to walk and we would drag him until he was glad to walk. By the time we reached the spot where the execution was to take place, a full three hundred Indians were on hand, but all remained peaceable until the rope was put around his neck, then they objected to his being hung; they wanted him shot as he had shot the men. But the headstrong leader of our party, a man named Anson Northrop, declared that Belcore should be hung and the Indians made no further objection. When the culprit found that he must hang he made a full confession and said he had shot the men, one in the yard and the other on the doorstep, and said that Fred Miller had offered him ten gallons of whiskey to

165

do the job. Fred Miller was then brought before the mob and sentenced to receive thirty-nine lashes on the bare back. Twelve black birch sprouts were brought for the whipping and Pat Collins was appointed to do the business and was told by the party that any blow that he failed to give full force would be given to himself by the mob, and you can judge the whipping the man got. After the whipping he was cut loose and given twelve hours to put as much territory as he could between himself and St. Croix Falls, and he made good use of his time, you can rest assured. The Indian was given five minutes to talk after witnessing the whipping from the barrel on which he was placed. He gave his people some good advice, after which the barrel was kicked out from under him and he was soon strangled to death. The Indians quietly dispersed and never made any complaint except as to the mode of the execution.

While I lived near Pocagemah Lake, Pat Collins, whose name appears as the whipper at the execution of Belcore, established a whiskey shop in a lumber camp. It was situated two miles above Pocagemah Lake, on the Snake River. At this time he had on hand three full barrels of whiskey besides the one he had on tap, which had been made from alcohol. This supply he expected to sell during the upcoming winter. About the first of November Collins left the shanty in charge of his Indian wife and a boy about fifteen years old, named Ira Slayton. He had been gone from the place a few hours when three Indians appeared and demanded whiskey of the boy, which he refused to give them. They went away saying they would get their guns and kill him if he did not comply. As soon as they were gone they boy closed the door and pulled the latchstring. The Indians returned shortly and began firing through the door, one bullet clipping a lock of hair from the head of Mrs. Collins. The woman and the boy now got close to the log walls to escape the balls, the boy getting close to the side of the door, and provided with the gun belonging to Collins, stood ready, should the door open, to sell himself as dearly as possible. Soon a bullet struck the latch and knocked it off and as the door came open the boy fired, sending the top of one Indians head to the happy hunting grounds. The other two ran for assistance and the boy skipped and got safely back to St. Croix Falls. The Indians went back to the shanty in large numbers. Surrounding it the broke in the heads of the barrels and soon were beastly drunk. They came to my place about midnight and demanded the boy, supposing he would come to me for protection. I was ignorant of what had taken place and did not know what they had come for until they asked for the boy. I then faced about 100 drunken Indians, yelling and whooping with all the vigor of their nature. I demanded to know what the row was about. "I never sold any whiskey to any of you, no will I harbor anyone who will, and I know nothing of this boy." Nevertheless they asked, yes, demanded the right to search, when I selected two whom I told might look around as much as they liked. They did so and reported to the mob that the boy could not be found. They then searched the barn where I kept horses for lumbermen and concluded they were on the wrong track, and gradually went back to the whiskey shop, where they remained until the runners they had sent out for the boy had returned. That night they had a number of ugly fights among them and animosities engendered there resulted in many fights and kills years afterwards.

When they received the news that the boy had escaped by way of St. Croix Falls they gave up the hunt, but always claimed the whites ought to surrender the boy to them.

This was the first and only time while among the Indians that I was frightened and had they been sober I should have had no fear on this occasion. The Indian the boy killed was a nephew of Chief Bi-a-jek, and after the excitement had cooled down somewhat, the old chief came to me in person and asked if I would make a rude coffin and go with him to bury the boy, which I did. The funeral was held between Pocagemah and Cross Lakes. Gun, pipe and all trinkets were buried with him, not because he would want them in the happy hunting grounds but because they were his own and no one had the right to use them after him.

CHAPTER XVII

———————— • ————————

A MURDER ON A TRAIL AT YELLOW LAKE YET A MYSTERY –
COLLAR AND SLEEVE BUTTONS OF THE MURDERED MAN – AN
INTRODUCTION TO THE BEAR FAMILY

In 1855 a man named McEwen came to me at La Pointe who told me he was from California formerly but was then located at St Paul, that he had been prospecting through this part of the country for some time for the purpose of finding a suitable location for business and to buy real estate but as the weather was becoming unfavorable for this work he had resolved to return to St Paul and wanted to know if I could furnish a couple of good, reliable men to pilot him as far as Yellow Lake for when once there he could get on alone over old lumber roads to St Paul. I furnished him with two men whom I considered reliable. They were two half breeds by the name of Gostelang, their first names being Belamy and Batese, and it transpired that they did their duty and left McEwen at Yellow Lake all right at a stopping place kept by Joseph Cobaux or Cavillion and that McEwen remained at this place two nights and a day. I further ascertained that Cobaux advised McEwen not to follow the tote road as he had intended but to go by trail to Clam Lake and from there to Wood Lake as it would shorten the distance some ten or twelve miles and that he would send a man with him as a pilot until he should again come to the tote road which he would do at a place called Knute Anderson's Meadow. Subsequent events show that McEwen took this advice but he was never again seen alive by his friends.

It seems that McEwen had written to a partner of his in St Paul prior to his departure that he would arrive there about a certain time and that his partner had become anxious about him after the time had expired. He wrote to me I answered him telling all I could which was his start and arrival at Yellow Lake. In a short time after, this friend of McEwen's whose name I cannot remember came to La Pointe to ferret out the mystery. I gave him what information I could and he set out promising to let me know from Yellow Lake what success he was having. He did so saying that McEwen had arrived at Yellow Lake and remained there two nights and the men that I had sent returned the next morning. I then sent two men to Yellow Lake who could talk both English and Chippewa and instructed them to talk with whites and Indians and get all the information they could and the route he had taken and find out if possible what became of the man. They ascertained at Yellow Lake from the Indians that Cobaux had sent a man with him by way of Clam Lake trail. The men followed. At Clam Lake they found where they had a fire and had cooked a meal. The next sign they found was at Wood Lake where they had occupied an old lumber camp. Here they found blood stains but a thorough search of the camp only revealed a tin box in which McEwen had carried his papers and minutes of land descriptions. The streams and lakes were now frozen over and snow had fallen and further search had to be abandoned until spring. A search was instituted then which resulted in finding his body in a little lake at the head of Wood Lake proper. The head had been cut with an axe or hatchet on the back part of it. Nothing by which he could be identified was left except his clothing. His collar button and shirt studs and a valuable finger ring which he told me were made of gold he had dug himself were missing. I do not think McEwen had any money about him except what might have been left from ten dollars which he borrowed from me. The collar button and shirt studs or similar ones were afterward seen in a shirt worn by a trader at St Croix Falls but there being no one who could identify them to a certainty we were compelled to be satisfied with our own conclusions, but from what we had seen of them and what he had said of them, we were more than satisfied that they were the property of Mr. McEwen.

In the spring of 1841 my first real good introduction to the bear family took place. It was in the logging camp of Mr. Page and less than one mile from the present city of Hudson, Wisconsin. The camp had been pretty well cleared out of its supplies, they having been moved down to the place where the drive would begin. Only a few papers, scaler's rule and time book and a keg part full of molasses were left behind. One afternoon after the landing had been broken *(Ice was out.)* and booming about completed, *(Booming refers many logs chained end-to-end and used to corral many other logs in order to float them downriver after ice out.)*, Mr. Page requested me to take a man and go to the camp and return in the morning, bringing the rule and papers and have the man bring along the keg of molasses. I took a young Indian about twenty years of age named Wa-sa-je-zik, and started for the camp. It was nearly dark when we started and we had a mile to walk over a muddy trail. The boy stripped some birch bark from an old wigwam near the road and made a torch to use as a light when we reached the shanty. When near the camp, he handed me the torch and picked up wood to make a fire. I lit the torch at the cabin and found the door partly open but went in followed by the boy who closed the door as he came through and dashed his armful of wood down at the fire place. At this we heard a rush alongside the camp at our left that nearly scared the life out of us and raising the torch we beheld two bears, who had doubtless been attracted to the cabin by the scent of the molasses. They made a rush for the door where they entered but it was closed and wheeling about they faced us, their eyes shining with a luster that we would much rather have seen in a painting.

But we were there; no door but the one the bears were guarding and no window where we could escape. We stood like statues for a while eyeing our companions, while the torch was fast burning away. The roof was made of shakes and the eaves were about 4 feet from the ground. Escape we must or we would soon be in the dark with our black companions. We expected any moment to be pounced upon, for every spring, bears, as a usual thing, are very hungry. It occurred to me that perhaps I could move the shakes enough to crawl through and handing the now-shortened torch to the boy and at the same time instructing him to keep it waving to hold the bruins at bay, I made a dash for the shakes and soon had a hole through which I could crawl and did and shouted to Wa-sa-je-zik to come. The lad went through that hole like and arrow and he was none too quick, for one of the bears espied the light of the Heavens through the hole I made and dashed for it, but missed his footing and fell back. By this time we had the shake kicked back into place and Messrs. Bruins were our prisoners. We camped outside that night and in the morning got a rifle and killed them both. We took the hides and best of the meat to the boys on the drive who had a regular powwow and feast to celebrate our adventure.

Imprisoned with Two Bears

I had several experiences with bear after this, but never again was caught in their den. A black bear is harmless except when wounded or cornered and then they are a wicked foe. I once wounded one and we had a lively promenade around an old pine stub until I got my hunting hatchet from my belt and dealt him several blows when he gave up the fight and we had no quarrel over gate receipts. He started away uttering a growl. I picked up my gun and finished loading it and soon had his hide as a trophy.

171

I did not meet Wa-sa-je-zik again until two or three years ago at Granite Falls on the Mississippi. He recognized me at once and began to relate the story and it seemed like meeting a long lost brother when our encounter with the bears had been revived.

Chapter XVIII

———— • ————

Now I will venture some opinions of my own that to me amount to certainties. It is generally believed by thinking people that wars were frequent between rival tribes of Indians before the discovery by Columbus. I cannot dispute it, but knowing so well the causes that have led to wars since 1835, and what I have learned by tradition and experience, I am forced to believe that if any such wars were had they must have been infrequent. I am fully convinced by old Indian tradition that disturbances between tribes before white men were known on the continent only occurred when disputes over territory could not be settled by council. I also believe that previous to 1492 the whole country that is now the United States and territories were completely inhabited by Indians and different tribes had large areas, probably in some cases as large as half a dozen of our present states; that they had boundary lines described by rivers, lakes and mountains, and that each and every boundary was known to all the other tribes. As the pursuit of game was their chief vacation it was necessary that their boundaries should be somewhat extended.

Since I have known them they would never settle down in the haunts of the largest game but two or three miles from their choicest hunting grounds, and in some locality where there was plenty of wood and water and on some high and healthy spot. Their care was not to unnecessarily disturb their game, as they desired it to multiply and be food for Indians forever. Now when white men came in the from Europe they must have an abiding place and

173

where could it be except in the dominion of some Indian tribe and as immigration swelled their ranks the Indians must move back. They could not move back far before they began to encroach upon the rights and possession of another tribe, and right here in my opinion the Indians Wars began and the same cause continuing could only produce the same effect and in greater proportion, as the country settled up from east to west. The whole front of a dozen or more tribes was assailed at the same time. Small tribes soon dwindled away or were merged into others and stronger ranks, until only a few tribes remain that have sufficient strength to become adversaries of each other or all combined to make a stand before the white race, which in military circles could be considered more than a mere skirmish. The Sioux and a few tribes west of them are all there are left of the former powerful tribes that have been scarred to the four winds of the earth, and but a very small portion of this extermination has been done by the whites. In fact it can safely be said that the Indians by their interment strife have fought the battles the white men certainly must have fought had the American Indians been all of one blood and one nation at the beginning of America's settlement, and it looks as if it was ordained that they should slaughter each other and thereby make the white man's entry into their country comparatively easy.

These wars, stirring up as they did a natural and the greatest characteristic of an Indian, which is revenge, helped along the extermination, which seems to have been and still is the ultimate result awaiting them. The true born Indian care nothing for his life after once being wronged except for the revenge he can get out of it. With no cause for revenge in his heart he is as peaceable and kind as any human being on earth. His word is his bond and he would not break it to save his life. But do him a dishonest act and he will never be your friend nor a friend to your children after you. The Indians are not complaining people; they put up with their lot as it falls to them without a murmur, provided that lot has been cast to them by the will of the Great Spirit or their own conduct. This I know to be the true Indian character. If by an accident caused by his own carelessness or want of prudence he is injured, you can no more get a complaint from him than could from a stone. Even your sympathy he does not want, nor will he receive it except by stolid silence and indifference. He seems imbued with the idea that each person should and must stand or fall upon his own individuality. No company business from him; no putting upon another a duty that belongs to himself; no reaping where he has not sewn, and no getting into the happy hunting ground in the canoe of his neighbor. Honor is his god. But let his discomfiture be brought about by the dishonest treachery of another and the remainder of his life is lived only for revenge. He doesn't want to forget a wrong and will not forget it, but will nourish it and cares not how soon he dies if he can only die in avenging that wrong or attempting to do it. Take this as the standard of Indian character back from time without date, when the first dishonorable act was committed against and Indian tribe, and you can readily see that for at least three hundred years, revenge has been their object and their only aim. An eye for an eye and a tooth for a tooth has always been Indian law. It is not recorded that Indians burnt prisoners at the stake until many years after white settlement began and I say it boldly and without fear of a contradiction that they learned of it from the whites. See the battles of Captain Mason with the Pequot in 1637. He burned their villages, their women and children without mercy and as they called it then, "by the will of God." From this and similar instances the Indians learned their lessons and they practiced it until their revengeful hearts were satisfied.

Among the Indians before white men had corrupted them there was no vice; they were a strictly moral people and the marriage tie was sacred; quarrels among them were very few but as with all classes of the human race, the incorrigible were found. I once knew a case where one Indian killed another with a knife and the family of the murdered man demanded his surrender by the chief, it being quickly done. These people marched him to the spot where he committed the deed and with the same weapon he had used on his victim, he was slain. Do you think the culprit murmured? Not he. Not a word of complaint did he utter nor for an instant shrink from the uplifted blade, but without a quiver and with his own hand held back his blanket to receive the blow, shouting: "How! How!" (Strike) After the affair the two families met and talked the matter over, the pipe of peace was smoked and thereafter no two families in the tribe were better friends. The deal had been an even one and although each family regretted the occurrence, the hatchet was buried. But had not the murderer been given up to them for sacrifice, time immemorial would have found these families at war with each other. In all cases of murder among Indians, the weapon used in the killing, be it club, knife or arrow, is carefully preserved and never used again, and hundreds of years thereafter, barring extermination of the tribe, the weapon can be produced and its story told.

The first lesson given the Indians by the white men were intended to impress upon their mind the necessity of giving up their old habits and conforming to those of the whites and to follow the example of their white brothers. As the Indian's memory is his record, the words of the white people were frequently talked over by them and kept fresh in their minds and all examples were carefully watched, because such examples they were expected to follow. Quick to observe, they had not long to wait before deception was apparent in the dealings of the white men and as to their action as examples, they could not follow them. The missionaries had no untutored among themselves to deceive, no wives and sisters to degrade by use of firewater, and as a consequence this all fell to the lot of the untutored Indian, and they soon learned that no honor was shown in the example set for them and no honor was expected in return. Thus the very foundation of Indian character was shattered and as they naturally looked to the white people as their superiors, their degeneration began and white people, instead of improving their morality, destroyed it.

Missionaries were sent among them to give them instructions as to a future life, which instructions, though they differed with their own, must be followed, because they were told if they did so they would become like white people in many ways; be better feed, be better clothed and in all respect better off. These religious teaching were very hard for them to embrace as theirs had been handed down to them from generation to generation by traditional means. They watched those teachers very closely, and it took not long to discover that the missionaries were but little better than the traders in matters of deal, for they exchanged trinkets and other articles with them for sugar and fur, the same as the traders did and they got no better bargains.

But as I am duty bound in these articles to be truthful, I must say that the Catholic missionaries must not be included with those of other denominations. I am not in the least prejudiced in saying so for the information of truthfulness in their dealings I get from the Indians themselves. But for the missionaries of other denominations I cannot say as much. Of my personal knowledge, I know on several occasions where they had received large consignments of clothing from benevolent institutions and societies for free distribution among the sick and needy, which they sold and traded for profit. One incident I will relate which came directly my way, in the winter of 1853, that shows one man least whose heart was true to his teaching. It was a very hard and cold winter and many Indians were poor and destitute, particularly so at Fond du Lac at the head of Lake Superior. By some means Father Baraga, a Catholic priest located at L'Anse Bay, Michigan, a distance by trail from Fond du Lac of about two hundred and fifty miles, heard of great suffering there and that one family in particular, a widow, with her children were all sick. He provided himself with such medicine as could be had and set out on snowshoes to make the journey in the dead of winter, with snow several feet deep. About the 20th of January 1854, I left La Pointe for Ontonagon, Michigan, some ninety miles away in the direction of L'Anse. About half way between La Point and Ontonagon I met Father Baraga on his way to Fond du Lac, as he said to assist the distressed and needy there, and I am quite positive that he would have perished that night but for our meeting. His snowshoes had given out and it would have been impossible for him to have proceeded far without them on account of the deep snow. Our party made it comfortable for him that night and one of my men repaired his snowshoes and in the morning returned with him on that perilous journey. Some months after I met him when he told me of his trip and how he had found the family sick and destitute; that he had given the medicine and otherwise provided for them, and when he left them they were doing well and were comfortable.

I do not mention this incident for the purpose of drawing a line between any two or more denominations that had missionaries in this country but to state the plain facts for history. Any denomination that secured such a martyr as Father Baraga would be fortunate indeed, for his manly and upright disposition would have prompted him to such acts wherever placed. I have been frequently told by the Indians of such acts of kindness as Father Baraga* displayed, but not to such a hazardous degree, were common with the Catholic missionaries. One thing is certain that while there were then to one missionaries here of other denominations not one succeeded in gaining the good will of the Indians or in establishing a congregation amounting to any considerable number, while the Catholics succeeded in establishing a congregation and building a church on Madeline Island, one of the Apostle group, more than two hundred years ago, and that church is still standing, a monument to the labors of Father Marquette.

Father Frederick Baraga, a Roman Catholic priest, arrived in New York from his Slovenia homeland in 1830. Ministering to German immigrants in Cincinnati, he studied the Native languages. In 1837, while posted in Michigan, he published the first Catholic prayer book written in the Ottawa language.

Long winter treks to visit Ojibwe people in Michigan, Wisconsin, and Minnesota, earned Baraga the title, "the Snowshoe Priest." In 1835 Baraga moved west to La Pointe, Wisconsin to minister to the Ojibwe and others near Madeline Island, a center for commerce then. Able to speak eight languages fluently added to his ability to serve the people there. In 1853, Baraga became the first bishop of the Roman Catholic Diocese of Sault Ste. Marie and returned there to complete his ministry.

In closing this work I wish to state my belief that spiritualism had its origin with the Indians. They have believed from time without date that certain ones among their number were clothed with the power of conversing with long departed friends, and through this source got information that was of much benefit to them. In fact no war or great undertaking would be begun without first invoking guidance from their deceased friends. This medium, as we call them, is termed by the Chippewa people Man-e-to-ca-so-ah-min-e. When the people wish to know certain things this man enters his wigwam alone. This wigwam is built entirely different from any other lodge in the band or tribe. He then prepares himself to ask the questions that his people wish to propound to the spirits. Many writers have confounded this medium with what is known as the "Medicine Man," but this is altogether wrong. The medicine man is a healer of the sick and is also looked upon and considered a very wise man, but is supposed to derive much of his information from the spirits through the efforts and power of this medium. After this medium has entered his wigwam for the purpose of conversing with the departed, many of the band will gather around the lodge to hear the answers which are many times received in two or three distinct voices which seem to come from above, each voice differing from the well-known voice of the questioner. I am willing to testify an oath that I have heard these voices a great many times

179

and have come to the conclusion that this medium is actually conversing with the spirits and in reality receives answers or that he is a very powerful ventriloquist, although a ventriloquist, as known to us, is a personage unknown to the Indians, and if any Indians have the power of ventriloquism or ever has had, it is and has been kept by the owners thereof a profound secret, not even coming to the surface in the great secret order and the ventriloquist secret, if such it was, could not be kept by the possessor from the other members of the order without violating their membership oath.

These are fact and I leave those who read this to draw their own conclusions.

Chapter XIX

———— • ————

THE CHIPPEWA LANGUAGE

I will now endeavor to give the reader some words and definitions of things unknown to the Indians before the advent of the white people among them and also of things always familiar to them. This tribe, as far back as I have ever been able to delve, never had a horse or pony, and when white men brought them they named them ba-ba-zhe-go-ga-zhe, meaning an animal with a solid or round hoof. When the cow became known among them it was named be-zhe-ga; ba-zhe-ga-wug is cattle. A moose is called moze, and the white people preserved nearly the Indian name. Ah-dik is elk; wa-was-kish is deer; ma-nish-to-nish is sheep; ah-nim-moze, a dog; ma-ying-gun, a wolf; wa-gooch, a fox; pesh-shu, a lynx; o-geak, a fisher; wa-ba-shush, a martin or sable; shong-qua-zhe, a mink; wa-shush, a rat; ah-mik, a beaver; ne-jik, an otter; ah-chit-a-moo, a squirrel and muk-wa, a bear.

An Indian never uses profane language, but when he wishes to use all the venom he can he calls the object of his wrath "mar-che-an-im," which means "the devil's dog."

Sco-ta-wa-boo is whiskey, sco-ta meaning fire and wa-boo a drink or tea.

Surprise a Chippewa and his first act will be to place his hand over his mouth. His expression on seeing a handsome woman is ka-gat-qua-nage-e-qua. Let him be surprised by his own thoughtfulness or want of skill he will put his hand over his mouth and shout "te-wa." Ke-sha-man-a-tou is the name of God. The good spirit is man-a-tou and mar-che-man-a-tou is the bad spirit or devil.

I will now give you some words and phrases used by them in designating different articles and other things, the accent always on the last syllable.

Different woods and timbers: The white birch or its bark is

called we-quas; sugar maple, nin-a-tick; sap is sis-e-ba-qut-ah-boo; sap boiled down to molasses they say is che-wah-ge-mis-e-gon and sugar is sis-e-gah-qut. White cedar is ge-zhik. A canoe made of birch-bark is we-quass-che-mon, but the word is no applicable to a boat of any other description. Paddle, ah-bo-eh. A pole used in pushing a canoe is con-da-ge-gon-auk. A pine tree, chin-quak; oak, me-tick-o-mich; tamarack, mus-ke-qua-tick. A combination word used to designate all evergreens except the two species of pine, is shin-go-beeg. One log, stick or tree is me-tick; me-tick-ohg, a collection of logs or trees. A forest is me-tick-o-goge.

A prairie is mush-go-day, and means a country formerly a forest which has been cleared by fire; a marsh or a swamp, mush-ke-gonk; natural meadows, mush-ko-se-wan-ing, mush-ko-se-wan is hay or standing grass. Ah-sin is a rock, while ah-sin-ege-cog means a rocky bottom or reef. A rock in a cliff is ah-she-bik.

Names they give to metals: Pe-wa-bik is iron; man-a-tou-wa-bik is steel; mes-qua-bik is copper; o-sa-wa-bik, brass; o-sa-wa-shu-ne-ah is gold either in coin or in its rough state; wa-be-ska-shu-ne-ah, is silver, either coin or metal; shu-ne-ah-ma-sin-ah-a-gon, paper money; o-sa-wah-bik-onse is their name for penny.

An iron stove they call ke-sa-be-kis-e-gon; a saw, gis-ke-bi-je-gon; and axe, wa-g-qut: ah-kik, iron kettle; ah-skik-o-mon-ah-kik, tin pail; a knife mo-quo-mon; pas-kis-e-gon is gun; a-skek-o-mon is lead: ah-new-eh, bullet; she-she-bun-win, shot; muk-ah-day is powder, the same word being applicable to black as a color; be-wah-nuk, a flint as used in a gun-lock. A needle was a wonderful thing with the Indians. It was so frail a thing and had such a delicate eye that it caused much amusement and they named it sha-bo-ne-gon, meaning that it had an eye to carry a thread. Pins were introduced about the same time and being so much the shape of the needle they named them o-ste-guan-sha-bo-ne-gon, meaning a needle with a head.

Che-mo-quo-mon is used in speaking of a white man and is also a name used to designate a large knife or sword. It was brought into use by seeing white officers with swords. As "che" meant a large and mo-quo-mon meant knife, so che-mo-quo-mon meant large knife, and thereby designated officers and soldiers from other pale-faced people, such as traders and missionaries, who were called ah-nin-e-wog, simply meaning men.

Among articles of clothing they designated a blanket, wa-be-wi-on; wa-be-e-gon, a flannel or clothing; man-a-tou-wa-gon – is a fine broad-cloth; wa-ba-ske-gon, muslin or white cotton goods; man-a-tou-me-nase, beads; moc-ah-cin-on, buckskin or moose hide moccasins; wa-was-kish-wi-on, a deer hide untanned, while an untanned moose hide was moze-wi-on, and either one after being tanned or dressed would be called bu-squa-gun; me-tick-qua-ke-cin, a boot or shoe; kit-da-ge-gon is calico.

In naming lakes and rivers the whites, in some cases preserved the Indian pronunciation. The following are the name of some of the most prominent lakes and rivers: The Indians call a lake soc-ka-a-gon, and a river ce-be. The name for Lake Superior is Cha-jik-o-ming, meaning the largest body of fresh water they knew of. The name of the Mississippi River, it will be noticed, has not been changed in any respect, there name being Mis-e-ce-be, he meaning of which is a grand and extensive water-course, the tributaries of which are almost numberless. They call the St. Croix River Ah-gich-che-ce-be meaning pipe-stem, as this river has a lake at its source and another at its mouth, one representing the smoker and the other the bowl of the pipe. Nim-ma-kah-gon means, in their tongue a lake where sturgeon are caught. O-da-bin-ich, means wild potatoes and the stream that empties into the St. Croix River above Stillwater, and called the Apple River by the whites, the Indian's name O-da-bin-ich-con-ce-be. Kin-ne-ke-nik-ce-be, a river which empties into the St. Croix Lake at Hudson, Wisconsin, the white people call the Willow River. Ka-ka-be-kong means he falls of a river. The Snake River they named Ka-na-be-go-ce-be, and the Kettle River Ah-kik-ah-ce-be. The river leading from the source of the St. Croix to Lake Superior the Indians named Wa-sah-gue-de-ce-be, meaning burnt river, and is now called by the whites, Brule, the French term for burnt. Ah-ga-wa-ce-be-one, is the name given by the Indians to the Montreal River, which divides Michigan and Wisconsin and the meaning of it is, "we hardly get started before the falls stop our navigation." Mus-ke-ce-be means Swamp River a, but it is now called by the whites Bad River. Sha-ga-wa-me-gunk is a peninsula dividing the bay at Ashland, Wisconsin, form the main lake, and a government lighthouse is now located there. Non-do-na-gon is the name of the river the whites call Ontonagon, and the Indians name means searching for a lost dish; the non-do meaning search and na-gon-meaning dish.

In the Chippewa language the earth is ah-ke-kong; a small territory is ah-kee; clay is wa-be-gun; sand, bing-que-ca; flying dust, bing-que; flying ashes, sco-ta-bing-que. Soil colors – white clay, wa-be-sa-be-gun; red clay, mus-squa-be-gun; yellow clay, o-sa-wa-be-gun. The word by which a color is designated is prefix to the one describing the material proper. White, wa-be-ska; red, ma-squa; blue, o-sou-wa-squa; yellow, o-sah-wa; black muck, muk-a-da-wa; mus-shuk-gunk-es-sha-ni-gua-sit, a sky color; ge-zhe-gunk, is the heavens; ge-she-que, is day; noon-gum, the present time; tip-pe-cut is night; noon-gum-tip-pe-cut, tonight; noon-gum-ge-zhe-gut, the present day.

Before white people came among them they knew no Sunday, nor the beginning or ending of weeks or months, but reckoned time by moons, winter and summer seasons; but now they have a name for Sunday – ah-num-e-a-ge-zhe-gut – which means "the day we go to church." They call the service at church, ah-num-e-a. New Year's Day is Nom-mik-wa-ta-tin or the meeting of two years. They call a priest, muk-wa-da-ah-coo-ne-a. Ah-num-ah-a-wa-co-me-cunk, means a church; ah-nin-e is a man; ah-nin-e-wug, a number of men; e-qua is woman; e-qua-wug, women; ah-be-no-gee, child; ah-be-no-gee-ng, children; ah-cue-wan-zee, an old man; che-mene-de-mo-ya, an old woman; o-skin-ah-way, a young man; o-ske-nage-e-qua, a young woman; ah-qua-nage-e-ua, a handsome young woman or girl; ah-qua-nage-ah-min-e, a handsome man; song-qua-da; brave; song-qua-da-a-nin-e, a brave man.

A human being is ah-nich-ah-na-be that is as a whole. Descriptive it is this: beginning at the feet, the Indian would say, a foot is o-sit, the leg is o-cot; the thigh is ob-wam, the hips o-chi-gun, the back o-bic-wan, the abdomen or stomach o-mis-cut, the arm o-nick, the hand o-minge, the neck o-qua-gun; the head is o-ste-quan, the ear o-do-uck, the nose o-josh, the mouth is o-doone, the eye is o-ske-zhic, the teeth is we-bit-dun, the tongue o-da-un-eau, the chin is o-da-mik-cun, the chest o-cah-ke-gun, the heart o-day, the blood mis-qua. The brain, which all Indians believe to be the source from which all Indians believe to be the source from which all knowledge emanates, they call we-nin-dip. One Indian, in speaking to another whom he considers above mediocrity in brainpower would say of him: Kat-get che-me-cha-ni-o-we-nin-dip. This mean he has got a very large brain. Nee-oss, my own flesh; ke-oss, your flesh; Nin, myself; kin, yourself; and win a third person; ah-nish-e-nah-big, two or three persons; che-ne-pe-wa-ah-nish-e-nah-big, means a great many people.

I never knew an Indian to grow a beard. The first chore in the morning, when a beard is showing itself, is to pluck every vestige of it out. I have often inquired why they did it, but could never get a satisfactory answer. The only reason seemed to be that it was not pretty. They have a name for it however, and call it me-soc-wat-one, the meaning of which word is the mouth hidden.

Now try to read this sentence: O-da-bin, ah-be-no-gee ma-we go-sha – go take the child, it cries.

The Indian count was thus: One, ba-zhic; 2, neich; 3, nis-swy; 4, ne-win; 5, nah-nun; 6, go-twas-swe; 7, neich-was-swe; 8, swa-swy; 9, shong-qus-swy; 10, me-da-swy; 11, me-da-swy-ah-she-ba-zhic; me-da-swy-ah-she-neich; and so on to twenty. You will observe that me-dah-swy means 10, ah-she means "and," the numeral being added to this until you reach twenty. Example: Nis-swy is 3; then me-da-swy-ah-she-nis-swy is 13; 20 is neich-tan-a;

21 is neich-tan-a-ah-she-ba-zhic, and so on to 30, which is nis-ce-me-tan-ah; 31, nis-ce-me-tan-ah-she-ba-zhic; 40 is ne-me-tan-ah; 50, na-ne-me-tan-ah; 60, go-twas-e-me-tan-ah; 70, neich-was-me-tan-ah; 80, swas-e-me-tan-ah; 90, shong-gus-e-me-tan-ah; 100, na-ning-go-twauk; 101, nane-go-twauk-ah-she-ba-zhic; 102, nane-go-twauk-ah-she-neich, and so on; 200, neich-wauk; 201, neich-wauk-ah-she-ba-zhic, and so on; 300, nis-wauk; 400, ne-wauk; 500, non-wauk; 600, go-twas-wauk; 700, neich-was-wauk; 800, swas-wauk; 900, shong-us-wauk; 1,000, me-dos-wauk, and so on.

Write the following in Chippewa: "An Indian killed one bear, two deer and one moose today," and it will read, "Noon-gum-ge-ne-sa ba-zhic muk-wa, neich wa-was-ka-zhe-gi-ah ba-zhic moze."

To continue with the names the Indians gave to the different species of the feathery flock, the American Eagle is called Che-me-ke-se, while me-ke-se is an ordinary eagle. Ah-zhe-jok; a sand-hill crane; ne-kuk, a goose or brant; zhe-zheep, a duck; zhe-zhe-buck, many ducks; ka-kik, hawk; co-co-co, owl; wa-be-na, grouse or prairie chicken; pe-na, partridge; o-me-me, pigeon, mumg-ua-ua, yellow hammer.

Madeline Island, in Lake Superior, derived its name from this bird, as it used to congregate there is great numbers. They named the island Mun-qua-na-ca-ning, but the Missionaries muddled it into Madeline.

Pe-na-she, a bird; pe-na-she-ug, many birds; ga-ga-ge, a crow; ma-ma, the large woodcock, by many historians called the Indian hen; twe-twish-ke-wah, a plover; che-zhe-zhe-buck, canvas back duck; nin-ah-zhe-buck, mallard; wa-week-ing-gronge-ge, the blue winged teal, meaning "their wings whistle in the air." Most other species they simply call zhe-zhe-buck; ba-ka-qua, domestic chicken; mis-e-say, a turkey.

Among the finny tribe they named the fish, which affords the followers of Isaac Walton so much pleasure, the brook trout, marsh-ah-may-guass, while a lake trout the named as nay-may-guass; a whitefish, ah-dik-gum-egg; catfish, ma-num-meg;

sturgeon, na-mae; walleyed pike, o-gah; pickerel, ke-no-zhe; muskellunge, mash-ka-no-zhe, and the perch o-ga-weg.

The Indian child now calls it father ne-bah-bah, and mother ne-mah-mah. Formerly it was noce for father and ning-ga for mother. Brother, ne-cieh; sister, ne-mis-eh, but it only applies to the brothers and sisters older than the speaker. Ne-she-way would apply to either brother or sister younger than the speaker. Ne-she-ma-que-we-zence means a boy; ne-she-ma-e-qua-zence, a girl; sah-sa-gah-e-nin-e means handsomely dressed or nice manners.

Their names for berries and fruits: Raspberries they call mis-que-me-nuk, meaning blood berries; blackberries, tuk-og-o-me-nuk; strawberries, o-da-me-nuk, shaped like a heart; cranberries, mus-ke-ge-me-nug; me-num, blueberries; a common apple, me-she-min; thorn apple, me-she-me-nace-suc.

The following isa miscellaneous collection of names and words which were in use almost daily, among which will be found the substantials of life introduced by the white race: Wheat-flour, or bread made from flour, bo-qua-zhe-qua; corn, min-dah-min; cornbread is min-da-min-ah-ba-qua-zhe-gun; o-be-nick, potatoes; che-a-ne-bish, cabbage; an-ne-bish, tea and after it is steeped it is called ah-ne-be-sha-boo; coffee is muk-a-da-ma-ske-ke-wa-boo; do-do-sha-boo is milk; mus-ke-ke-wa-boo is medicine; the mus-ke-ke the medicine and wa-boo the drink; do-do-sha-bo-ba-me-day is butter, meaning, properly, grease from milk; we-oss is fresh meat; be-she-ke-we-oss is beef; co-kush-we-oss is pork; wa-wash-kesh-we-oss, venison; moze-we-oss, fresh moose meat; muk-wa-we-oss, bear meat; ah-dik-we-oss elk meat; mac-in-ton-ish-we-oss, mutton; o-da-bon, sleigh or wagon; de-be-sa-o-dak-bon, wagon or car with wheels; ne-cun-ah, a road or trail; sko-da-o-da-bon-me-cun-ah, a railroad; ah-sho-gun, a bridge; ah-sho-ga, across a bridge or water; be-mich-ca, he crosses in a boat; this shore, o-das-o-gon; the other shore, ah-gon-mink; to row a boat is ah-sha-boo-ya, while ba-ma-sha is sailing a boat; ba-mo-za, walking; be-me-bat-to, running; ke-she-ca, run fast; ba-pin, to laugh; ma-we, to cry; ge-git-o, speak;

ke-nooch, speak to those people. Both the later words are commands. Was-wa means a fire hunt; wa-swa-gun is torchlight; was-squaw-nane-ge-gun is lamp or candlelight; the sun is called ge-ses; the moon, tip-e-ge-ses; a star, ah-nung; ah-nung-goog, many stars; me-shuk-qut, clear sky; ah-nuk-qut, cloudy sky; num-me-keeg is thunder; num-me-keeg-wa-sa-tage is lightening.

Although the format and length differ, this chapter bears resemblance to the portion of John Falcon Tanner's memoir, dictated to a friend and published in 1831. The Tanner book was quite successful, being published in New York, London, Paris, Russia, and Germany.

Fourteen years after he wrote it, Tanner found himself wrongly accused of the murder of Henry Schoolcraft's brother, James. John Tanner disappeared and was thought dead by many. In truth, he secluded himself on an island in Lake Namakagon and, far from anyone who might recognize him, lived a hermit's life for the last four decades of his life.

The fact that both men lived in the same region at the same time and each dictated their memoir to another and included English-Ojibwe translations may indicate they were well acquainted.

Biographical

I was born in the State of Alabama in the year 1820, and at the age of ten years, having had less than three weeks of schooling, I was decoyed away from home by a man named Thomas, who was engaged in horse racing, traveling all over the southern states.

In the summer of 1833 we went to New Orleans, Louisiana where I was injured by a fall from a horse, and just after this and before I had recovered from that injury, I was taken sick with a fever, which lasted for a number of weeks. Mr. Thomas and his party left me there with directions to follow as soon as I was able. They went on to Holly Springs, Mississippi. I started in about four weeks and reached Holly Springs, but had left my bed too soon and there had a relapse, and from that time until spring was not able to do any work.

I was then moved to Decatur, Ala, and a short time afterwards to Athens, where I met Mr. Thomas, who said: "Perhaps you had better go home, for probably you will never be able to ride a horse again." He also stated that he had written to my oldest brother about a month before and told him that my health was bad and that I would have to lay by and have good care for some time to come, but said he had received no reply to his letter and would not be surprised to see my brother at any time, and hoped he would come, for he did not like to see me start alone to make the journey in the condition I was. "Besides," he says, "you have been with me three years, and your salary for this time is all due, which I will pay you at any time," but said he did not think it would be safe for me to carry it, and would pay me enough for current expenses and put the remainder in the bank subject to my order if my brother did not come to meet me. I told him I would like to go to Huntsville, as I had a friend there whom I would like to see. He paid my stage fare to Huntsville and told me to come back to Athens, as he would be there two or three weeks. After the visit I came back to Athens.

I owned a horse at this time, which was in the possession of

189

Mr. Thomas. He asked me one day shortly after my return from Huntsville: "How much do you suppose I owe you?" I told him what the agreement was – to pay me $50 per month and extras that were allowed to riders in the races they won, besides there was the difference between the value of the horse I had brought with me and the one I now had.

"That is correct," says he. "I owe you now just $2,600. I have deposited it in the bank." He handed me the certificate of deposit for it, then took me to the bank and told the cashier I was the party to whom the money is to be paid. He next took me to a clothing store and made me a present of two suits of clothes, and also of a watch to remember him by, and remarked: "I am very sorry you can ride no more, for you are the most successful rider that ever lived, and if you are ever able to ride again come to me and you shall have a place as long as I have the place to give anybody."

We returned to the hotel where we were stopping when he told me he had arranged with the landlord to pay my bill until I was ready to go home, and that he had reserved money enough from my salary to pay my fare.

During all the time I had been with Mr. Thomas I was known by an assumed name, so that my mother would not find out where I was.

Mr. Thomas and I walked out upon the porch of the hotel just as the stagecoach was driving in from Huntsville. Three passengers alighted, one of whom was my oldest brother. He did not recognize me, on account of being so reduced by bad health, but he recognized Mr. Thomas immediately, and soon was aware that I was in his presence. The excitement incident to this meeting with my brother, and the good treatment I had received from Mr. Thomas, quite unbalanced me and caused me a backset that confined me to my bed for three or four days, and during that confinement physicians told me I had better leave that climate and go either west or north.

It was decided to do this as soon as I was able to travel, and we set out for the west instead of going home. I rode a horse and my brother walked as far as Florence, Alabama, where we took a steamboat down the Tennessee River for Paducah, Kentucky. There we were obliged to halt for a few days for me to recuperate and receive medical treatment. When we left here it was by steamboat for St. Louis, Missouri. We spent the winter of 1834 and most of the year 1835 in that city. My health improved by little. During the season of 1835 we learned that a boat was going up river to Prairie du Chien, and thinking it might benefit my health, my brother and I took passage and witnessed the peace treaty which was consummated that year by General Cass with the different tribes of Indians.

We returned on the boat to St. Louis and the same fall went to Hannibal, Missouri, where we stayed until 1837. During the time I made the acquaintance of Major Walker, who was one of the parties on the part of the government to make a treaty at St. Peter, Minnesota. I took this trip up the river, but remained on the boat, not being able to go through with Mr. Walker and returned to Hannibal.

At times I felt better, and always best during the trips up river. I had a constant cough both day and night, and this, with the chills and fever, prevented me from gaining strength. Doctors pronounced me in the last stages of consumption. Fortunately for me I visited Dr. Peek, then residing in Hannibal, an old physician who had about retired from practice. He made an examination of my case and told me he thought my lungs were all right and believed a change in climate would benefit me, and if that would not, medicine would do me no good. Upon his recommendation I went up the Mississippi again to the St. Croix pineries, taking a man with me to help get back into the woods to rough it and to live or die there. When I parted with my friends at Hannibal none expected to see me again alive.

At Prairie du Chien I engaged a half-breed by the name of Ben Young, who had been raised with Chippewas and spoke

English tolerably well.

I landed at Lake St. Croix, where the city of Hudson now stands, on the second day of July 1840. The place was then called Page's Landing. Mr. Page was on board the boat I came up on, having been below to purchase supplies for his camp. He assisted me in getting ashore and also having my cabin built in the woods, back of the present city of Hudson. I remained in that camp until about the middle of January 1841, and lived on wild meat, with no tea or coffee, and but little bread, seeing nobody except my man and one hunter whose name was Peter Bushu, a Canadian half-breed.

By the first of January I was able to run through the woods every day to hunt, and my health was gaining rapidly. I gave up my shanty about the middle of January and spent the remainder of the winter in the camp of Mr. Page. My man was teaching me the Chippewa language, and by spring I was able to converse quite freely. During the time I kept up constant communication with my brother, and when navigation opened I made a flying trip to Missouri, my brother having written me that he was going to California. I returned immediately to the Northwest, which has been my home since that time.

###

APPENDIX

The following is a letter from Chief Buffalo to Luke Lea, Commissioner of Indian Affairs in Washington. It was dictated to Benjamin Armstrong after consultation with the chiefs of the other Lake Superior Ojibwe bands.

To the Hon. Luke Lea
Commissioner of Indian Affairs
Washington, D.C.

Our Father:
We send you our salutations and wish you to listen to our words. We the Chiefs and head men of the Chippeway Tribe of Indians, feel ourselves aggrieved and wronged by the conduct of the U.S. Agent John I. Watrous and his advisors now among us. He has used great deception towards us in carrying out the wishes of our Great Father in respect to our removal. We have ever been ready to listen to the words of our Great Father whenever he has spoken to us, and to accede to his wishes. But this time, in the matter of our removal, we are in the dark. We are not satisfied that it is the President that requires us to remove. We have asked to see the order, and the name of the President affixed to it, but it has not been shewn us. We think the order came only from the Agent and those who advise with him, and are interested in having us remove.
We will now tell you the words of the Commissioner spoken to us when our lands were sold at La Pointe. "Your Great Father," he said, "does not want the land to cultivate, it is only the mineral on it which he wants. The Whites do not

wish to come and occupy your country now—until they want it you will be permitted to live and hunt on your land as before. So far as you may live on land which will be wanted by the miners and you will have to remove (onto) one side; but if you are not in the way of the whites, and live on terms of friendship with them, it will be a great while before you will be required to remove. I don't believe that you or I will ever see the day when you will be troubled about your lands."

He said that we and our children after us might be permitted to live on our land fifty years or even a hundred if we lived on friendly terms with the Whites. It is true, our Father, that some of our countrymen have had trouble with the whites; but this is not true of us who live on the Lake. We have never shed the blood of the Whites; nor killed their cattle; nor done them any injury; and we are not in their way. And why do we now hear this order to remove? We do not understand it. Stuart, the Commissioner, promised us when the treaty was made that our payment should be made at La Pointe for twenty- five years. But now the man you have sent to be our agent has removed our payment to a distant place. The Commissioner (Stuart) promised us too. Carpenters, Farmers, Blacksmiths and Teachers, to work for us and teach us how to build houses—cultivate the soil and become wise like the Whites. These the Agent has now taken away. It is when we think of the promises made to us by the Comm. who bought our lands, and think too, of the conduct of our present Agent that we cannot believe that he is *acting according to the instruction of our Great Father, in trying to affect our removal.*

We wish to speak now of our payment at Sandy Lake, how we suffered and were deceived there by our Agent. This is what our Agent told us. "Come, my children, come to Sandy Lake and you shall have plenty to eat and be fat and I will make your payment quick."

We went, but did not find him there. His Secretary and Mr. Warren were there to take care of the goods, but he had gone down the River to get the money. Instead of having a good supply of provisions to eat, we had but little; and the pork & flour furnished us had been soaked in the water, and was so much damaged that we could not eat it. It was this that caused so much sickness among us. After being kept there two months waiting for our payment, the Agent at length arrived and paid us our goods, but our money we did not get at all. By this time the rivers had frozen and we had to throw away our canoes and go to our distant homes with our families on foot. As the Agent did not supply us with provisions we were obliged to sell our blankets and buy on credit with the traders, that our children might be kept from starving and we have something to eat during our journey home. When we left for home we saw the ground covered with the graves of our children and relatives. One hundred and seventy had died during the payment. Many, too, of our young men and women fell by the way, and when we had reached home and made a careful estimate of our loss of life, we found that two hundred and thirty more had died on their way home. This is what makes us so sad to think that the payment should be removed to that place.

We will now speak of what has taken place this summer. In the Spring the Agent wrote to the Chief at La Pointe, telling him not to let his young men plant at Bad River—that he was going to plant for them at Fond du Lac. In the summer he came himself, and ordered us to arise quickly and go to Eon du Lac. We asked him by what authority he requested us to remove. He said it was the order of the Great Father himself, and if we did not promptly obey we should soon see soldiers here to compel us to go. He said we were not required to go any farther than Fon du Lac, or to our own land, and if we would go there, he promised us, that when we should arrive, we should find our money ready for us, and that farms should be opened, and stores of provisions be laid in, and everything be provided, by which we should be made comfortable and happy. He wished us to go to Fon du Lac with our families and go to Sandy Lake for our payment. We said we should not go there—When we die we will lay our bones at La Pointe. We told him if he would pay us well, we would go to Fon du Lac and no farther. He said he would pay us our money at Fon du Lac, both our last year's payment and this year's, but the goods had been ordered to Sandy Lake and could not be carried to Fon du Lac. He promised our Chief Buffalo that he should go to Washington to see our Great Father that he might hear with his own ears his words and tell him all about our affairs. He said he himself would go with our Chief, pay his expenses to Washington and back again, and would take good care of the Indians and see that they were well fed during our Chief's absence. We went to Fon du Lac but were not fed well. Our rations did not fulfill his pledges we should have full liberty to return again to our homes. We did not see them fulfilled. And when we saw that everything was contrary to what we expected, and to what the Agent had promised, we arose and returned home. But not until he had left, and there was no more hope of our expectations being fulfilled.

Believe these words, our Father, which we have spoken about our Agent that it is in consequence of what he has done that we are so poor. Our women and children do indeed cry, our Father, on account of their suffering from cold and hunger. You, our Father, are at the head of all authority, and you have it in your power to redress all our grievances. We wish to have our future payments made at La Pointe as they formerly were. We wish to have our Farmers, Carpenters, Blacksmiths, & Teachers restored to us, and we be permitted to remain here where we were promised we might live, as long as we were not in the way of the Whites. We wish to be remunerated for the losses we have suffered at Sandy Lake. We ask for not one shilling more than any honest man will say we ought to receive. And finally, that our affairs may be properly investigated and justice be done to us, we wish that a delegation of our own choice, in connection with any that you may wish to send for, may be permitted to visit Washington. Especially would we like to have our friend and half breed child Wm. W. Warren go. In his truth and friendship we have confidence, he is well acquainted with our affairs, and he has ever advised us to listen to the words of our Great Father.

One thing more. The Indians are especially displeased at seeing the Agent so intimate with the traders. The goods and money of the Indians are deposited in their stores. They are the constant advisers of the Agent and, we fear, extensively control his conduct. We wish our goods and money could be deposited somewhere else and the Agent have for his counsellors a more disinterested class of persons.

Chief Great Buffalo

Dr. John A. Anderson, while president of the Lac Courte Oreilles College, presented the following address on the 130th anniversary of the signing of the 1854 Treaty of La Pointe. The ceremony took place on Madeline Island, September 30, 1984.

FULFILLMENT OF THE 7TH PROPHECY

Grandfather - Great Spirit, we are gathered here today on this island now known as Madeline in a spirit of remembrance and thanksgiving. For those of us here who are Ojibwa it is a pilgrimage back‾to our roots. We remember that the historic signing of the Treaty of La Pointe took place here on this day 130 years ago and that the Ojibwa Reservations of Red Cliff, Bad River, Lac Courte Oreilles, and Lac du Flambeau were created as a result. For this we are deeply thankful.

We recall also the thousands of Ojibwa people who once inhabited this island and who in about the year 1491 and continuing for over 350 years thereafter called this island their home. Here these people, our ancestors the Anishinabi, planted their gardens of corn, beans, and squash and fished these waters of Gitchi Gumi for ciscos, trout, and whitefish. It was here also that they married, conducted religious ceremonies, lived out their lives, and were buried. Is it any wonder that we consider this land and its surroundings sacred? From here messengers were sent out to other tribes, our warriors seeking to prove their manhood began their journey from this site, and trappers in quest of furs utilized this place as their headquarters. Soon this island came to be known as the capitol of the Ojibwa Nation. Formerly it was a refuge and sanctuary for our people when they first came into these parts and were harassed by war parties of the Sioux and Fox Tribes. As our people grew in strength and numbers, we began to settle the mainland along this great Chequamegon Bay and we set up villages at Red Cliff, Odanah and beyond.

But what was it that brought us here a distance of some 1800 miles from our homeland in the East which lay along the mouth of the St. Lawrence River? Was it a search for wealth, was it conquest, or was it hunger for more territory? It was none of these. Historians' opinions withstanding, we came here in the main to fulfill a prophecy of one of our tribal elders, a medicine man, who warned our people that they were to make a long and dangerous journey to the west or suffer the ravages of sickness and death and perish. This information .was given to him in a dream after a long fast while he was deliberating the future of his people. He told the Ojibwa that they were to follow the .guiding light of the Megis - a sacred shell which represents the Medawewin religion. This shell he-said would show them the way. The migration began sometime in the early twelve hundreds and continued for a period of over 200 years. During the journey our tribe set up stopping places at Montreal, Lake Huron, and

Sault Ste. Marie before arriving at this island which they called Mo-ning-wun-a-kaun-Ing— the home of the golden breasted woodpecker. At each of the principal stops the Medawewin lodge was set up and ceremonies were held to help give the people long life and wisdom through the use of medicines and a code of conduct. Part of the prophecy which brought the Ojibwa to these parts foretold the time when our culture would become almost totally extinct, the coming of the whiteman to these shores and the growth of a grain in the water, which we call mahnomen, which would be found at the end of our people's journey. Another prediction known as the 7th Prophecy foretold of how the Ojibwa would by returning to their old homesites recapture their culture, assert their independence and leadership, and become more spiritual in nature. By so doing, they were told that they would once again become a proud, happy and prosperous people. We are living today at the time of the 7th Prophecy and today, as we gather for this treaty conference, we should know that this gathering is part of the process of fulfillment.

We must learn today at this meeting from Chief Buffalo's experience of 132 years ago in 1852 when he and Chief Oshoga made the long and arduous journey to Washington, D.C., a distance of over 1500 miles, mostly by birchbark canoe, with 4 of their warriors and an interpreter by the name of Benjamin Armstrong. Buffalo was 93 years old at the time. Their mission was to secure the occupancy and use of this territory, our ancestral homeland, for themselves and their descendants for all time. What a mission— what a challenge—what an assignment-for a man of Buffalo's advanced years.

It was Buffalo who persuaded President Fillmore to countermand the removal order which President Zachary Taylor had issued in 1850 which would have relocated the Ojibwa people of Wisconsin to Sandy Lake, Minnesota. Buffalo used all his skill as a leader and diplomat to prevent his tribe the Ojibwa from being removed to Minnesota. For example, after smoking and sharing the pipe of peace with all assembled at this critical meeting with the President, he called on Chief Oshoga a powerful orator to present the Ojibwa's case. In addition, before coming to Washington, he had sent out runners to all of his fellow tribesmen to inquire if any of them had given cause through some unfriendly act to cause the removal. He also presented various petitions signed by many citizens of the State of Wisconsin and Michigan objecting to the removal of the Ojibwa without just cause, and finally he garnered the support of several renowned politicians in his day including Senator Briggs of New York to support him in his efforts.

The rest of the story is Buffalo's gift to us - for aren't we still living in the State of Wisconsin and are we not commemorating and celebrating today at this conference the fruits of his efforts?

Now then, what ought this assemblage do to ensure the fulfillment of the 7th Prophecy *which states we must retrace our steps and recapture our rituals and cultural heritage— assert our leadership—and reestablish our spiritual ties with our creator? I have a few ideas. First, we must find the Great Spirit's presence in every flower and bush and in every tree and rock and we must join hands with other people on this continent who also honor and respect our mother the earth. Secondly, we must make available to ourselves every tool of the media we can muster to tell our story thus developing a communication and public relations system which is second to none. Thirdly, we must continue to develop good leadership and educate ourselves and our people in the ways of contemporary society so that our educators, social workers, healthcare personnel, businessmen, attorneys, politicians, and statesman alike can best represent our cause .and our people. Fourthly, we must learn to play the game of politics, acquainting ourselves with the many facets of diplomacy which are involved in the process. Fifth, the Wisconsin Bands of Ojibwa need to formulate a federation and alliance much like the Minnesota Chippewa Tribes in order to better communicate their needs, consolidate their strength and increase their influence. Sixth, we must pray and ask the Great Spirit to assist us in our endeavors today and every day as we seek to recapture the spirit of our ancestors and to rekindle the flame of our nation's heritage. Seventh, we must give thanks to he-who made us Ojibwa so that by honoring him we can count on his presence in our deliberations as we here gathered today, with his help make plans for the future of his people and our tribe the Ojibwa.*

And so, Great Spirit - Grandfather, it was a prophecy that led our Ojibwa people here to this island almost 500 years ago and it was our ancestors' courage and unwavering spirit that allowed them to make this difficult journey. Today then, with thankfulness, we gather here together in your presence to commemorate this, the 130th anniversary of the signing of the 1854 Treaty of La Pointe. We ask that you - motivate us - inspire us - and protect us as we, your people the Anishinabi, go forth from this island, our ancestral home, to lead our people and to fulfill our destiny.

(Submitted by Dr. John A. (Little Bird) Anderson, D.L. for exclusive use in this text.)

Duluth Herald

Weather
A little cooler
High Wednesday in 30s
Date on Page 7B

One 86th Year—No. 131.

Tuesday, November 20, 1979

20¢

Indians mull reviving claim to Duluth

Who Really Owns Downtown Duluth and Park Point?
James A. Brakken

Historians agree that in 1852 Benjamin Armstrong helped avert a war between the Great Lakes Ojibwe and the U.S. government. He did this by guiding Chief Great Buffalo and five Ojibwe dignitaries from La Pointe, Wisconsin, to Washington, D.C., and by helping them convince President Fillmore to honor U.S. treaty commitments to the Lake Superior Ojibwe.

Chief Buffalo and the other leaders wanted to show Armstrong their appreciation. Their first choice was to reward Armstrong with some of the money promised them in their government allotment. Armstrong refused this, knowing the Ojibwe people needed the money to survive. The elders, determined to show their gratitude, then offered land for a home—one square mile—anywhere within their lands he wished. In fact, they insisted this be written into the Treaty of 1854. The U.S. treaty negotiators agreed to their request and, although the insertion in Article 2 does not specify Armstrong's name or the location of the land, it is clear that Buffalo had the right to award him this gift.

As Armstrong's memoir shows, he and Buffalo went "landlooking" by canoe to the mouth of the St. Louis River. There he laid claim to his mile-square section of land. Buffalo had a document prepared that specified the metes and bounds with Benjamin Green Armstrong as the owner. Over time he lost this land due to a combination of setbacks. They included his blindness and the resulting medical expenses, several poor business decisions, and the faltering economy during the following decades. Later court cases failed to solve problems with the deed.

Nevertheless, the Treaty of 1854 clearly shows Great Buffalo had the right to give Armstrong the land and the claim was made. Because Armstrong never received the promised payment for his land, some historians believe it remains his. If so, his descendants are the rightful owners.

When Benjamin Armstrong claimed his mile-square Minnesota Point, he had no idea that it would become what is now called Park Point, including a large part of downtown Duluth, Minnesota. He could not have predicted his land would become a major commercial center, an outstanding recreational area, a thriving city. Nor would he have guessed it would be the gateway to one of the busiest port cities on the Great Lakes. Thousands of ships carry cargo in and out of the harbor through this single keyhole, once owned by Benjamin Armstrong.

The *Duluth Herald* carried this story Nov 20, 1979.

When the Treaty of La Pointe was signed, Chief Buffalo insisted on reserving a square mile of land for Armstrong in payment for his services. Armstrong related later he, Chief Buffalo and four other Indians rowed to Duluth to select his parcel. Just west of Minnesota Point they stood on a rock ledge and mentally marked off a parcel running easterly from where they stood and one mile back from the bay. The area had not yet been surveyed, so there was no way of describing it accurately in the Treaty at La Pointe. It was generally conceded, however, it covered an area west of Lake Avenue that subsequently became part of downtown Duluth.

In his memoir, Armstrong says the land description appears in the treaty. If so, it must be on a page not included in the official document. What appears doesn't offer a specific description.

And being desirous to provide for some of his connections who have rendered his people important services, it is agreed that the chief Buffalo may select one section of land, at such place in the ceded territory as he may see fit, which shall be reserved for that purpose, and conveyed by the United States to such person or persons as he may direct.

Armstrong said, *"I will be satisfied with one mile square, and let it start from the rock which we have christened Buffalo Rock, running easterly in the direction of Minnesota Point, taking in a mile square immediately northerly from the head of St. Louis Bay."*

According to Armstrong's recollection, Agent Gilbert wrote the specific metes and bounds beginning with, *"starting from a rock immediately above and adjoining Minnesota Point, etc."*

So, are Benjamin Armstrong's descendants the rightful owners of his mile-square section? Downtown Duluth? Park Point? Maybe. Will the courts ever make a final decision? Not likely. It seems the original document, even the wording in the treaty itself, did not meet the necessary legal requirements of a valid, authentic deed.

This may never be settled in the courts, leaving it to followers of history and Indian culture to forever wonder. Meanwhile, the descendants of Benjamin Armstrong can proudly walk through downtown Duluth, pointing out building after building, and saying, "That's mine. That's yours. That's mine," yet never have to pay a penny of the property tax or replace a fallen shingle.

Downtown might have new landlord

BY SUSAN STANICH
Staff writer

Richard Lee Armstrong thinks there's a slim possibility he owns downtown Duluth.

That's right. Owns.

The country-western singer from Winona is a direct descendant of Benjamin Armstrong, the adopted son of Kitchi Waishke, "The Great Buffalo," who in the mid-1850s was given by the government a portion of what is now Duluth.

The Great Buffalo — also known as Chief Buffalo — gave it to Benjamin Armstrong.

"I guess he sold it to somebody, and he never got payment for it," Richard Armstrong, 41, said.

Richard Armstrong

The land was not given to Benjamin Armstrong until after an all-night council of Lake Superior chiefs, at which Buffalo argued that Armstrong's services as interpreter to the Ojibwe people deserved a gift.

The old chief, then in his

See Landlord Page 11A

209

An Uncanny Similarity between Memoirs
James A. Brakken

My study of Benjamin Armstrong, a steadfast friend to the Chippewa people, began after in-depth research into the life of Chief Namakagon, also known as Mikwam-mi-migwan or Ice Feathers, a legendary figure in Bayfield and Sawyer counties, in northwest Wisconsin. Prior to living in Wisconsin, he was known as Shaw-shawa nay-baysay or Swift Sparrow and also known as John Falcon Tanner, an adventurer, war hero, and author from southern Manitoba, northern Minnesota, and Sault Ste. Marie, Michigan.

My understanding of the relationship between Armstrong and Tanner caused me to research the lives of both men, including their memoirs. I found many similarities between these writings, including the fact that neither Benjamin Armstrong nor John Tanner could write their own life stories. This, because of Armstrong's failed vision when his book was written, and Tanner's inability to read or write when his book was completed. Both men dictated their tales to friends who recorded their words. And both men ended their books with pages filled with Ojibwe language translations. Was this simply a strange coincidence? Could it be that Namakagon inspired Armstrong to write his own memoir—modeled after the Tanner memoir—including the Ojibwe to English translations? It had worked for Tanner. Extremely successful in the United States, Tanner's book also won international acclaim after being printed in London, Paris, Germany, and Russia. Did John Tanner—Chief Namakagon—encourage Armstrong to write his life story, both men hoping for a similar outcome?

The similarity between the two books is uncanny, causing many to believe these men were close friends and willing to share their experiences—perhaps even their secrets—with each other.

Additional Notes

The image on this book's cover is purported to have been painted from sketches done in La Pointe during the September, 1854, treaty negotiations. The unknown artist took liberties when painting the attire by including a Sioux headdress, probably thinking this would enhance the image. Ironically, the Ojibwe and Sioux were enemies. No Ojibwe would have worn a Sioux headdress then.

The book used by the author in creating this annotated edition of the Armstrong memoir is an original, produced in Ashland, Wisconsin, by Arthur W. Bowron in 1892. Armstrong's signature appears inside. The recipient of the book was Joseph Raymond Feldsmith, an Ashland resident. The book remains in private ownership.

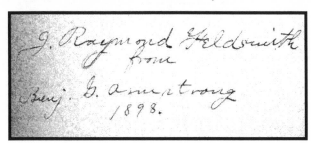

Some of the images provided by the Marr and Richards Engraving Company for the Armstrong book were later used in other publications. The above is a combination of Marr and Richards images. It appeared in the August 5, 1871, issue of *Harper's Weekly.*

The Marr and Richards engraving (below right) was made from the original 1854 photograph (left) of the treaty allotment distribution at La Pointe.

As noted on page 18, Chief Buffalo gave Benjamin Armstrong the pipe created for and used at their council with President Fillmore. The pipe remained with Armstrong's descendants for generations prior to being given to the Red Cliff band. Below is a copy of the estimated auction value of the pipe as appraised by Christie's of New York.

CHRISTIE'S

CHRISTIE, MANSON & WOODS INTERNATIONAL, INC.

Date: Sep. 10, 1995

Regional Property # PBI1695

ID #

(Contact information masked by author.)

Telephone: (   )   Day
           (   )   Night

This temporary receipt will be replaced with a formal Property Receipt, which may reflect different descriptions and values, once this property has been examined by Christie's specialist(s).

Item Number	Quantity	Description	Department	Reserve Agreed/Suggested	Provisional Value
1	1	Buffalo pipe-28" w/bowl 33-34"			500,000

sending to Hadley Freeman for examination - *in the American Indian, African and Oceanic Art Dept*

Christie's Is Not Responsible for Picture Frames

Special Instructions:

Consignor hereby appoints Christie's as consignor's attorney-in-fact and grants to Christie's a special power of attorney for the limited purpose of executing a consignment agreement in the event the consignor or the consignor's authorized agent or representative shall have failed to execute a consignment agreement by the day preceding the date on which the Property shall be offered for sale.

Consigned By:

Received By: Marjorie McKinley

(4/93)

Consignor Charges:
Commission:
Insurance: CMW - 1½%, Owner
Shipping: Owner, CMW
Illustration:
Other:

Contract Signed
Attach if Yes ☐   ☐
            Yes   No

CLIENT COPY

213

TREATY WITH THE CHIPPEWA, 1854.

Sept. 30, 1854.
10 Stats., 1109.
Ratified Jan. 10, 1855.
Proclaimed Jan. 29, 1855.

Articles of a treaty made and concluded at La Pointe, in the State of Wisconsin, between Henry C. Gilbert and David B. Herriman, commissioners on the part of the United States, and the Chippewa Indians of Lake Superior and the Mississippi, by their chiefs and head-men.

Cession to the United States by the Chippewa of Lake Superior.

ARTICLE 1. The Chippewas of Lake Superior hereby cede to the United States all the lands heretofore owned by them in common with the Chippewas of the Mississippi, lying east of the following boundary-line, to wit: Beginning at a point, where the east branch of Snake River crosses the southern boundary-line of the Chippewa country, running thence up the said branch to its source, thence nearly north, in a straight line, to the mouth of East Savannah River, thence up the St. Louis River to the mouth of East Swan River, thence up the East Swan River to its source, thence in a straight line to the most westerly bend of Vermillion River, and thence down the Vermillion River to its mouth.

Relinquishment to Chippewas of Mississippi by Chippewas of Lake Superior.

The Chippewas of the Mississippi hereby assent and agree to the foregoing cession, and consent that the whole amount of the consideration money for the country ceded above, shall be paid to the Chippewas of Lake Superior, and in consideration thereof the Chippewas of Lake Superior hereby relinquish to the Chippewas of the Mississippi, all their interest in and claim to the lands heretofore owned by them in common, lying west of the above boundry-line.

Reservation for Chippewa of Lake Superior.

ARTICLE 2. The United States agree to set apart and withhold from sale, for the use of the Chippewas of Lake Superior, the following-described tracts of land, viz:

1st. For the L'Anse and Vieux De Sert bands, all the unsold lands in the following townships in the State of Michigan: Township fifty-one north range thirty-three west; township fifty-one north range thirty-two west; the east half of township fifty north range thirty-three west; the west half of township fifty north range thirty-two west, and all of township fifty-one north range thirty-one west, lying west of Huron Bay.

2d. For the La Pointe band, and such other Indians as may see fit to settle with them, a tract of land bounded as follows: Beginning on the south shore of Lake Superior, a few miles west of Montreal River, at the mouth of a creek called by the Indians Ke-che-se-be-we-she, running thence south to a line drawn east and west through the centre of township forty-seven north, thence west to the west line of said township, thence south to the southeast corner of township forty-six north, range thirty-two west, thence west the width of two townships, thence north the width of two townships, thence west one mile, thence north to the lake shore, and thence along the lake shore, crossing Shag-waw-me-quon Point, to the place of beginning. Also two hundred acres on the northern extremity of Madeline Island, for a fishing ground.

The Treaty of 1854

Articles of a treaty made and concluded at La Pointe, in the State of Wisconsin, between Henry C. Gilbert and David B. Herriman, commissioners on the part of the United States, and the Chippewa Indians of Lake Superior and the Mississippi, by their chiefs and head-men.

ARTICLE 1.

The Chippewas of Lake Superior hereby cede to the United States all the lands heretofore owned by them in common with the Chippewas of the Mississippi, lying east of the following boundary-line, to wit: Beginning at a point, where the east branch of Snake River crosses the southern boundary-line of the Chippewa country, running thence up the said branch to its source, thence nearly north, in a straight line, to the mouth of East Savannah River, thence up the St. Louis River to the mouth of East Swan River, thence up the East Swan River to its source, thence in a straight line to the most westerly bend of Vermillion River, and thence down the Vermillion River to its mouth.

The Chippewas of the Mississippi hereby assent and agree to the foregoing cession, and consent that the whole amount of the consideration money for the country ceded above, shall be paid to the Chippewas of Lake Superior, and in consideration thereof the Chippewas of Lake Superior hereby relinquish to the Chippewas of the Mississippi, all their interest in and claim

214

to the lands heretofore owned by them in common, lying west of the above boundry-line.

ARTICLE 2.

The United States agree to set apart and withhold from sale, for the use of the Chippewas of Lake Superior, the following-described tracts of land, viz:

1st. For the L'Anse and Vieux De Sert bands, all the unsold lands in the following townships in the State of Michigan: Township fifty-one north range thirty-three west; township fifty-one north range thirty-two west; the east half of township fifty north range thirty-three west; the west half of township fifty north range thirty-two west, and all of township fifty-one north range thirty-one west, lying west of Huron Bay.

For the La Pointe band, and such other Indians as may see fit to settle with them, a tract of land bounded as follows: Beginning on the south shore of Lake Superior, a few miles west of Montreal River, at the mouth of a creek called by the Indians Ke-che-se-be-we-she, running thence south to a line drawn east and west through the centre of township forty-seven north, thence west to the west line of said township, thence south to the southeast corner of township forty-six north, range thirty-two west, thence west the width of two townships, thence north the width of two townships, thence west one mile, thence north to the lake shore, and thence along the lake shore, crossing Shag-waw-me-quon Point, to the place of beginning. Also two hundred acres on the northern extremity of Madeline Island, for a fishing ground.

3d. For the other Wisconsin bands, a tract of land lying about Lac De Flambeau, and another tract on Lac Court Orielles, each equal in extent to three townships, the boundaries of which shall be hereafter agreed upon or fixed under the direction of the President.

4th. For the Fond Du Lac bands, a tract of land bounded as follows: Beginning at an island in the St. Louis River, above Knife Portage, called by the Indians Paw-paw-sco-me-me-tig, running thence west to the boundary-line heretofore described, thence north along said boundary-line to the mouth of Savannah River, thence down the St. Louis River to the place of beginning. And if said tract shall contain less than one hundred thousand acres, a strip of land shall be added on the south side thereof, large enough to equal such deficiency.

5th. For the Grand Portage band, a tract of land bounded as follows: Beginning at a rock a little east of the eastern extremity of Grand Portage Bay, running thence along the lake shore to the mouth of a small stream called by the Indians Maw-ske-gwaw-caw-maw-se-be, or Cranberry Marsh River, thence up said stream, across the point to Pigeon River, thence down Pigeon River to a point opposite the starting-point, and thence across to the place of beginning.

6th. The Ontonagon band and that subdivision of the La Pointe band of which Buffalo is chief, may each select, on or near the lake shore, four sections of land, under the direction of the President, the boundaries of which shall be defined hereafter. And being desirous to provide for some of his connections who have rendered his people important services, it is agreed that the chief Buffalo may select one section of land, at such place in the ceded territory as he may see fit, which shall be reserved for that purpose, and conveyed by the United States to such person or persons as he may direct.

7th. Each head of a family, or single person over twenty-one years of age at the present time of the mixed bloods, belonging to the Chippewas of Lake Superior, shall be entitled to eighty acres of land, to be selected by them under the direction of the President, and which shall be secured to them by patent in the usual form.

ARTICLE 3.

The United States will define the boundaries of the reserved tracts, whenever it may be necessary, by actual survey, and the President may, from time to time, at his discretion, cause the whole to be surveyed, and may assign to each head of a family or single person over twenty-one years of age, eighty acres of land for his or their separate use; and he may, at his discretion, as fast as the occupants become capable of transacting their own affairs, issue patents therefor to such occupants, with such restrictions of the power of alienation as he may see fit to impose. And he may also, at his discretion, make rules and regulations, respecting the disposition of the lands in case of the death of the head of a family, or single person occupying the same, or in case of its abandonment by them. And he may also assign other lands in exchange for mineral lands, if any such are found in the tracts herein set apart. And he may also make such changes in the boundaries of such reserved tracts or otherwise, as shall be necessary to prevent interference with any vested rights. All necessary roads, highways, and railroads, the lines of which may run through any of the reserved tracts, shall have the right of way through the same, compensation being made therefor as in other cases.

ARTICLE 4.

In consideration of and payment for the country hereby ceded, the United States agree to pay to the Chippewas of Lake Superior, annually, for the term of twenty years, the following sums, to wit: five thousand dollars in coin; eight thousand dollars in goods, household furniture and cooking utensils; three thousand dollars in agricultural implements and cattle, carpenter's and other tools and building materials, and three thousand dollars for moral and educational purposes, of which last sum, three hundred dollars per annum shall be paid to the Grand Portage band, to enable them to maintain a school at their village. The United States will also pay the further sum of ninety thousand dollars, as the chiefs in open council may direct, to enable them to meet their present just engagements. Also the further sum of six thousand dollars, in agricultural implements, household furniture, and cooking utensils, to be distributed at the next annuity payment, among the mixed bloods of said nation. The United States will also furnish two hundred guns, one hundred rifles, five hundred beaver-traps, three hundred dollars' worth of ammunition, and one thousand dollars' worth of ready-made clothing, to be distributed among the young men of the nation, at the next annuity payment.

ARTICLE 5.

The United States will also furnish a blacksmith and assistant, with the usual amount of stock, during the continuance of the annuity payments, and as much longer as the President may think proper, at each of the points herein set apart for the residence of the Indians, the same to be in lieu of all the employees to which the Chippewas of Lake Superior may be entitled under previous existing treaties.

ARTICLE 6.

The annuities of the Indians shall not be taken to pay the debts of individuals, but satisfaction for depredations committed by them shall be made by them in such manner as the President may direct.

ARTICLE 7.

No spirituous liquors shall be made, sold, or used on any of the lands herein set apart for the residence of the Indians, and the sale of the same shall be prohibited in the Territory hereby ceded, until otherwise ordered by the President.

ARTICLE 8.

It is agreed, between the Chippewas of Lake Superior and the Chippewas of the Mississippi, that the former shall be entitled to two-thirds, and the latter to one-third, of all benefits to be derived from former treaties existing prior to the year 1847.

ARTICLE 9.

The United States agree that an examination shall be made, and all sums that may be found equitably due to the Indians, for arrearages of annuity or other thing, under the provisions of former treaties, shall be paid as the chiefs may direct.

ARTICLE 10.

All missionaries, and teachers, and other persons of full age, residing in the territory hereby ceded, or upon any of the reservations hereby made by authority of law, shall be allowed to enter the land occupied by them at the minimum price whenever the surveys shall be completed to the amount of one quarter-section each.

ARTICLE 11.

All annuity payments to the Chippewas of Lake Superior, shall hereafter be made at L'Anse, La Pointe, Grand Portage, and on the St. Louis River; and the Indians shall not be required to remove from the homes hereby set apart for them. And such of them as reside in the territory hereby ceded, shall have the right to hunt and fish therein, until otherwise ordered by the President.

ARTICLE 12.

In consideration of the poverty of the Bois Forte Indians who are parties to this treaty, they having never received any annuity payments, and of the great extent of that part of the ceded country owned exclusively by them, the following additional stipulations are made for their benefit. The United States will pay the sum of ten thousand dollars, as their chiefs in open council may direct, to enable them to meet their present just engagements. Also the further sum of ten thousand dollars, in five equal annual payments, in blankets, cloth, nets, guns, ammunitions, and such other articles of necessity as they may require.

They shall have the right to select their reservation at any time hereafter, under the direction of the President; and the same may be equal in extent, in proportion to their numbers, to those allowed the other bands, and be subject to the same provisions.

They shall be allowed a blacksmith, and the usual smithshop supplies, and also two persons to instruct them in farming, whenever in the opinion of the President it shall be proper, and for such length of time as he shall direct.

It is understood that all Indians who are parties to this treaty, except the Chippewas of the Mississippi, shall hereafter be known as the Chippewas of Lake Superior. *Provided*, That the stipulation by which the Chippewas of Lake Superior relinquishing their right to land west of the boundary-line shall not apply to the Bois Forte band who are parties to this treaty.

ARTICLE 13.

This treaty shall be obligatory on the contracting parties, as soon as the same shall be ratified by the President and Senate of the United States.

In testimony whereof, the said Henry C. Gilbert, and the said David B. Herriman, commissioners as aforesaid, and the undersigned chiefs and headmen of the Chippewas of Lake Superior and the Mississippi, have hereunto set their hands and seals, at the place aforesaid, this thirtieth day of September, one thousand eight hundred and fifty-four.

Henry C. Gilbert,
David B. Herriman,
Commissioners
Richard M. Smith, Secretary

La Pointe Band:
Ke-che-waish-ke, or the Buffalo, 1st chief, his x mark.
Chay-che-que-oh, 2d chief, his x mark.
A-daw-we-ge-zhick, or Each Side of the sky, 2d chief, his x mark.
O-ske-naw-way, or the Youth, 2d chief, his x mark.
Maw-caw-day-pe-nay-se, or the Black Bird, 2d chief, his x mark.
Naw-waw-naw-quot, headman, his x mark.

Ke-wain-zeence, headman, his x mark.
Waw-baw-ne-me-ke, or the White Thunder, 2d chief, his x mark.
Pay-baw-me-say, or the Soarer, 2d chief, his x mark.
Naw-waw-ge-waw-nose, or the Little Current, 2d chief, his x mark.
Maw-caw-day-waw-quot, or the Black Cloud, 2d chief, his x mark.
Me-she-naw-way, or the Disciple, 2d chief, his x mark.
Key-me-waw-naw-um, headman, his x mark.
She-gog headman, his x mark.

Ontonagon Band:
O-cun-de-cun, or the Buoy 1st chief, his x mark.
Waw-say-ge-zhick, or the Clear Sky, 2d chief, his x mark.
Keesh-ke-taw-wug, headman, his x mark.

L'Anse Band:
David King, 1st chief, his x mark.
John Southwind, headman, his x mark.
Peter Marksman, headman, his x mark.
Naw-taw-me-ge-zhick, or the First Sky, 2d chief, his x mark.
Aw-se-neece, headman, his x mark.

Vieux De Sert Band:
May-dway-aw-she, 1st chief, his x mark.
Posh-quay-gin, or the Leather, 2d chief, his x mark.

Grand Portage Band:
Shaw-gaw-naw-sheence, or the Little Englishman, 1st chief, his x mark.
May-mosh-caw-wosh, headman, his x mark.
Aw-de-konse, or the Little Reindeer, 2d chief, his x mark.
Way-we-ge-wam, headman, his x mark.

Fond Du Lac Band:
Shing-goope, or the Balsom, 1st chief, his x mark.
Mawn-go-sit, or the Loon's Foot, 2d chief, his x mark.
May-quaw-me-we-ge-zhick, headman, his x mark.
Keesh-kawk, headman, his x mark.
Caw-taw-waw-be-day, headman, his x mark.
O-saw-gee, headman, his x mark.
Ke-che-aw-ke-wain-ze, headman, his x mark.
Naw-gaw-nub, or the Foremost Sitter, 2d chief, his x mark.
Ain-ne-maw-sung, 2d chief, his x mark.
Naw-aw-bun-way, headman, his x mark.
Wain-ge-maw-tub, headman, his x mark.
Aw-ke-wain-zeence, headman, his x mark.
Shay-way-be-nay-se, headman, his x mark.
Paw-pe-oh, headman, his x mark.

Lac Court Oreille Band:
Aw-ke-wain-ze, or the Old Man, 1st chief, his x mark.
Key-no-zhance, or the Little Jack Fish, 1st chief, his x mark.
Key-che-pe-nay-se, or the Big Bird, 2d chief, his x mark.
Ke-che-waw-be-shay-she, or the Big Martin, 2d chief, his x mark.
Waw-be-shay-sheence, headman, his x mark.
Quay-quay-cub, headman, his x mark.
Shaw-waw-no-me-tay, headman, his x mark.
Nay-naw-ong-gay-be, or the Dressing Bird, 1st chief, his x mark.
O-zhaw-waw-sco-ge-zhick, or the Blue Sky, 2d chief, his x mark.
I-yaw-banse, or the Little Buck, 2d chief, his x mark.
Ke-che-e-nin-ne, headman, his x mark.
Haw-daw-gaw-me, headman, his x mark.
Way-me-te-go-she, headman, his x mark.
Pay-me-ge-wung, headman, his x mark.

Lac Du Flambeau Band:
Aw-mo-se, or the Wasp, 1st chief, his x mark.
Ke-nish-te-no, 2d chief, his x mark.
Me-gee-see, or the Eagle, 2d chief, his x mark.
Kay-kay-co-gwaw-nay-aw-she, headman, his x mark.
O-che-chog, headman, his x mark.
Nay-she-kay-gwaw-nay-be, headman, his x mark.
O-scaw-bay-wis, or the Waiter, 1st chief, his x mark.
Que-we-zance, or the White Fish, 2d chief, his x mark.
Ne-gig, or the Otter, 2d chief, his x mark.
Nay-waw-che-ge-ghick-may-be, headman, his x mark.
Quay-quay-ke-cah, headman, his x mark.

Bois Forte Band:
Kay-baish-caw-daw-way, or Clear Round the Prairie, 1st chief, his x mark.
Way-zaw-we-ge-zhick-way-sking, headman, his x mark.
O-saw-we-pe-nay-she, headman, his x mark.

The Mississippi Bands:
Que-we-san-se, or Hole in the Day, head chief, his x mark.
Caw-nawn-daw-waw-win-zo, or the Berry Hunter, 1st chief, his x mark.
Waw-bow-jieg, or the White Fisher, 2d chief, his x mark.
Ot-taw-waw, 2d chief, his x mark.
Que-we-zhan-cis, or the Bad Boy, 2d chief, his x mark.
Bye-a-jick, or the Lone Man, 2d chief, his x mark.
I-yaw-shaw-way-ge-zhick, or the Crossing Sky, 2d chief, his x mark.
Maw-caw-day, or the Bear's Heart, 2d chief, his x mark.
Ke-way-de-no-go-nay-be, or the Northern Feather, 2d chief, his x mark.
Me-squaw-dace, headman, his x mark.
Naw-gaw-ne-gaw-bo, headman, his x mark.

Wawm-be-de-yea, headman, his x mark.
Waish-key, headman, his x mark.
Caw-way-caw-me-ge-skung, headman, his x mark.
My-yaw-ge-way-we-dunk, or One who carries the Voice, 2d chief, his x mark.

John F. Godfroy, Interpreters.
Geo. Johnston, Interpreters.
S. A. Marvin, Interpreters.
Louis Codot, Interpreters.
Paul H. Beaulieu, Interpreters.
Henry Blatchford, Interpreters.
Peter Floy, Interpreters.

Executed in the presence of—
Henry M. Rice,
J. W. Lynde,
G. D. Williams,
B. H. Connor,
E. W. Muldough,
Richard Godfroy,
D. S. Cash,
H. H. McCullough,
E. Smith Lee,
Wm. E. Vantassel,
L. H. Wheeler.

Recommended Reading

History of the Ojibway People William W. Warren

The Chippewa: A History of the Great Lakes Woodland Tribe over Three Centuries Walker D. Wyman and Kurt Leichtle

Life with the Ojibwe: A Northern Land Howard D. Paap

Wild Rice and the Ojibway People Thomas Vennum, Jr.

La Pointe: Village Outpost on Madeline Island Hamilton N. Ross

Ojibwe Journeys: Treaties, Sandy Lake and the Waabanong Run Charlie O. Rasmussen

Treaty Rights: The Reserved Rights of Wisconsin's Chippewa Indians in Historical Perspective Ronald N. Satz

The Chief Namakagon Trilogy James A. Brakken

Madeline Island & the Chequamegon Region John O. Holzhueter

People and Places: A Human History of the Apostle Islands Dr. Jane C. Busch

History, Tradition and Adventure in the Chippewa Valley William W. Bartlett

Treaty Rights Great Lakes Indian Fish and Wildlife Commission

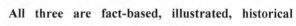

DARK - A CAMPFIRE COMPANION

56 very scary short stories & delightfully frightening poems. Spine-tingling tales of ghosts, dragons, ne'er-do-wells, and monsters—each waiting to raise goosebumps. Every story is morbidly illustrated by long-dead master artists of the macabre. Chilling, yet wonderful fireside reading. A "must-have" for every cabin bookshelf and home library. Ages 12 and up.

THE MOOSE & WILBUR P. DILBY
Plus 36 Fairly True Tales from Up North.

Thirty-seven short stories straight from the heart & the heart of the north. All fairly true, more or less. Some are sad, some shocking, most are hilarious. Small town tales of baseball, fishing, and hunting, tavern tales, jokesters, murderers, gangsters, and flimflam men. Lost treasure, lumberjacks, and legends of the north. Includes a 1-act play and several short stories based on the Chief Namakagon trilogy. Written for adults but fine for age 12. **Features *two* 1st place award-winning stories.**

SAVING OUR LAKES & STREAMS:
101 Practical Things You Can Do Today

A handbook for all who care for our lakes and streams. Simple tips, ideas, and articles from award-winning conservationist and author, James Brakken. Foreword by Dan Small, host of Wisconsin Public TV's "OUTDOOR WISCONSIN." 200-pages, 101 tips, 75 articles, 75 photos. Discounted at BadgerValley.com. All ages. Great fundraiser! Ships free. (Up to 33% off & factory-direct shipping to conservation groups, lake associations, & lake districts.) Profits help support efforts to protect and preserve Wisconsin's waters.

Secure <u>online ordering</u> or <u>download an order form</u> at <u>BadgerValley.com</u> where shipping is free!

BADGER VALLEY PUBLISHING
45255 East Cable Lake Road
Cable, Wisconsin 54821 715-798-3163
Email TreasureofNamakagon@Gmail.com

Badger Valley can publish YOUR book, too!
Now accepting new book proposals.

The Treasure of Namakagon
James Brakken's "flagship" lumberjack novel.
Book 1 in the award-winning Chief Namakagon trilogy:

2nd PLACE WINNER out of 10,000 worldwide entries in the 2013 *Amazon Breakthrough Novel Award* competition!

A young lumberjack, his Indian mentor, and a lost silver mine—a fact-based tale of timber, treasure, and treachery in America's 19th century wilderness. Following a daring rescue from a dangerous child-labor scheme in 1883 Chicago, an orphan is plunged into the peak of lumberjack life in far northwestern Wisconsin. There, an Ojibwe chief teaches him respect for nature and shows him to hidden treasure—an actual mine, lost when the chief died in 1886 and yet to be rediscovered.

You'll meet young Tor Loken whose family owns a wilderness lumber camp. You'll join the fight when a sinister timber tycoon takes control of the river, threatening the Lokens' future and the lumberjacks' dollar-a-day pay. You'll be in the cook shanty before dawn for breakfast, then out into the cuttings where, knee deep in snow, you'll help harvest giant pine logs. Hitch the Clydesdales to the tanker. Ice the trails for the giant timber sleighs. Take the train to town but keep one eye peeled for hooligans seeking an easy swindle.

Back in the bunkhouse, spin a yarn with colorful lumberjack friends. Next, it's a Saturday night of merriment in town. Dress warmly, though. It's a three hour sleigh ride back to camp at twenty below zero.

Come spring, you'll drive the timber down a thundering, icy river, jumping log to log as they rush downstream, danger around each bend. Finally, payday! Time to celebrate. Keep your pocketbook buttoned up, though. Scoundrels are eager to separate you from your winter wages.

Put on your red wool mackinaw. Grab your pike pole. You are about to plunge into 19th century lumberjack life *The Treasure of Namakagon*, a thrilling adventure, thick with twists and turns, researched and illustrated by an author who lives there.

And, yes, the boy wins the girl's heart.

Tor Loken and the Death of Chief Namakagon

Lace your calked boots and button your mackinaw once again. You are about to plunge into a twisting, turning, thrilling north woods mystery: *Tor Loken and the Death of Chief Namakagon.*

Based on the suspicious death of Chief Namakagon in 1886, this tale depicts a time when rugged lumberjacks and miners brought civilization and wealth to Wisconsin's wilderness, while corrupt, ruthless opportunists devoured all they could.

Following a devastating blizzard, Namakagon's body is discovered near a secluded silver mine. Only nineteen-year-old Tor Loken can prove murder. Suspicious accidents soon plague his father's lumber camp. Tor and his sweetheart, Rosie, risk their lives to capture the killer and protect the tribal treasure. With you, they will solve the dark mystery surrounding Namakagon's murder in this fast-paced, fact-based thriller by the award-winning Wisconsin author whose research now unlocks the truth.

History tells us Chief Namakagon traded silver for supplies in Ashland in the 1880s. Several miners tried to get him to disclose the source of his silver. One man came close but, when a large bear blocked their trail, Namakagon took this for a bad omen and refused to continue. Following a fierce 1886 blizzard, Namakagon's remains were found along a trail that may have been very near his silver cache. Many suspect he met with foul play. Suspicions remain regarding the cause of his death. The location of the lost silver is still unknown.

In this mystery-adventure, Tor loses his mentor during this snowstorm. Tor is determined to solve the mystery of Namakagon's death. Suspicious accidents plague the Loken camp as Tor and Rosie risk all to stop the murderer.

Learn more about the rich history of the lumberjack days, help solve the mystery, and gather your own clues about the likely location of the legendary silver mine of Chief Namakagon.

243 pages. Illustrated. Written for adults though suitable for age twelve and up. **Maps to the 19th century Marengo silver fields, the likely location of Chief Namakagon's lost silver mine, are included in this novel.** This is a thrilling read and a book you will treasure in more ways than one! Available at select outlets and BadgerValley.com.

Grab a paddle and step into your birch bark canoe. You're off to the early 1800s and a fascinating, factual dramatization of the early life of Old Ice Feathers. It is a novel you won't be able to put down.

Book 3 in the trilogy:
The Secret Life of Chief Namakagon

When his friend and mentor dies in 1886, young Tor Loken learns of Namakagon's previous life. But why, four decades earlier, did he isolate himself in this uninhabited northern Wisconsin wilderness? Was Namakagon running from a troubled past?

Now James Brakken's research reveals Namakagon's life *before** he came to his northern Wisconsin home. His is an amazing true-life adventure—a tale of a child abduction by renegades, then 30 years living as an Ojibwe. Caught in the middle of a bloody war between the Hudson's Bay Company and the North West Fur Company, his people reject him. He tries living among the Whites but is unable to adjust. Loved by few and despised by many, he can't find his niche in life—a life torn in two by others. All odds are against him until he meets a doctor who helps him write a book about his life with the Indians. But even his highly successful book cannot stop his downward spiral.

Then, accused of murder in 1846, he flees and begins a new life, that of an Indian hermit in northwest Wisconsin where he becomes Ice Feathers and discovers a secret silver mine. (A map in this book gives the best clue yet to the lost mine's likely whereabouts.)

These adventure-filled pages unveil Chief Namakagon's secret and offer a captivating, stand-alone novel written for all readers who enjoy a fusion of thrilling fiction and fascinating history. This illustrated novel is suitable for readers age twelve and up.

*Since northern Wisconsin was settled in the 1880s, nobody knew that Chief Namakagon was actually a man who disappeared after being accused of a Michigan murder in 1846. When, in 2014, James Brakken's research verified the "original" identity of Chief Namakagon, he solved a 168-year-old cold case that historians have pondered for more than a century.

The Early Life and True Identity of Chief Namakagon
James Brakken
If it waddles like a duck and quacks like a duck …

When, in 2008, I began *The Treasure of Namakagon,* I did not intend to write a sequel, much less a trilogy. But research for book one led me to these two conclusions: 1, the chief really did refuse to disclose where he was getting silver. And, 2, his death involved foul play. Compelled to share what I discovered about his silver mine and the suspicious facts surrounding his death. I wrote *Tor Loken and the Death of Chief Namakagon,* a fact-filled murder mystery.

My research soon had me wondering why, in the mid-1840s, this man came to a remote, uninhabited lake in northern Wisconsin to live a hermit's life. Why did he isolate himself in this distant place? And how was it he could speak English, extraordinarily uncommon of Natives then?

I imagine the November, 1880 arrival of the railway turned his life on end, especially when newspaperman, George Thomas, stepped off the train and sought out the only English-speaking, long-time resident of the area. The reporter's interview helped answer some of my questions: According to Thomas, Namakagon came from Sault Ste. Marie decades earlier. Why? Because a dream revealed a fire and a death. Thomas wrote that this dream made Namakagon fear he'd be executed for a murder he did not commit.

By itself, this statement shed no light on my search for his previous life—until, that is, I traveled to the Sault where a deeper investigation revealed a murder *had* occurred there—in 1846. Fearing execution, the accused man fled—*a statement nearly identical to that given by Namakagon to George Thomas!*

I exposed many more clues and convincing details, but positive proof came while scouring the old land records, looking for the location of his silver mine. *The official records, buried for decades, disclosed the "early" identity of Chief Namakagon.* Eureka! I'd solved a *168-year-old cold case*—the solution to the 1846 disappearance of an innocent man wanted for a cold-blooded murder. The official government land records, along with the sheer number of clues, statements, and facts provided by professional historians, were clear evidence that the hermit of Lake Namakagon was, indeed, a fugitive who hid for forty years in the Wisconsin wilderness. I'd unveiled compelling, reliable verification of Namakagon's early life.

So, research for my fact-based murder mystery, *The Death of Chief Namakagon,* led me to write *The Secret Life of Chief Namakagon,* a book about the first half of his life. It's a fascinating, wilderness adventure based on his own words and those of historians—historians who, by the way, knew only part of his colorful life. My first two Chief Namakagon books shed light on the final half of his intriguing life and still-suspicious death.

Secret is a window into the world of a woodsman with an amazing history, an adventurer, a war hero who evaded death many times, a celebrated author forced to turn fugitive and become Mikwam-mi-Miguan, or Ice Feathers, the legendary hermit we now call Chief Namakagon.

Take pleasure in sharing his journey and learning his story in book three of the trilogy, *The Secret Life of Chief Namakagon.*

~~~

Enjoying a Badger Valley book? Three ways you can help.

Indy authors, unlike writers tied to brick and mortar publishing houses, must rely on our readers to stimulate interest in our books. If you enjoyed this book, you can ... 1. Give it 5 stars at Amazon. (Search: James Brakken books.) 2. Ask your local library to order a copy. 3. Tell your friends, neighbors, and co-workers.

Thanks for your interest and support!

Coming soon to BadgerValley.com and select northern Wisconsin outlets: A new novel by James Brakken, Bayfield County's award-winning author of historical fiction.

ALIAS RAY OLSON

The 1939 Chequamegon Forest Manhunt

A double homicide in Hayward leads a posse of 200 deputies & the FBI on Wisconsin's largest manhunt. An eye-opening, fact-based novel. Thrilling historical fiction at its best by James Brakken.

Watch for it soon. Pre-orders accepted at BadgerValley.com, where we pay the sales tax and shipping is free.

What readers say about James Brakken's writing:

"Wonderfully written .... Compelling" *"A good piece of writing with suspense and action ..."* **Jerry Apps, award-winning Wis. author.**

"Weaving mystery into history, James Brakken's writing vivifies the tumultuous nature of 19th-century life in the legendary north woods." **Michael Perry, NYT bestselling Wisconsin author**

"Open with caution. You won't want to put this one down." **LaMoine MacLaughlin, President, Wisconsin Writers Association**

"A fascinating tale ... *"Rip-roaring action ..."* *"So well-written."* *"Difficult to put down; a great read."* **Publisher's Weekly Magazine**

"The writing style of this piece is its greatest strength." *"The flow of the words is like an old fashioned song."* **Amazon Books**

"It's the dialog and characters that drive The Treasure of Namakagon, a book that, if the audience for (adventure novels) was more like it was in the 1950s, would likely be sitting at or near the top of the best seller's lists. It appears as if author James A. Brakken is determined to make a go of this series, and ... he's made at least one fan of this reader." **Judge at 22nd Writer's Digest Book Awards**

"James Brakken has captured all of the current science, technology, and leadership necessary to preserve our lakes and streams." **Mary Platner, Founder and Past-president of WAL.**

"Brakken has provided a timely handbook for citizens ready to play their role in realizing the state's Public Trust Doctrine." **Eric Olson, Director, UW Extension Lakes**

"A twisting, thrilling mix of mystery, adventure and legendary treasure. Wisconsin history buffs will find this book a treasure in itself. An exciting adventure for all ages." **Waldo Asp, AARP Chairman**

"In scene after scene, the reader is surrounded by the beauty of pristine woods and lakes, rooting for the good guys to beat out the greedy." **A. Y. Stratton, author of Buried Heart**

"I liked it!" **Larry Meiller, Wisconsin Public Radio host.**

About the Author

The writing career of Bayfield County author, James Brakken, began in college when his "Muskie Madness," the story of a fishing trip with his father was published in a 1974 *Boy's Life Magazine*. More articles followed in *Sports Afield*, *Outdoor Life*, and *Field & Stream*.

His first novel, *The Treasure of Namakagon*, features a boy in an 1883 northern Wisconsin lumber camp and a legendary lost silver mine. The suspicious 1886 death of Chief Namakagon and the 1846 disappearance of a murder fugitive led to two more in the trilogy, *Tor Loken & the Death of Chief Namakagon* and *The Secret Life of Chief Namakagon*.

Treasure won 2nd place out of 10,000 worldwide entries in the 2013 Amazon Breakthrough Novel Awards. Brakken also received the 2013, 2014, and 2016 Lake Superior Writers Award and the coveted Wisconsin Writers Association Jade Ring Award for a short story in his collection, *The Moose and Wilbur P. Dilby plus 36 Fairly True Tales from Up North*. The author earned statewide recognition for conservation as reflected in his self-help book, *Saving Our Lakes & Streams: 101 Practical Things You Can Do Today*.

To fulfill his desire to accurately portray Native American history in his books, Brakken went to a friend, Dr. John Anderson, a retired professor of Native American Studies and a former tribal chairman of the Lac Courte Oreilles band of Great Lakes Ojibwe. Known by many as Little Bird, Professor Anderson shared his thoughts with the author. Both men committed to offering readers a fresh look at the 1892 memoir of Benjamin Armstrong. This annotated edition of *Early Life Among the Indians* is their effort to bring Armstrong's story to light.

Of James Brakken's writing, *Publisher's Weekly Magazine* and *Amazon Books* said, "Difficult to put down. ... A great read," and "the flow of words is like an old fashioned song." Brakken publishes his own books, as well as those of other authors. They are available at BadgerValley.com where shipping is free.